LIVING WITH GRIEF

ETHICAL DILEMMAS AT THE END OF LIFE

EDITED BY
KENNETH J. DOKA, BRUCE JENNINGS, AND CHARLES A. CORR

Foreword by Jack D. Gordon, Chairman, Hospice Foundation of America

D0066945

HFA

HOSPICE FOUNDATION
OF AMERICA

Supported in part by the Foundation for End-of-Life Care

This book is part of HFA's *Living With Grief* ® series.

Ordering information:

Call Hospice Foundation of America: 800-854-3402

Or write:
Hospice Foundation of America
1621 Connecticut Avenue, NW #300
Washington, DC 20009

Or visit HFA's Web site:
www.hospicefoundation.org

Managing Editor: Amy Tucci
Assistant Managing Editor: Kate Viggiano
Cover Design: Patricia McBride
Typesetting and Design: Pam Page Cullen
Cover Image: Science et charite ©2005 Estate of Pablo Picasso /
    Artists Rights Society (ARS), New York

Publisher's Cataloging-in-Publication Data
(Prepared by Quality Books Inc.)

Ethical dilemmas at the end of life / edited by Kenneth J. Doka,
    Bruce Jennings, and Charles A. Corr ; foreword by Jack D. Gordon.
        p. cm. -- (Living with grief)
        Includes bibliographical references and index.
        LCCN 2004112043
        ISBN 1-893349-06-3

        1. Terminal care. 2. Terminal care--Moral and
    ethical aspects. 3. Grief--Psychological aspects.
    4. Terminally ill--Psychology. 5. Death--Psychological
    aspects.   I. Doka, Kenneth J., 1948- II. Jennings, Bruce,
    1949- III. Corr, Charles A. 1937- IV. Series.

    R726.8.E84 2005   179.7
                                 QBI04-800145

■ DEDICATION ■

To Dame Cicely Saunders
whose vision begat hospice
and whose deep moral sensitivities
framed its ethics

■ CONTENTS ■

■ FOREWORD ■

Jack D. Gordon
Chairman, Hospice Foundation of America

M ost of us make many decisions every day without thinking of the
ethical component of the issue. We simply rely on our own training
and experience to factor that into the decision where applicable. But when
we come to decisions about our own life as it nears its end, or decisions
made before in the contemplation of death, and when we have to make
decisions for loved ones, we generally make that decision consciously.
We ask, "What is the right thing to do?" And we call upon that set of prior
decisions and our moral and spiritual beliefs and life experiences to arrive
at a decision we feel to be correct. When making the decision for another
we must try to understand his or her beliefs and wishes, and remember
what the dying person may have expressed as a wish or request.

As you might suspect, this is probably the most difficult decision for
any of us to make either for another or for one's self. Some of the time a
physician or often a nurse participates in the decision. Most often, they
have little or no prior relationship to the person, but they have a great deal
more experience in this situation. On the other hand, medical education is
premised on curing the patient, so very little time is spent by doctors or
nurses in learning how to deal with a patient's death, and how to tell
survivors. Even less time is spent on how to relate to family and loved ones
at the time of impending death, or how to communicate to a family that
death has occurred.

One of the purposes of this book and the Hospice Foundation's
teleconference on the same subject is to provide health professionals and
the general public some information that will add to their understanding
of the often-inevitable situation. Death is a universal experience from
which none of us is exempt. All of us will be forced to face our own and,

in the course of events, the deaths of persons we are connected to in some way. When the dying person is one we cherish, we will ask— "What is the best course for us to take? What guidance is there from our own moral compass?" This book contains several descriptions of real life situations and issues that it would do us well to ponder and decide how we would have acted.

Hospice personnel are faced with these questions daily and have been trained to respond. Hospices are always one of the best—if not *the* best—organization in a community to turn to when confronting dying as well as grief and bereavement. It is the Foundation's mission to help these hospice workers as well as the variety of health workers, emergency medical personnel, physicians and nurses, and really everybody become better able to be of greater help in this common, but deeply disturbing, human experience.

■ ACKNOWLEDGMENTS ■

In editing this book, it is both a responsibility and a pleasure to thank all those whose help and support was a great gift. It was wonderful to work with co-editors Charles Corr and Bruce Jennings. Both offered their unique perspectives, ideas, and insights. My son Michael and his wife Angelina, my grandson Kenneth, and my godson Keith are always a source of joy and respite. This has been a year when two dear friends and neighbors— Margot Kimball and Herb Webber—died. They will be deeply missed. Other members of my intimate network of friends and family, including Kathy Dillon; my sister Dorothy and my brother Franky; and all of their families as well as neighbors, friends, and others including Dylan Rieger, Jim and Karen Cassa, Paul Kimball, Don and Carol Ford, Allen and Gail Greenstein, Jim and Mary Millar, Linda and Russell Tellier, Terry Webber, Fred and Lisa Amori, Eric Schwarz, Lynn Miller, and Larry Laterza, are especially appreciated. I also want to thank the College of New Rochelle, especially administrators and colleagues President Stephen Sweeny, Vice President Joan Bailey, Dean Nancy Brown, and Division Chair Marie Ribarich, who nurture such a supportive environment. Mary Whalen and Vera Mezzaucella offer invaluable administrative and secretarial assistance. Colleagues at the college as well as in the Association of Death Education and in the International Work Group on Death, Dying and Bereavement provide constant friendship, support, and stimulation.

—Kenneth J. Doka

I can gladly second Ken Doka's comments. It has been a pleasure and a stimulating learning experience to work with him and Charles Corr on this book, and with Amy Tucci of the Hospice Foundation of America as well. I am also grateful to the contributors in this volume who have written deeply and well under very onerous time constraints. May the patients and families served by the hospice and end-of-life care systems of this country be the ultimate beneficiaries of the wisdom and insight these authors have shared with us.

—Bruce Jennings

I am especially grateful to Kenneth Doka for his friendship, encouragement, and critical interactions over many years. In this book, and in many other worthwhile projects, it has always been gratifying to work with the leadership and staff of the Hospice Foundation of America. For my chapter in this book, I owe particular thanks for guidance and advice to Margaret Coolican, founder of the National Donor Family Council, and to Catherine Paykin of the National Kidney Foundation. In all of my professional work and my personal life, I am deeply indebted to Donna Corr—colleague, friend, spouse, and helpmate.

—Charles A. Corr

In addition, we as editors need to acknowledge and thank Jack Gordon, the chairman of the Hospice Foundation of America (HFA), who lent his counsel, experience, and wisdom as well as contributing a foreword. The very teleconference that this book supports is a testament to his vision. David Abrams, the president of HFA, offered suggestions at each stage of the process. These comments always kept us grounded in the real world of hospice. Amy Tucci dove right in as new managing editor—quickly proving her incalculable value. Lisa McGahey Veglahn and Kate Viggiano provided assistance that allows HFA to annually produce a book on a Herculean schedule. Sophie Viteri Berman, Robert Lee, Donna Hines, and Karen Higgins kept everything else operating at high levels of efficiency, making all of this possible. And how can we not acknowledge Cokie Roberts, who always is so willing to contribute her time and energy to make the teleconference the event it has become.

True Ryndes, the executive director of the National Hospice Work Group, an association of the nation's largest hospices, merits special thanks. He and his association labored to produce the case vignettes that ground this book in the real-life dilemmas that hospices constantly face.

Of course, we need to thank all the contributing authors who met impossible deadlines with understanding and grace as well as their thoughtful insights and ideas. One author deserves special mention: ElizaBeth Beyer completed her chapter even as her teenage son, Seth Webb Beyer, entered hospice care. We hope this book, then, is seen as part of his enduring legacy of courage and strength. ▪

Editor's note: The Terri Schiavo case is mentioned a number of times by authors of this book. At press time, the U.S. Supreme Court declined to intervene in the case, allowing a lower court ruling to stand that would allow Terri Schiavo's husband, Michael Schiavo, the right to disconnect her feeding tube. Terri Schiavo suffered severe brain damage in 1990 when her heart stopped beating. She left no written directive. This case began as a legal battle in 1993 between Michael Schiavo and Terri Schiavo's parents, Robert and Mary Schindler, and appeared to reach its climax in 2003 when Michael Schiavo won a court decision ordering that his wife's feeding tube be removed. Her parents opposed his decision. The feeding tube was reinserted six days later, after the Florida Legislature passed "Terri's Law." The Florida Supreme Court ruled that "Terri's Law" was an unconstitutional effort to override court rulings. The U.S. Supreme Court refused without comment to review that decision.

SECTION I

Historical, Spiritual, and Cultural Perspectives

As historians of ethics look back on the past fifty years, one of the most significant conclusions they may draw is that, in this period, the cultural consensus on when life begins and ends shattered. Current technology has outpaced a societal consensus on how that technology should be understood and employed. The current bitter debates and litigation over both abortion and end-of-life decisions reflect that cultural lag.

In hospice and end-of-life care, the old ethical conundrums over whether a patient should be told or when treatment is futile, have now been replaced by much more nuanced and complex debates about what constitutes aggressive treatment, when treatment is ineffectual, and who is empowered to make these decisions. These decisions not only affect a society's legal and political debates, they are a daily reality of hospice and palliative care. Such decisions, too, influence more than the nature of an individual's death. They radically shape surviving family members' and friends' experience of that death, sometimes painfully complicating grief.

For those reasons, the leadership of the Hospice Foundation of America decided to focus on end-of-life ethics as the topic for the 2005 Living with Grief ® Teleconference and accompanying book.

Ethics can be understood as beliefs about what constitutes appropriate and right actions in given situations and circumstances. Ethics derives from values or core beliefs that are in turn shaped by religious, cultural, and historical experiences. Ethics also involves questioning and critically scrutinizing prevailing values and beliefs in light of philosophical analysis and human reason.

This first section explores that larger context. Werth begins this section with an analysis of the major philosophical principles—nonmaleficence, beneficence, autonomy, justice, and fidelity—that underlie end-of-life ethics. His chapter makes clear that the application of these principles in any given circumstance may be fiercely debated, as interpretation of these principles may vary and conflict. Consequently, Werth offers a paradigm for resolving these conflicts. Nonetheless, it is these principles that do define and frame that debate.

These principles are shaped by larger religious, spiritual, cultural, and ideological perspectives. Two chapters, one by Cohen, and one by Tiano and Beyer, explore how these perspectives affect end-of-life decision making. Both chapters offer practical information that delineates how varied cultural and religious groups have applied their own principles to specific and current ethical issues. Both chapters also reinforce two critical points that lie behind these choices. The first is that each of these perspectives—whether spiritual, religious, cultural, or ideological—has to consider whether the focus should be on the dying individual or, more broadly, on a larger unit such as the family, tribe, or society. That question forms the ethical debate. Second, these perspectives are themselves fashioned by experiences with death. In some cases, death may be part of everyday experience, while in others, deaths are more removed—encountered primarily by older persons and separated from public view.

Both chapters further explore ways historical experience shapes ethical perspectives. Tiano and Beyer, for example, note that the unique historical experience of African Americans, which includes slavery, pervasive racial discrimination, historically disparate medical care, and the Tuskegee syphilis experiments, have made African Americans suspicious not only of hospice and palliative care but also of a host of end-of-life decisions such as advanced directives. These chapters move beyond a racial focus to provide both a reminder and a model for caregivers and ethicists to consider how historical experience and cultural attributes of any group influence their responses to ethical decisions.

This is illustrated in the San Diego Hospice case study. Buckholz offers the first of the ethical case studies contributed by various hospices throughout the country. These case studies attempt to ground the discussion of ethical dilemmas in the daily moral struggles of hospice care. While names and details have been modified to protect privacy, these cases are direct submissions from hospices sharing the daily ethical concerns that they continually face. Buckholz asks a central question. Modern medical practice is based upon informed consent. How far can and should hospices go to accommodate the wishes of families? How flexible and culturally sensitive can health services be in acquiescing to the demands of varied cultural mandates? Some would say that informed consent allows the ability to choose not to be informed at all. Can that decision, however, be made by surrogates—even in cultures that take a protective stance toward communicating bad news?

Ethics and law are related. Like ethics, laws derive from larger values shaped by shared history and larger ideological, spiritual, religious, and cultural perspectives. Like ethics, laws dictate appropriate and right actions—this time backed by legal sanction. Yet the relationship is really quite complex. Sometimes, such as during the civil rights struggles, ethical conduct may require defiance of law. In other cases, the laws may be silent.

Still, laws both reflect and define ethical debate. Meisel and Jennings are sensitive to this complex relationship. In their chapter, they explore how medical practice has informed and shaped the laws even as the laws have influenced and framed medical practice.

Underlying Meisel and Jennings's chapter is the notion of change. As the pace of technology changes, new realities emerge that will affect end-of-life care, and will have to be reflected in both ethics and possibly ultimately in laws.

Thus, the ethical debate never ends. ■

CHAPTER 1

Philosophical Principles of Ethical Judgments

James L. Werth, Jr.

Professionals who provide clinical services in end-of-life situations will likely be faced with a variety of complicated issues and decisions. As outlined in this book, issues include how, where, and when people die; how to talk about dying; and conflicts in end-of-life situations. Decisions associated with all of these areas occur within legal and cultural contexts that must be taken into account. Similarly, there are ethical aspects to many of these decisions; however, unlike the legal and cultural aspects (which are essentially immutable), ethical considerations are more contextual and decisions may be more variable. In other words, two different providers who are working with a single dying person must follow the same laws and take the same cultural characteristics of the person into account, but what these two professionals consider to be ethical issues, how they solve ethical dilemmas, and the decisions at which they arrive might be very different (though equally acceptable). This variability may increase if the providers are from dissimilar cultural backgrounds.

When presented with an ethical issue, there are a variety of ways of deliberating and resolving what to do. Regardless of the steps involved and the order in which they are considered, there must be a foundation. Because of the significant influence of Beauchamp and Childress's (1979) work in medicine and bioethics and Kitchener's (1984) adaptation of their ideas for psychology, one common foundation for many professionals working in end-of-life care may be the ethical meta-principles of autonomy, nonmaleficence, beneficence, justice, and (for some) fidelity. A provider's values, whether rooted in a spiritual/religious belief system, ethnic background, and/or some other influences, will interface with these four (or five) meta-principles and therefore affect how they are considered and weighted when the provider is faced with an ethical dilemma. In addition, the contextual factors associated with the situation may significantly affect the courses rejected and selected. As a result, any attempt to declare that a given decision in a particular situation is ethical or unethical is likely doomed to failure. On the other hand, outlining a process for ethical decision making and, in particular, specifying the core elements to consider may be useful.

The purpose of this chapter is to describe a set of principles that can be used in making ethical judgments and demonstrating how they may apply in end-of-life situations that medical and mental health professionals experience. Although the focus is on "philosophical" principles, the author is a practicing psychologist who has been working with chronically and terminally ill individuals for more than a decade, and therefore the principles will be discussed primarily from a practical or applied standpoint as opposed to a theoretical or ideal perspective. The chapter begins with an overview of one decision-making model and then moves to defining and describing the five ethical meta-principles that providers should consider when evaluating ethical dilemmas in end-of-life situations. Incorporated within the discussion of each principle are examples of how it may be implicated in end-of-life situations.

ETHICAL DECISION-MAKING

When faced with the need to make an ethical judgment, one certainly may merely choose the first idea that comes to mind or defer to another individual. However, a professional who wishes to maximize the chances of making the best decision possible given the circumstances, enhance the possibility of providing optimal care to the dying person and/or loved ones, and protect herself or himself from repercussions if someone is unhappy with the events that take place and/or the outcome, should follow some sort of decision-making model. Further, the importance of consultation and documentation (as well as documentation of the consultation) throughout the decision-making process cannot be overemphasized. Following a model is helpful, but if the professional does not consult with another person, there is the possibility that, especially in as delicate an area as end-of-life decision-making, the professional's own perspective may overshadow those of the dying individual and/or loved ones, and this may compromise care and decision making. Thus, consultation increases the likelihood that the ethical decision making process and outcome will meet or surpass the standard of care. Contemporaneous documentation of the review process, consultation, and implementation of the plan will provide evidence that the provider did her or his utmost to serve the client, even if the outcome is negative.

One model that has been used in end-of-life situations (see Barret, Kitchener, & Burris, 2001b; Eversole, Kitchener, & Burris, 2001) was described by Barret, Kitchener, and Burris (2001a). Their model has nine steps, listed below. For the purposes of this chapter, the focus will be on steps 5, 7d, and 7e.

1) Pause and identify your personal responses to the case.

2) Review the facts of the case.

3) Conceptualize an initial plan based on clinical issues.

4) Consult agency policies and professional ethical codes to see if your plan is congruent with them.

5) Analyze your plan in terms of the five ethical meta-principles (autonomy, beneficence, nonmaleficence, fidelity, and justice).

6) Identify legal issues.

7) Refine your plan so that it:
   a. Is most congruent with your personal values,
   b. Advances clinical issues as much as possible,
   c. Permits you to operate within agency policies and professional ethics codes,
   d. Minimizes harm to the client and relevant others,
   e. Maximizes all other ethical principles to the extent possible, and
   f. Allows you to operate within the law.

8) Choose a course of action and share it with your client.

9) Implement the course of action, then monitor and document the outcomes.

Werth (2002; see also Werth & Kleespies, in press) recommends that professionals involved in end-of-life care use this model when faced with ethical dilemmas. Ideally, a provider will take the time to imagine the types of situations that may arise and work through the process before being faced with a dilemma, because sometimes a decision must be made in the moment and there is not time to fully consider a wide variety of possible implications and potential courses of action.

ETHICAL META-PRINCIPLES

An ethical dilemma occurs when a person is faced with two or more apparently equally acceptable or reasonable alternatives (Kitchener, 2000). As the model above indicates, there are many aspects to consider when attempting to decide which option to choose. Many of these considerations are determined by outside forces (e.g., agency policies, state or federal laws, professional ethics codes), and some may be quite idiosyncratic (e.g., the provider's personal values, the facts of the situation). The ethical meta-principles seem to fall somewhere in between the two, for although they can technically be defined in a way that transcends the context and the individuals involved, their application in particular situations may change if even minor alterations are made to the issue under consideration. Further, not only may the application change, the relative importance of the various meta-principles may vary in different situations or among different individuals involved in the same situation. However, as the model indicates, nonmaleficence is typically viewed as the most important of the five. Therefore, the discussion below begins with nonmaleficence and is followed by beneficence (because of its conceptual association with the former) and then autonomy (because of its significance within the United States and especially in the health and mental health systems, although there are cultural implications, as will be outlined below and in other chapters), justice (especially relevant in today's cost-conscious environment), and fidelity (of significant importance in professional or fiduciary relationships). The material in this section is drawn from a number of sources, including Beauchamp and Childress (2001), Kitchener (1984, 2000), Kitchener and Barret (2001), and Battin (1994).

Nonmaleficence

The principle of nonmaleficence is often interpreted as "do no harm," which is fine in an ideal or theoretical world. However, in actual practice, the principle can more accurately be thought of as *minimizing* harm to as many interested parties as possible. Further, just as there is tension among the meta-principles, there may be different ways of viewing each principle, depending on the perspective from which one examines them (e.g., the perspective of the dying person, a loved one, a service provider). This is especially clear with nonmaleficence. For example, in an end-of-life situation, if there are disagreements about what course of action to take within the dying person's circle of loved ones or between loved ones and health care providers, unless a mutually agreeable solution or compromise can be reached, someone will be "harmed" by the resulting decision.

At times there is also the sense that the issue is not necessarily about minimizing all harm but, more pointedly, harm intentionally inflicted by the provider. However, this too is more ideal than realistic, for whenever a professional does or does not do something, any harm that results may not be "intended" (although it may be foreseen), but the actions leading to the harm are intentional. For example, if a decision is being made about keeping a comatose person on a ventilator or withdrawing the treatment (regardless of the reason for the withdrawal, whether because of an advance directive, a surrogate's decision, or use of the "futility" rationale), the results—which someone may interpret as "harm" in some way—are due to an intentional action (or set of actions) by the professional.

Further complicating the issue is that the likelihood of harm being perceived is increased if providers ignore the possibility that different values (e.g., based on religious or spiritual beliefs) or cultural backgrounds (e.g., African Americans' history with the medical system) will affect interpretations of the issues at hand. For some people, "suffering" is not necessarily bad, while for others, minimizing suffering is the most important goal. Similarly, for some, withholding or withdrawing treatment is tantamount to murder, while for others it is more harmful to keep someone alive on machines. A tremendous amount of research has shown that health care professionals' perspectives on treatments may differ significantly from nonproviders' views, possibly owing to the preexisting values and personality characteristics of those who enter medical and mental health fields as well as the values transmitted to them during their professional education.

Unfortunately, the relativity of harm is such that no clear rules can be promulgated, and it would even be difficult to set forth a decision tree when examining situations for the degree of harm. Thus, although nonmaleficence can be considered the bottom line, minimizing harm is often difficult, tricky, and context-dependent. However, professionals are advised to keep the goal of minimizing harm in mind, while also realizing that their own view of what is harmful may be inconsistent with the perspectives of other involved parties, especially if cultural differences exist.

Beneficence

In general, most people do not have a legal responsibility to help others. They may believe they have a moral responsibility, but the duty to "do good" is more internally than externally based in most situations. However, health and mental health professionals do have a duty to attempt to do good once they have entered into a professional relationship with an individual. Yet, just as it is difficult to define harm when speaking of nonmaleficence, it is often hard to determine what is "good" when discussing beneficence. What is perceived as "good" or "more good" is often dependent upon one's perspective and background.

Kitchener and Barret (2001, p. 51) highlighted the tension within the areas of beneficence and nonmaleficence as well as between these two principles when they said that, "At a minimum, beneficence requires that [providers] balance the goods that [may] result from their actions against the harm." They illustrated this balancing through the example of the famous *Tarasoff v. Regents of the University of California* (1976) decision, indicating that the court balanced the social goods of protecting potential victims versus the harms that might arise for the client because of taking some action (e.g., breaking confidentiality). Similar considerations regarding the balance of individual harms and societal good in the end-of-life arena could be the intertwined areas of cost of care during the last month or year of life and the possibility of rationing resources, and/or decisions based on medical "futility."

Thus, although beneficence is a separate principle from nonmaleficence, in reality the issues of doing good and minimizing harm must often be considered in concert. Balancing the amount and extent of good versus similar considerations in terms of harm can be complicated, especially in situations that literally involve life and death. Just as is the case with nonmaleficence, providers who do not consider cultural issues or who do not consult with others are likely to create more difficulties and minimize the chances of doing good.

Autonomy

The importance of autonomy within the majority U.S. culture and within the health and mental health environments cannot be overemphasized. Self-determination is a foundation for the way such critical issues as providing informed consent and assessing decision-making competence have been interpreted by the courts and implemented in practice.

Closely associated with the principle of autonomy in the majority culture is the idea of respect for the person. European Americans, especially men, tend to believe it is respectful to increase a person's autonomy or control. This perspective is not necessarily shared by members of other cultural groups or even by European American women. For these people, interdependence and shared decision making may be more important, and maximizing individual autonomy may actually not be the most respectful of the person and her or his best interests—from her or his perspective. Given these considerations, respect should be redefined in terms of the person's decision as opposed to the primacy of autonomy. Unfortunately, because many of the people in power, including those who are often decision makers in medical and mental health settings, are European American men, they may force their own values on others under the guise of "maximizing self-determination."

One way autonomy can be maximized without ignoring the importance of individual cultural values is by examining the process of decision making as opposed to the result. This idea has been discussed in the literature on legal competence (or, clinically speaking, "capacity") and health care decisions. The current standard of care in this area maximizes autonomy by focusing on how a person went about making a decision as opposed to whether the professional agrees with the decision (Grisso & Appelbaum, 1998). Thus, it actually can be respectful of autonomy to allow a person to decide to give up decision-making power and defer to others, such as the eldest child or a partner. On the other hand, it likely would be disrespectful of autonomy for a provider to overrule a competent person's decision to withhold or withdraw treatment just because the professional disagrees with the choice. Yet, just as the dying individual and loved ones should have their autonomy respected to the greatest degree possible, so should the providers, which may lead to the need to refer to another professional if disagreements over treatment decisions are unresolvable.

Regarding competence, one difficult area is decision making by children and adolescents—when is a nonadult able to make autonomous decisions in situations that may result in death (e.g., Powell, 1984)? Similar concerns have been expressed for people who have never had decision-making competence (e.g., someone with profound mental retardation), may be losing their competence (e.g., someone in the early stages of dementia), or who have lost competence and whose current actions seem to imply a different perspective from what was expressed before incompetence.

Perhaps the areas associated with autonomy where the tension is most obvious in the current end-of-life literature are related to whether there can be such a thing as "rational suicide" and whether it can be acceptable to aid a client in hastening death. These issues are discussed elsewhere in this book and have been the subject of intense debate in other books and journal articles and therefore will not be expanded upon here. However, it should be noted that there has been recent discussion of whether the clinical issues associated with decisions about "rational suicide" or "assisted suicide" are different from other decisions that may hasten death, such as withholding or withdrawing treatment (Quill, Lo, & Brock, 1997; Werth, 2000, in press-b). Further, concern has been expressed about the rationale for decisions of "medical futility" and their implications for vulnerable groups such as persons with disabilities (Werth, in press-a). All of these situations involve the issue of how to maximize autonomy of all the parties involved, along with balancing the principles of nonmaleficence and beneficence.

Justice

The principle of justice essentially refers to fairness regarding treatment of others and how goods and services are distributed. Issues of justice should be at the forefront of health and mental health providers' minds, given the significant issues associated with the cost of care, the vast numbers of individuals who have no or inadequate insurance, and discrimination in service provision. However, given the capitalistic nature of U.S. society, it can be difficult to balance concerns for justice with concerns for remaining fiscally solvent. In any event, the issues of who should receive treatment, what type of treatment, where, when, and for how long are all associated with the principle of justice.

One aspect of end-of-life care that has received attention is the amount of money expended during the last year or month of life. Issues of justice are implicitly, if not explicitly, a part of such discussions. Depending on one's perspective, it can be just or unjust to support efforts at curative care up until a person dies. A complicating factor in such analyses is the cultural belief system of the individuals involved. Because African Americans, for example, are more likely than European Americans to "want everything done" when they are ill (Werth, Blevins, Toussaint, & Durham, 2002), decisions to limit treatment or coverage for treatment based on life expectancy may be perceived as just by European Americans or by those who come from a financial perspective, but may be viewed as unjust and even discriminatory by African Americans and civil libertarians.

Issues of justice and discrimination are not only implicated in paying for services, they are also a part of other aspects of treatment provision (Werth et al., 2002). For example, substantial research indicates that members of ethnic minority groups are at a significant disadvantage when it comes to receiving optimal care for pain, treatment of life-threatening conditions, and referral for hospice care. Similarly, older adults may not be offered the same kind or degree of care as younger individuals.

Thus, although justice is supposed to be an underlying ethical principle, there are major barriers within U.S. society and its health care system, as well as among treatment providers themselves, to maximizing the fair distribution of services to all dying individuals and their loved ones. However, the presence of such barriers does not absolve professionals from attempting to act justly; in fact, the principle of justice would indicate that providers actually have the responsibility to work proactively to reduce the impact of these barriers. In doing so, the professionals likely will also be maximizing the principles of nonmaleficence, beneficence, and autonomy.

Fidelity

Although Beauchamp and Childress (2001) do not include fidelity as a core principle, instead relegating it to an aspect of the professional relationship, Kitchener (1984, 2000) decided that it deserved to be considered a meta-principle, given the importance of trust and loyalty in professional relationships. Because health and mental health professionals enter into fiduciary relationships with clients, they are expected to give precedence to clients/patients over people with whom they do not have such relationships.

Thus, in general, responsibilities to clients/patients take precedence over responsibilities to others and to society. As noted above, there are some exceptions and some balancing needs to take place, but usually the principle of fidelity means the professional must act to maintain and enhance the trust of the client/patient. The primary ways this is done are through truth-telling and maintaining confidentiality.

In end-of-life situations, truth-telling has not always been, and still may not be, the norm. There have been changes over time regarding the revelation of actual diagnoses and perceived prognoses. Combining the principles of fidelity and autonomy, and conforming to the expectations associated with informed consent, there has been a move toward informing people of their medical conditions, their available treatment options, and the implications of choosing or not choosing particular options (e.g., side effects). One aspect of this trend is the professionals' sense of the amount of time the individual may have related to experiencing symptoms and their exacerbation/elimination and/or time left to live. Although prognosis is not an exact science, research has indicated that physicians may not give the patient the most accurate information available, for a variety of reasons (Christakis, 1999). This lack of prognostic awareness has been demonstrated to have significant effects on treatment decisions and other decisions that may affect a person's self-perceived quality of life (Weeks et al., 1998).

Truth-telling is also important in terms of the types of treatments the professionals are willing or unwilling to provide and the types of decisions they will or will not support. For example, a person has the right to know whether a given provider will agree to provide terminal sedation in the event of uncontrollable suffering or will accept a decision by a competent individual to withhold or withdraw food and fluids. As was mentioned earlier, perhaps the most controversial area here is associated with "assisted suicide" in particular and hastening death more generally.

Another key component of fidelity is maintaining confidentiality. Of course, people must be informed of the limits of confidentiality in order to make informed decisions about what to reveal to providers, but once they have given informed consent, the choice about what they say is theirs. In end-of-life situations, although the provider may disagree with a person's decisions to talk to other people or not and what information, if any, to share with different people, the choices of a competent person should be respected. The dynamics of a circle of family, friends, and loved ones may mean that a person does not want to involve others at all or wants to do so in a different way than the provider believes she or he would want to do in a similar situation. For example, a gay man dying of an AIDS-related condition may refuse to inform his parents of his situation for any number of reasons, including rejection by them for his sexual orientation and illness or fear that they will challenge his wishes regarding advance directives and visitation. It is his right to make this decision, even if the provider is concerned that the parents will have a more difficult time grieving as a result of being excluded from their son's dying process.

In general, fidelity is one of the most basic aspects of the professional's relationship with clients/patients. But in end-of-life situations, the provider may find it challenging to adhere to the implications of this principle, especially regarding truth-telling and confidentiality. Yet, by examining issues of fidelity in concert with the other meta-principles of nonmaleficence, beneficence, autonomy, and justice, professionals can enhance the likelihood that their actions will foster trust and loyalty in the relationship.

Summary

The five ethical meta principles discussed here form the foundation for making judgments in clinical situations, including providing end-of-life care. Although it may be difficult to decide how to balance the principles, especially given the many perspectives involved and the influences of values and cultural background, providers who keep these principles in mind, and consult with knowledgeable colleagues, increase their chances of providing optimal care to dying individuals and their loved ones.

CONCLUSION

The philosophical principles of nonmaleficence, beneficence, autonomy, justice, and fidelity have significant implications for practice in end-of-life situations. These meta-principles supplement and complement professional ethics codes, agency policies and procedures, and state and federal laws. They are influenced by the provider's own values and cultural background and must be interpreted and implemented in light of the values and culture of the dying person and her or his loved ones. Because of the variability inherent in how the principles can be applied in a given situation, professionals should strongly consider following a specified decision-making model and are advised to incorporate consultation (and documentation) throughout the decision-making process.

Providing services to people who are dying and their loved ones can be a truly remarkable and life-affirming experience. However, there is the potential for strong emotions and beliefs to play a part in how the dying process unfolds. As a result, providers will likely face ethical dilemmas related to the type of care to provide, disagreements among people involved in the situation, and the involvement of the professional's own values. The five ethical meta-principles described in this chapter and elsewhere can help to increase the likelihood that the resolution of these dilemmas will minimize harm, maximize good, respect autonomy, maximize justice, and enhance fidelity, leading to the highest quality of life and best dying process possible. ■

James L. Werth, Jr. received his PhD in Counseling Psychology from Auburn University in 1995 and his Masters of Legal Studies from the University of Nebraska-Lincoln in 1999. He was the 1999-2000 American Psychological Association William A. Bailey AIDS Policy Congressional Fellow where he worked on aging and end-of-life issues in the office of United States Senator Ron Wyden (D-OR). He has been employed as an Assistant Professor in the Department of Psychology at The University of Akron since August 2000; he is also the pro bono psychologist for the local HIV services organization where he provides counseling and supervises graduate students. He has authored/co-authored over 50 articles and book chapters, edited/co-edited five special journal issues, and written/edited three books on end-of-life matters and/or HIV disease. He is the only person to have served on all of the American Psychological Association's major end-of-life work groups.

REFERENCES

Barret, B., Kitchener, K. S., & Burris, S. (2001a). A decision model for ethical dilemmas in HIV-related psychotherapy and its application in the case of Jerry. In J. R. Anderson & B. Barret (Eds.), *Ethics in HIV-related psychotherapy: Clinical decision making in complex cases* (pp. 133–154). Washington, DC: American Psychological Association.

Barret, B., Kitchener, K. S., & Burris, S. (2001b). Suicide and confidentiality with the client with advanced AIDS: The case of Phil. In J. R. Anderson & B. Barret (Eds.), *Ethics in HIV-related psychotherapy: Clinical decision making in complex cases* (pp. 299–314). Washington, DC: American Psychological Association.

Battin, M. P. (1994). *The least worst death: Essays in bioethics on the end of life.* New York: Oxford University Press.

Beauchamp, T., & Childress, J. (1979). *Principles of biomedical ethics.* Oxford, England: Oxford University Press.

Beauchamp, T., & Childress, J. (2001). *Principles of biomedical ethics* (5th ed.). New York: Oxford University Press.

Christakis, N. A. (1999). *Death foretold: Prophecy and programs in medical care.* Chicago: University of Chicago.

Eversole, T., Kitchener, K. S., & Burris, S. (2001). Multiple roles with a dying client: The case of Pat. In J. R. Anderson & B. Barret (Eds.), *Ethics in HIV-related psychotherapy: Clinical decision making in complex cases* (pp. 277–297). Washington, DC: American Psychological Association.

Grisso, T., & Appelbaum, P. S. (1998). *Assessing competence to consent to treatment: A guide for physicians and other health professionals.* New York: Oxford University Press.

Kitchener, K. S. (1984). Intuition, critical evaluation and ethical principles: The foundation for ethical decisions in counseling psychology. *The Counseling Psychologist, 12*(3), 43–55.

Kitchener, K. S. (2000). *Foundations of ethical practice, research, and teaching in psychology.* Mahwah, NJ: Lawrence Erlbaum Associates.

Kitchener, K. S., & Barret, B. (2001). Thinking well about doing good in HIV-related practice: A model of ethical analysis. In J. R. Anderson & B. Barret (Eds.), *Ethics in HIV-related psychotherapy: Clinical decision making in complex cases* (pp. 43–59). Washington, DC: American Psychological Association.

Powell, C. J. (1984). Ethical principles and issues of competence in counseling adolescents. *The Counseling Psychologist, 12,* 57–68.

Quill, T. E., Lo, B., & Brock, D. W. (1997). Palliative options of last resort: A comparison of voluntarily stopping eating and drinking, terminal sedation, physician-assisted suicide, and voluntary active euthanasia. *JAMA, 278,* 2099–2104.

Tarasoff v. Regents of the University of California, 13 Cal.3d 117, 529 P.2d 553 (1974), vacated 17 Cal.3d 425, 551 P.2d 334 (1976).

Weeks, J. C., Cook, F., O'Day, S. J., Peterson, L. M., Wenger, N., Reding, D., et al. (1998). Relationship between cancer patients' prediction of prognosis and their treatment preferences. *JAMA, 279,* 1709–1714.

Werth, J. L., Jr. (2000). How do the mental health issues differ in the withholding/withdrawing of treatment versus assisted death? *Omega, 41,* 259–278.

Werth, J. L., Jr. (2002). Legal and ethical considerations for mental health professionals related to end-of-life care and decision-making. *American Behavioral Scientist, 46,* 373–388.

Werth, J. L., Jr. (in press-a). Concerns about decisions related to withholding/withdrawing life-sustaining treatment and futility for persons with disabilities. *Journal of Disability Policy Studies.*

Werth, J. L., Jr. (in press-b). The relationships among clinical depression, suicide, and other ways that death may be hastened. *Behavioral Sciences and the Law.*

Werth, J. L., Jr., Blevins, D., Toussaint, K., & Durham, M. R. (2002). The influence of cultural diversity on end-of-life care and decisions. *American Behavioral Scientist, 46,* 204–219.

Werth, J. L., Jr., & Kleespies, P. M. (in press). Ethical considerations in providing psychological services in end-of-life care. In J. L. Werth, Jr. & D. Blevins (Eds.), *Psychosocial issues near the end of life: A resource for professional care providers.* Washington, DC: American Psychological Association.

CHAPTER 2

Religious, Spiritual, and Ideological Perspectives on Ethics at the End of Life

Cynthia B. Cohen

The power of medicine to sustain life has grown steadily since the 1960s. The spread of the use of such life-prolonging medical technologies as respirators and artificial nutrition and hydration has made the time and circumstances of death increasingly a matter of human choice and control. As a result, concern has been growing in our society, especially among those who are aging, that individuals will eventually die in pain and suffering, dependent on machines. The basic question is, ought we to do what we can do? That is, should we sustain the lives of those near death for as long as possible, or should we recognize that there is a time to let go and allow them to die in peace and comfort?

Religion has served for centuries as one of the major standard-bearers on matters of life and death. Therefore, it is not surprising that when these sorts of questions arose in the 1960s and 1970s, religious groups had the resources with which to respond. Many religious bodies have developed specific views about these questions and are in a position to shape the beliefs of their members and others about the ethics of making difficult decisions near the end of life. It follows that if we are to respond adequately to the beliefs and feelings of patients who face death and their families, we need to understand the responses of the religious bodies to which many belong to certain ethical issues arising near the end of life. Our purpose here is not to describe the views of every known religious tradition about such matters, but to focus on themes and issues that cut across the teachings of many religious traditions, pointing out their commonalities and their differences.

This chapter has an additional purpose. In the 1960s, religious thinkers were joined by physicians, scientists, lawyers, and politicians in wrestling with difficult questions about the ethical use of life-sustaining treatments. As they mixed with one another, some began to clash openly, resulting in a passionate and increasingly polarized debate about appropriate treatment for the critically ill and dying. Our second purpose is to trace how the ferment among a variety of groups caught up in ideological divisions about end-of-life matters has influenced many religious bodies, and how, in turn, these religious bodies have influenced politics, medicine, and the law. We will consider ways in which the views of religious groups were reinforced by social currents and how these views could factor into the thinking of patients, families, and health care providers.

WHO SHOULD MAKE TREATMENT DECISIONS

Toward the end of the 1960s, two Protestant theologians, Paul Ramsey (1970) and Joseph Fletcher (1954, 1979), initiated a public debate about end-of-life issues that set the tone for later discussions. Among the major questions they explored was who should decide what sort of treatment to provide to those who are seriously ill and near death.

Ramsey argued that individual freedom of choice is important, but that people are more than choosers. They are also "members of one another"—members of families and communities, some of which are not of their own choosing. Decisions about difficult matters near the end of life are not exclusively individual matters, he declared, but should incorporate the shared beliefs and values of those within the circle surrounding patients. With this in mind, he held that choices about treatment should be made by patients in company with their families, physicians, and religious counselors.

Fletcher, in contrast, viewed freedom as the capacity of individuals to will what they choose without constraint or coercion. He contended that decisions about treatment should be made by individual patients, for they have their own conceptions of the good and should be free to manage their treatment on that basis. Individual freedom of choice was at the heart of Fletcher's approach.

Clearly, they differed in that Ramsey took into account the familial, religious, and social setting that he believed is integral to the moral identity of individuals. Fletcher saw patients as discrete individuals who are entitled to control their own lives according to their beliefs, values, personality, and style. Many religious commentators weighed in on Ramsey's side, for his view of persons as social creatures, rather than self-defined atoms, was more in keeping with theirs. Yet they recognized that it was important to understand the respects in which Ramsey and Fletcher were of a common mind. Even though they gave different weight to patient's family and social setting, both theologians underscored the moral significance of human freedom and both declared that in the end, the patient should be the final decision maker.

In the first major legal case in the country to address the use of life-sustaining treatment, the Supreme Court of New Jersey followed the road paved by Ramsey. In the case of Karen Ann Quinlan (In re Quinlan, 1976), the court made the father of a young woman in a persistent vegetative state who had been maintained on a respirator for some time the decision maker for his daughter. In its decision, the court emphasized the role of families and religious communities in making treatment choices for their incapacitated members. Interestingly, it did not seek to learn what Ms. Quinlan herself would have wanted done about the respirator that was enabling her to breathe. It was her identity as a social being—a person who was intimately connected to those who had raised her and cared for her— that the court honored. This decision was consistent with Ramsey's view, although he was not cited by the court in the Quinlan case.

The mixed public response to this court decision jolted many religious groups into refining statements they already had formulated regarding end-of-life issues and developing new ones, particularly regarding the question of who should decide whether to provide or withdraw life-sustaining treatment from critically ill patients. Ramsey's thought can be seen behind several of the policies and statements that they subsequently developed. These policies stress the interconnectedness of patients with families and religious and social communities. For instance, a commission of the Evangelical Lutheran Church states, in language reminiscent of Ramsey, that

> [t]he patient is a person in relationship, not an isolated individual. His or her decisions should take others into account and be made in supportive consultation with family members, close friends, pastor, and health care professionals (Evangelical Lutheran Church in America, 1992).

Similarly, Episcopal commentators observe that "patients are free to choose their form of treatment, but are bound to do so in ways that are rooted in their lives in community and in God's purposes" (Cohen & Smith, 2004, p. 34). Roman Catholic thinkers also acknowledge that persons are integrally connected with family and community, and maintain that competent patients have the authority to make final decisions about their treatment (O'Rourke & Boyle, 1999). Islamic thought moves along these same lines in that it maintains that competent persons are responsible for making final treatment decisions. When patients do not have decision-making capacity, a leading Muslim commentator indicates, decisions should be made by close family members or religious and lay leaders in the community, who act as guardians for the patient (Sachedina, 2004). Each of these traditions holds that the family and community surrounding patients should be closely involved in treatment decisions, but that ultimately it is patients who should make the final choice about treatment or nontreatment when possible.

Although the Quinlan case did not, as is often mistakenly believed, make the preferences of the patient the standard for treatment decisions, when the public saw pictures of a comatose woman maintained on a ventilator—presumably indefinitely—it reacted with concern and even horror. Many began to call for the legalization of advance directives for health care. These documents enable individuals to express their preferences about end-of-life care in advance of serious illness, when they have the capacity to make decisions. A movement known as the "patients' rights" movement, whose aim was to put patients in charge of their own medical treatment, received an immense boost from the Quinlan case. States began to pass laws providing for the use of such advance directives as "living wills" and durable powers for health care, and today such laws have been adopted in every state. Moreover, in 1990, Congress passed a federal law requiring all health care facilities receiving Medicare or Medicaid funding to inform patients of their right to develop advance directives for medical treatment. Thus, although the Quinlan court took a position that echoed Ramsey's view of the individual as a social being, the right of individuals to make their own treatment choices, so important in the thought of Fletcher, came to the fore after Quinlan.

Here, too, many religious groups have entered the fray and actively supported the use of advance directives. The Evangelical Lutheran Church, the United Church of Christ, and the Islamic tradition, to name just a few, approve of the use of advance directives. Indeed, the Episcopal Church has published a book that specifically informs members about how to develop advance directives for health care and also provides a religious service for a time when life-sustaining treatment is withdrawn (Committee on Medical Ethics, 1995).

WHETHER TO WITHHOLD OR WITHDRAW LIFE-SUSTAINING TREATMENT

It is not just who should make end-of-life treatment decisions, but also what treatment patients approaching death and their families should receive that has been of concern to various religious bodies. The phrase "the right to die" began to be heard more frequently in the 1970s and 1980s as the patients' rights movement expanded. It referred to the right of patients to stop life-prolonging treatment that was considered no longer beneficial. While many religious groups were sympathetic to the concept behind the right to die, some were concerned that this movement might encourage the wrongful removal of life-sustaining treatment. These groups entered into the public policy arena to voice opposition to bills in state legislatures that would allow the use of advance directives and the withdrawal of certain life-sustaining treatments from patients deemed near death.

A significant concern of many religious groups was whether stopping treatment for patients near the end of life would amount to killing. Most of them have reached the conclusion that forgoing the use of life-sustaining treatment for patients nearing the end of life is a way of allowing them to die, rather than killing. Continued treatment in such cases, they maintain, will provide patients little or no benefit, since it cannot reverse their underlying progression toward death. When treatment is discontinued in such instances, it is the disease, rather than the withdrawal of treatment, that leads to the patient's death.

Some religious groups that accept this view have been influenced by a distinction made originally within the Roman Catholic tradition between "ordinary" treatment—treatment that is more beneficial than burdensome to a patient—and "extraordinary" treatment whose burdens outweigh its benefits (Tollefsen & Boyle, 2004). It is obligatory to provide ordinary treatment, but it is permissible to remove or not begin extraordinary treatment. It is important to recognize that the difference between ordinary and extraordinary treatment is not between usual and unusual treatment. What is at issue is not how usual it is to use a certain medical technology, but whether its use is beneficial or burdensome to the specific patient. The sorts of burdens that may be taken into consideration include whether the patient's condition can be reversed, whether the treatment would create great pain and suffering for the patient, whether it would be seriously disfiguring, and whether it might bankrupt the patient and his or her family.

A wide range of religious bodies in this country accept the distinction between ordinary and extraordinary treatment. For example, Stanley Harakas, an Orthodox Christian thinker, states that "When, however, the major physical systems have broken down, and there does not seem to be any reasonable expectation that they can be restored, Orthodox Christians may properly allow extraordinary mechanical devices to be removed" (Harakas, 1990). The Islamic view is that it is permissible for the patient, either through a prior living will or his or her immediate family or supreme legal authority (*hakim al-shar'*), to refuse any treatment that prolongs the process of dying (Sachedina, 2004). This view is consistent with the reasoning behind the distinction between ordinary and extraordinary treatment, although those specific terms are not used.

Protestant denominations, almost without exception, consider whether treatment would be proportionately beneficial (ordinary) or disproportionately burdensome (extraordinary) for patients who are terminally ill. The United Methodist Church, for instance, states, "There is no moral or religious obligation to use these when they impose undue burdens or only extend the process of dying. Dying persons and their families thus have the liberty to discontinue treatments when they cease to be of benefit to the patient" (United Methodist Church, 2000). Many other Protestant bodies agree with this view, although some tend to define terminal illness more narrowly than others.

There are differences within Judaism about whether to recognize the benefits and burdens of treatment to those who are approaching death and, indeed, just when someone can be said to be approaching death. Traditional Jewish sources draw a line between sustaining a person's life, which is required, and prolonging the process of dying, which is not. Thus, J. David Bleich, an Orthodox rabbi, urges that medical treatments should be administered to patients as long as there is reason to think that they will save their lives (Bleich, 1979). Only when patients have reached the state of *goseis*, or are on their deathbed, which occurs three days before death according to Orthodox Jewish teaching, can aggressive medical treatment be ended.

The Reform branch of Judaism, however, rejects a reading of the tradition that maintains that human life must be sustained until near the point of death. Elliott N. Dorff, a Reform rabbi, holds that the definition of *goseis* should take account of the fact that we can maintain patients on machines for long periods of time. *Goseis*, he argues, should be used to refer to those who have an irreversible, terminal illness (Dorff, 2000). Once they have been so diagnosed, aggressive medical treatment may be ended, even if it is effective in maintaining vital organs. The paramount concern in determining the course of therapy for those who are *goseis* or terminally ill, Dorff holds, should be patient benefit. In this approach, the Reform tradition implicitly accepts a distinction between ordinary and extraordinary care. Some Conservative and Orthodox rabbis have also moved in this direction (Goldfarb, 1976; Jakobovits, 1975).

The Hindu tradition accepts that life-sustaining treatment may be withdrawn from those near death for a different reason. Death, in this tradition, is a passage to another life, and how individuals face illness and death will help determine the conditions of their next life. Those who are dying should be allowed to go peacefully, since medical technology that sustains life is of little value to them. They can take solace as they die in the expectation of rebirth (Crawford, 2004).

Religious groups became increasingly involved in publicly advocating their beliefs about the use of life-sustaining treatment. They differed not so much about whether to withdraw such treatment from the dying as about which treatments could be withdrawn and whether the power to withdraw them could lead to abuse. They contacted lawmakers and congressional committees to express their views and filed amicus briefs in relevant legal cases. A particularly vexing issue they confronted was whether to remove tube feedings from patients near death.

WHETHER TO FORGO ARTIFICIAL NUTRITION AND HYDRATION

Many of those who might readily be prepared to stop technological treatment for a dying person are inclined to feel differently about stopping artificial nutrition and hydration (providing food and fluids intravenously or through a nasogastric or stomach tube). In part, this is because they are uncertain whether tube feedings amount to a form of medical treatment that can be withdrawn when no longer beneficial or a form of care that they are always obliged to provide. Feeding family, friends, and strangers has been a potent symbol of what it means to care for one another, and they are therefore reluctant to end it (Callahan, 1988). They view the provision of nutrition as morally necessary, whether it is provided by means of a simple cup and spoon or an invasive line into the stomach. Others emphasize the fact that the nutrition and hydration in the situations at issue are provided by a technological means, not by hand; this is the crucial moral factor for them. If it would be right to stop medical treatment for a specific patient near death, they maintain, it would be equally acceptable to stop artificial nutrition and hydration.

The public debate about the use of artificial nutrition and hydration for those who are seriously ill became especially heated when the United States Supreme Court handed down another famous legal decision, concerning Nancy Cruzan, a young woman in a persistent vegetative state (*Cruzan v. Director, Missouri Department of Health*, 1990). It affirmed the constitutional right to refuse life-sustaining medical treatment, but ruled that in Ms. Cruzan's case, evidence that she would have wanted to have artificial nutrition and hydration withdrawn did not meet the standards of evidence of the state of Missouri. Her treatment therefore had to continue, the court ruled. This case heightened the growing fear of many that they might be kept alive in pain and suffering by machines and tubes if they should suffer a devastating illness. When a friend subsequently provided evidence to a Missouri state court that Ms. Cruzan's earlier oral statements indicated that she would not wish to be kept alive by artificial means, the state court ruled that the tube feedings could be withdrawn. Ms. Cruzan subsequently died. Her death led to major demonstrations by those who maintained that withdrawing artificial nutrition amounted to starving her to death. Representatives of certain religious bodies were prominent among those protesting.

Religious objections to the withdrawal of artificial nutrition and hydration played a role in another case that has gained great publicity. In 2003, the relatives of Terri Schiavo, a young woman who had suffered a brain injury in 1990 and exhibited no cognitive function, had a serious dispute about her treatment that triggered actions by officials in all three branches of Florida's state government. Her husband had been appointed her guardian, and in 1998 he asked that her feeding tube be removed. The lower courts in Florida ruled in favor of removing the feeding tube, and the Florida Supreme Court refused to reverse this decision (*Schindler v. Schiavo*, 2003). This decision precipitated major protests from a range of groups, including some religious bodies, on grounds that tube feedings are no different from feedings with a cup and spoon and ending them would amount to starving her to death. The protest level and political pressure was so great that in 2003, at the request of the governor, the Florida legislature passed a statute that applied only to Mrs. Schiavo. It empowered the governor to overrule the court and order that her feeding tube be reinserted. This law is currently being appealed on grounds that it is unconstitutional.

Such events have made the question of whether to provide or forgo artificial nutrition and hydration for those nearing the end of life increasingly contentious. This is especially the case for many religious traditions, in which feeding people has deep spiritual significance. Thus, it is not surprising that they are deeply divided about this question and feel called to address it in public.

Within the Roman Catholic tradition, the question of whether to withhold or withdraw artificial nutrition and hydration from patients in various circumstances has not been definitively answered. The U.S. Bishops' Pro-Life Committee stated in 1992, "We hold for a presumption in favor of providing medically assisted nutrition and hydration to patients who need it, which presumption would yield in cases where such procedures have no medically reasonable hope of sustaining life or pose excessive risks of burdens." However, others within this tradition are strongly opposed to the withdrawal of tube feedings, particularly when patients are in a persistent vegetative state. Some Roman Catholic commentators consider the withdrawal of such feedings a form of intentional killing (Grisez, 1989). This question has been raised repeatedly in public, especially in connection with several legal cases in the United States. In 2004, the Pope stated in a speech that did not carry the authoritative weight of an encyclical that patients in a persistent vegetative state must be provided with nutrition and hydration. "The administration of food and water, even when delivered using artificial means, always represents a natural method of preserving life and not a medical act," he declared. He went on to say, "Its use, furthermore, should be considered, in principle ordinary and proportionate, and as such morally obligatory . . . " (Wooden, 2004). Some take this statement to mean that tube feedings and other forms of artificial nutrition and hydration are always to be considered "ordinary" forms of care and hence required. However, others maintain that it does not mean that the use of a feeding tube is obligatory in every circumstance (Thavis, 2004).

Some Protestant groups state unequivocally that it is wrong to consider the provision of food and water by medical means to be extraordinary care. Thus, the Southern Baptist Convention discourages any designation of food and/or water as "extraordinary care" for patients (Christian Life Commission Board, 1987). Similarly, Gilbert Meilaender, a commentator from the Lutheran Church-Missouri Synod, denies that the provision of food and drink, by whatever means, is medical care. "It seems, rather, to be the sort of care that all human beings owe each other" (Meilaender, 1984, p. 12).

The Islamic tradition is of one mind with these Protestant groups in that it condemns the withdrawal of artificial nutrition and hydration from patients. The Islamic Medical Association of North America holds that when treatment becomes futile and is no longer mandatory, "the basic human rights of hydration, nutrition, nursing and pain relief cannot be withheld" (Medical Ethics Committee, 1997, p. 100). These are "ordinary life needs" that are not to be categorized as treatment (Hathout, 1994).

However, those in several other Protestant denominations hold that there are times when tube feedings can be burdensome or extraordinary because they create pain and suffering in patients near death who may be unable to assimilate such feedings. For instance, an End-of-Life Task Force of the General Convention of the Episcopal Church observed about the use of life-sustaining treatment for those approaching death,

> Certainly, depriving the weak of needed food and drink is a paradigmatic case of individual and social sin within the Christian tradition. Even so, we must recognize that having a synthetic protein compound pumped directly into the intestine by skilled medical personnel is not the same as eating and drinking with friends. It is a qualitatively different act from feeding a patient with a cup and a spoon. Therefore, the task force maintains that sustaining a person by artificial nutrition and hydration constitutes a medical intervention . . . . As a form of medical treatment, it may be declined or ended when it is burdensome or futile (Cohen et al., 2000, p. 43).

The Evangelical Lutheran Church (1992) has come to a similar conclusion.

Sharp disagreements persist today among different religious bodies about the conditions under which it is ethical to withdraw artificial nutrition and hydration. This issue has become one of the major focal points of conflict and confrontation in the right to die debate. Religious groups have come down on both sides of this debate, and some, triggered by the Cruzan and Schiavo cases, have brought their respective statements and policies into the political struggles surrounding this issue.

WHETHER TO PROVIDE ASSISTED SUICIDE AND EUTHANASIA

An equally contentious question has emerged over the last several decades: Should physicians provide terminally ill patients with drugs that they can use to end their lives or kill dying patients who request euthanasia? In asking this question, the right to die movement has gone beyond issues related to the withdrawal of life-sustaining treatment to consider those associated with actions that would directly end the lives of patients. Some religious groups that have decried both assisted suicide and euthanasia have fought to oppose the legalization of these practices. They were particularly affronted by several events in the 1990s that centered on physician-assisted suicide.

At that time, Dr. Jack Kevorkian tapped into the fears of an aging society about losing control of care at the end of life with his well-publicized acts of assisting patients to kill themselves by means of his "suicide machine." Those who feared a slow death accompanied by the steady loss of mental faculties saw assisted suicide as a way of taking control of their lives—and their deaths. Some who had heard of Kevorkian contacted him to ask for assistance in ending their lives, and this resulted in the deaths of several people.

In the wake of the publicity given to Kevorkian's acts, including one involving euthanasia, for which he was convicted of murder and sent to prison, several states passed laws prohibiting assisted suicide. The state of Oregon, in contrast, conducted a referendum that resulted in the legalization of assisted suicide for the first time in the United States. In a 1997 ruling, the U.S. Supreme Court refused to interfere with these state laws, leaving the door open for other states to enact laws for or against assisted suicide (*Vacco v. Quill*, 1997; *Washington v. Glucksberg*, 1997). Some religious bodies were prominent in their opposition to Kevorkian's acts and the Oregon law allowing physician-assisted suicide.

The major religious traditions teach that it is wrong to kill oneself or another and therefore generally reject assisted suicide and euthanasia. The debate between the two Protestant theologians, Ramsey and Fletcher, in the 1970s once again foreshadows the main positions of various religious traditions on this issue.

Ramsey asserted that it is wrong as a matter of principle to choose assisted suicide or euthanasia. Our lives are not our own to do with as we please, but are a gift that we should not thrust back into the face of the Creator. To end the lives of those near death through assisted suicide or euthanasia is to abandon them (Ramsey, 1970). Fletcher, in contrast, held that we should not follow a set of abstract moral principles that ignore the plight of the individual person, but instead should do that which produces the best, most loving consequences for that person (1966). Among the choices that individuals could appropriately consider as they came near the end of their lives, Fletcher asserted, was whether to take their own lives or to ask others to do this for them.

Many religious traditions oppose assisted suicide and euthanasia on grounds akin to those set out by Ramsey. What is at stake is not a matter of individual choice, as Fletcher would have had it, but of divine dominion over life, they declare. Thus, the Roman Catholic Church, even more starkly than Ramsey, condemns assisted suicide and euthanasia and equates them with murder (Sacred Congregation for the Doctrine of the Faith, 1980). The Jewish tradition also strongly opposes assisted suicide and euthanasia. All four branches of Judaism maintain that

> The sanctity of human life prescribes that, in any situation short of self-defense or martyrdom, human life be treated as an end in itself. It may thus not be terminated or shortened because of considerations of the patient's convenience or usefulness, or even our sympathy with the suffering of the patient. Thus euthanasia may not be performed either in the interest of the patient or of anyone else (Feldman & Rosner, 1984).

Physicians, in particular, may do nothing positive to hasten death, not even close a patient's eyes (Freehof, 1969).

Assisted suicide and euthanasia are viewed as wrong in the Islamic tradition as well (Medical Ethics Committee, 1997). Allah is the creator of life and is the one who decides when it should end. Mercy killing and assisted suicide for reasons of compassion are unacceptable. "When means of preventing or alleviating pain fall short, this spiritual dimension can be very effectively called upon to support the patient who believes that accepting and standing unavoidable pain will be to his or her credit in the hereafter . . . " (Hathout, 1994).

Although the Protestant tradition also generally rejects assisted suicide and euthanasia, it has been reluctant to condemn those who take their own lives. The accepted view that emerged out of the Reformation was that those who commit suicide should be entrusted to God (Ferngren, 1989). Yet the Protestant tradition is more divided about this issue than many other religious denominations.

The Lutheran Church-Missouri Synod exemplifies those Protestants who take a stand against the use of euthanasia without exception. It asserts that this practice is contrary to God's word and will and therefore cannot be condoned. "[S]uffering has a positive purpose and value in God's economy and is not to be avoided at all costs" (Lutheran Church-Missouri Synod, 1979, p. 61). The Disciples of Christ Church at first seems to move in the direction of leaving this question a matter of individual choice, for it refuses to "provide a systematic blueprint" for personal behavior because doing so would abridge individual freedom. However, it goes on to assert that it is murder to shorten life, even at an individual's request. It states that the reasons often cited for allowing euthanasia—that a patient is suffering and is terminally ill—are nullified by the positive significance of suffering in the Bible (Cummins, 1981).

In the past few decades, however, several Protestant churches have issued statements that appear to signal that they are more open to euthanasia, and presumably assisted suicide, for terminally ill patients in extreme pain. For instance, the Presbyterian Church stated that

"Active euthanasia" is extremely difficult to defend morally. There are, however, extreme circumstances in which we may have to at least raise the question of a fundamental conflict of obligations . . . the conflict between doing no harm and protecting from harm has reference to one and the same individual (Presbyterian Church in the United States, 1995).

Methodists participating in a dialogue with Roman Catholic representatives in 1986 held that under certain circumstances euthanasia "might be an ethically permissible action" (United Methodist Church and National Conference of Catholic Bishops, 1986).

Other Protestant denominations have rejected assisted suicide and euthanasia on different grounds from those presented thus far. A task force of the Episcopal Church, for instance, states about those who face extreme pain and suffering near death,

The End of Life Task Force does not support the cruel extension of such suffering but instead calls out for its alleviation. Where there are drugs available to hand to a despairing person near death so that he or she can commit suicide, there are also drugs available to provide to that person that will afford relief from pain and allow a peaceful death . . . there should be no need for anyone to undergo radical suffering near the end of life. The way in which to address such terrible suffering is to eliminate it, rather than eliminate the person who undergoes it (Cohen et al., 2000, p. 57).

The task force here rejects two beliefs: that assisted suicide and euthanasia should be denied because extreme suffering deepens the Christian life, and that assisted suicide and euthanasia provide the only available means of alleviating severe pain at the end of life. Instead, it maintains that gratuitous suffering can twist, rather than enrich, the Christian life and that medicine has the means to alleviate extreme pain at the end of life and should use them, making assisted suicide and euthanasia unnecessary.

Hindu thought is wary of acts that would destroy life, such as assisted suicide and euthanasia. One Hindu commentator rejects euthanasia because it would interrupt the working out of karma, which has its origins in ignorance about the nature of reality, in the patient's life. Unless a person's karma terminates with natural death, it will have to be purged in the next life (Desai, 1989). However, another commentator maintains about Hindu thought that

> [I]n rare cases it is morally permissible for a spiritually elevated person to [choose the precise moment of his death] . . . with the help of a doctor, should he find himself terminally ill and in persistent pain. The individual knows that today the mind can control his body, but tomorrow his body will control his mind. Excruciating suffering may rob him of the equanimity he cherishes for his final moments of life. Euthanasia ensures a merciful death . . . (Crawford, 2004, p. 206).

On similar grounds, Buddhist thought maintains that it would be futile to request euthanasia. A human life does not end in physical death but continues, and its karma, both good and bad, is carried with it into the future, making assisted suicide and euthanasia irrelevant (Lesco, 1986).

One of the more effective arguments of religious groups opposed to assisted suicide and euthanasia was that such acts would be unnecessary if adequate hospice care were available to more of those who are terminally ill. Many religious traditions have wholeheartedly endorsed hospice, taking it as self-evident that when terminally ill persons receive assurance that they will enter hospice care, with its physical, psychological, social, and spiritual dimensions, they are less apt to want to kill themselves or be killed. Indeed, the state of Oregon has increased access to hospice since passing the act legalizing assisted suicide, and fewer than 1% of terminally patients in that state have requested assisted suicide on average each year, in part because they know that they can have access to hospice.

Although it was considered socially taboo in the 1970s to discuss hospice care, when some within the right to die movement began to promote assisted suicide and euthanasia as a way of ending life in the 1990s, this brought hospice as an alternative into public view and conversation. In the philosophy of hospice, we find, in an interesting final twist, that the views of Ramsey and Fletcher turn round to join one another, in that both were sympathetic to the hospice movement and argued that dying persons should not be abandoned.

DYING WELL AS A CIVIC ISSUE

Since the 1970s, religious groups have addressed ethical issues that arise for those approaching death in ways that have anticipated and illuminated the concerns of their members. They have generally accepted the withdrawal of life-sustaining treatment from those who are terminally ill, although they have differed in how they define terminal illness and when to withdraw treatment. Their statements about stopping treatment have served to allay the fears of many of their members that they might die attached to machines. Their views about forgoing artificial nutrition and hydration in those approaching death, which range from complete prohibition to complete acceptance, have served to assure their followers that they have carefully considered this question and responded with sound theological answers. Further, nearly all religious groups advocate the use of adequate pain relief for those near the end of life, so that their members need not picture themselves dying in great pain and misery. They are essentially unified in their rejection of assisted suicide and euthanasia, although several denominations leave room for these practices in the exceptional situation where a dying person would face great pain if his or her life were not ended speedily. Again, their members can find definitive answers from their religious leaders on this question so that they are not left hanging in uncertainty. Moreover, members are reassured by the strong support that religious denominations have given to hospice care.

Several religious bodies in the United States have played an active role in bringing their positions to the attention of the public, particularly when controversial events and legal decisions related to end-of-life care have roiled public debate. They have attempted to tailor their explanations of their positions to secular concerns while being true to their deepest beliefs. As their views have come to public attention, it has become obvious that their positions about several end-of-life issues exhibit the pluralism char-acteristic of American religiosity. For this very reason, religious positions about end-of-life issues do not tend to translate well into legislation, which requires a certain degree of agreement. Nevertheless, religious bodies have often enriched public conversation with ways of thinking and believing that touch on many people's deepest convictions. Unfortunately, at other times, reflecting the larger cultural struggles within our society, they have helped to polarize that conversation, for they have presented their positions in ways that are not open to the voices of those who dissent. When that occurs, many people stop listening, stop discussing, and lose sight of important considerations related to care for those approaching the end of life.

The ethical issues that arise at the end of life are weighty enough to be treated with something more than dueling hyperbole. A significant strength of our society has been that it adapts to changing conditions as a result of open and receptive discussion. The various religious groups in our country can play a prominent role in efforts to restore civility and balance to public conversations about end-of-life issues. They can help to restore civil public dialogue and the kind of politics in which debate and tolerance of opposing views are respected. This does not mean that they should forgo challenging prevailing views and arguments, but that they must engage the shared values of our society of diverse faiths and needs. ■

Cynthia B. Cohen, PhD JD, is Senior Research Fellow at the Kennedy Institute of Ethics at Georgetown University in Washington, D.C. She received a doctorate in philosophy from Columbia University, a law degree from the University of Michigan, and an undergraduate degree from Barnard College. Her publications include five books that she has authored or edited and over 100 articles on ethical issues that arise at the beginning and end of life and several in between. Dr. Cohen is a member of the Working Group on Research on the Nearly and Newly Dead at Emory University, the Working Group on Human Dignity of the American Association for the Advancement of Science, the Stem Cell Oversight Committee of the Canadian Institutes of Health, and the Human Genetics Committee of the National Council of Churches. She is an elected Fellow of The Hastings Center in New York and has been awarded an Honorary Doctor of Humane Letters degree by Virginia Theological Seminary.

REFERENCES

Bleich, J. D. (1979). The obligation to heal in the Judaic tradition: A comparative analysis. In F. Rosner & J. D. Bleich (Eds.), *Jewish bioethics* (pp. 1–44). New York: Sanhedrin Press.

Callahan, D. (1988). Commentary on too sick to eat: The case of Joseph. In C. B. Cohen (Ed.), *Casebook on the termination of life-sustaining treatment and the care of the dying* (pp. 56–58). Bloomington and Indianapolis, IN: Indiana University.

Christian Life Commission Board, Southern Baptist Church. (1987). *Policy and procedures manual of the Christian Life Commission of the Southern Baptist Church* (p. 3). Retrieved on August 20, 2004, from http://www.sbc.net.

Cohen, C. B., & Smith, D. H. (2004). Bioethics in the Episcopal tradition. In J. F. Peppin, M. J. Cherry, & A. Iltis (Eds.), *The annals of bioethics: Religious perspectives in bioethics* (pp. 31–51). London and New York: Taylor and Francis.

Cohen, C. B., Heller, J. C., Jennings, B., Morgan, E. F. M., Scott, D. A., Sedgwick, T. F., & Smith, D. H. (2000). *Faithful living, faithful dying. Anglican reflections on end of life care.* Harrisburg, PA: Morehouse.

Committee on Medical Ethics, Episcopal Diocese of Washington. (1995). *Before you need them: Advance directives for health care.* Cincinnati, OH: Forward Movement.

Crawford, C. (2004). Hindu bioethics. In J. F. Peppin, M. J. Cherry, & A. Iltis (Eds.), *The annals of bioethics: Religious perspectives in bioethics* (pp. 189–209). London and New York: Taylor and Francis.

Cruzan v. Director, Missouri Department of Health, 110 S. Ct. 2841 (1990).

Cummins, D. D. (1981). *Handbook for today's disciples. Cited in Active euthanasia, religion and the public debate* (p. 55). Chicago: The Park Ridge Center.

Desai, P. N. (1989). *Health and medicine in the Hindu tradition.* New York: Crossroad.

Dorff, E. N. (2000). End-stage medical care: Halakhic concepts and values. In A. Mackler (Ed.), *Life and death responsibilities in Jewish biomedical ethics* (pp. 309–337). New York: The Jewish Theological Seminary of America.

Evangelical Lutheran Church in America Church Council. (1992). *End of life decisions.* Retrieved August 20, 2004, from http://www.elca.org/socialstatements/endoflifedecisions/

Feldman, D.M., & Rosner, F. (Eds.) (1984). *Compendium on medical ethics* (6th ed.). New York: Federation of Jewish Philanthropies of New York.

Ferngren, G. B. (1989). The ethics of suicide in the Renaissance and the Reformation. In B. A. Brody (Ed.), *Suicide and euthanasia: Historical and contemporary themes* (pp. 155–181). Dordrecht, Netherlands: Kluwer.

Fletcher, J. (1954). *Morals and medicine.* Boston: Beacon.

Fletcher, J. (1966). *Situation ethics: The new morality.* Philadelphia: Westminster.

Fletcher, J. (1979) *Humanhood: Essays in Biomedical Ethics.* Buffalo, NY: Prometheus Books.

Freehof, S. B. (1969). Responsa 77, Allowing a terminal patient to die. *American Reform responsa, 79,* 118–121. New York: Central Conference of American Rabbis.

Goldfarb, D. C. (1976). The definition of death. *Conservative Judaism, 30,* 10–22.

Grisez, G. (1989). Should nutrition and hydration be provided to permanently unconscious and other mentally disabled persons? *Issues in Law and Medicine, 5,* 165–170.

Harakas S. (1990). *Health and medicine in the Eastern Orthodox tradition.* New York: Crossroad.

Hathout, H. (1994). Islam and euthanasia. *Journal of the Islamic Medical Association, 26,* 152–154.

In re Quinlan, 355 A.2d. 647 N.J. (1976).

Jakobovits, I. (1975). *Jewish medical ethics.* New York: Bloch.

Lesco, P. A. (1986). Euthanasia: A Buddhist perspective. *Journal of Religion and Health,* 55–64.

Lutheran Church-Missouri Synod, Commission on Theology and Church Relations, Social Concerns Committee. (1979). *Report on euthanasia with guiding principles. Cited in Active euthanasia, religion and the public debate.* (1991). (pp. 59–62). Chicago: The Park Ridge Center.

Medical Ethics Committee, Islamic Medical Association of North America. (1997). Care at the end of life and euthanasia. *Journal of the Islamic Medical Association, 29,* 100–101.

Meilaender, G. (1984). On removing food and water: Against the stream. *Hastings Center Report, 14,* 11–13.

O'Rourke, K., & Boyle, P. (1999). *Medical ethics: Sources of Catholic teachings* (3rd ed.). Washington, DC: Georgetown University Press.

Presbyterian Church in the United States, 121st Assembly. (1995). The nature and value of human life. In *In life and death we belong to God* (pp. 43-45). Louisville, KY: Presbyterian Distribution Services.

Ramsey, P. (1970). *The patient as person.* New Haven, CT and London: Yale University.

Sachedina, A. (2004). Islamic bioethics. In J. F. Peppin, M. J. Cherry, & A. Iltis (Eds.), *Annals of bioethics: Religious perspectives in bioethics* (pp. 153–171). London and New York: Taylor and Francis Group.

Sacred Congregation for the Doctrine of the Faith. (1980). Vatican declaration on euthanasia. *Origins, 10,* 154–157.

Schindler v. Schiavo (In re Guardianship of Schiavo) 851 So. 2d 182 (Fla. 2d DCA 2003); review denied, 855 So. 2d 621 (Fla. 2003) (table decision).

Thavis, J. (2004, April 7). Experts say Pope's speech on feeding tubes settles some key issues. *Catholic News.* Retrieved August 27, 2004, from http://www.catholicnews.com

Tollefsen, C., & Boyle, J. (2004). Roman Catholic bioethics. In J. F. Peppin, M.J. Cherry, & A. Iltis (Eds.), *Annals of bioethics: Religious perspectives in bioethics* (pp.1–20). London and New York: Taylor and Francis Group.

United Methodist Church. (2000). Faithful dying. In *The book of discipline of the United Methodist Church – 2000.* United Methodist Publishing House. Retrieved August 26, 2004, from http://www.umc.org/interior.asp?mid=1734

United Methodist Church, General Commission on Christian Unity and Interreligious Concerns, & National Conference of Catholic Bishops, Bishops' Committee for Ecumenical and Interfaith Affairs. (1986). *Holy living and holy dying.* Cited in *Active euthanasia, religion and the public debate.* (1991). (pp. 65–66). Chicago: The Park Ridge Center.

U.S. Bishops' Pro-Life Committee. (1992). Nutrition and hydration: Moral and pastoral reflections. *Origins, 21*, 705–712.

Vacco v. Quill, 117 S.Ct.2293 (1997).

Washington v. Glucksberg, 117 S.Ct.2258 (1997).

Wooden, C. (2004, March 25). Pope: Patients must get nutrition, hydration as long as possible. Catholic News Service. Retrieved August 27, 2004, from http://www.catholicherald.com/cns/cns04/patients/htm

CHAPTER 3

Cultural and Religious Views on Nonbeneficial Treatment

Noel Tiano and ElizaBeth Beyer

Reflecting on the uncertainty of the time of death develops a mind that is peaceful, disciplined, and virtuous, because it is dwelling on more than the superficial stuff of this short lifetime.
—Dalai Lama, *This Life Is Precious . . . and Fleeting*

According to Jewish legend, one day, Rabbi Yehudah the Prince became gravely ill. His students, worried about losing their beloved teacher, began to pray fervently for his recovery. Some time later, a perceptive handmaiden noticed that the prayers being offered for the rabbi actually increased his suffering and were a hindrance to his passing. So she climbed up to the roof of the House of Study and threw a jar to the ground, smashing it into tiny pieces. Startled by the sudden noise, the students stopped praying for an instant. It was at that very moment that the soul of Rabbi Yehudah departed and went to heaven (Talmud, Ketubot 104a).

Today, there is an overwhelming number of interventions to cure diseases and extend life. In the early 1900s, the average life expectancy was 50 years. People died quickly because of infectious diseases, accidents, and war. With the discovery of antibiotics and improved sanitation, the average life expectancy has increased to 76.9 years in 2000, with women living longer than men by an estimated 5.4 years (Emanuel, von Gunten, Ferris, & 2003a). Unfortunately, amid rapid advances in medical science, there has also been a radical shift in values—toward a more death-denying culture. And with a daunting forecast that more than 90% of Americans, while living longer, will also be undergoing more chronic and protracted life-threatening illnesses, the question is, are we really prolonging life, or are we merely prolonging the dying process? Are we victims of our own successes? Perhaps, like the wise handmaiden, we need to cease to see death as the enemy, and embrace our mortality as an essential part of our shared human experience.

This chapter deals with cultural and religious perspectives on some modern medical treatments that are not beneficial in improving the patient's medical status at the end of life. The term "nonbeneficial treatment" is preferred here over "medical futility," owing to the lack of consensus on the latter's definition, and a growing development of institutional (American Medical Association, 1999) and community-wide policies such as in Houston, Denver (Youngner, 2004), and San Francisco (Bay Area Network of Ethics Nonbeneficial Treatment Working Group, 1999). The issues of health care rationing and resource allocation are oftentimes raised in conjunction with the futility debate. While these are legitimate concerns, especially with millions of Americans currently having little or no insurance, they are different issues and will not be addressed here.

During the past several decades, the pendulum of bioethics has swung from concerns about medical paternalism to patient autonomy. Freedom to make choices is a cherished American value. Unfortunately, autonomy has also been used as the trump card for maintaining biological function through nonbeneficial treatments, insistence on brand name over generic medications, and at times, assisted suicide. Ideally, one's preferences need to be *balanced* with the other ethical principles of beneficence, nonmaleficence, and justice, as well as the virtues of compassion, care, and a communitarian understanding of societal responsibility.

AUTONOMY

Autonomy recognizes "the human capacity for self-determination and puts forward a principle that the autonomy of persons ought to be respected" (Miller, 2004, p. 246). Miller adds that autonomy is used to justify rights to privacy, confidentiality, informed consent, disclosure of diagnosis, and refusal of treatment (p. 249). The concept denotes that a reasonable and competent person has a right to make his or her own decisions without external coercion.

Though dealing ostensibly with contraception, the U.S. Supreme Court established a "right to privacy" under the Fourth Amendment in *In re Griswold v. Connecticut* (1965). Similarly, in *Roe v. Wade* (1973), while concerning itself primarily with abortion, the Court confirmed the right to autonomy over one's body. The New Jersey Supreme Court extended the right of privacy to matters of refusing treatment and withdrawing life-sustaining treatment in *In re Quinlan* (1976), and suggested the use of ethics committees in an advisory capacity in future cases. In April 1975, 21-year-old Karen Ann Quinlan ended up in a hospital and was later determined to be in a persistent vegetative state (PVS). The following year, the court granted her father guardianship, and the family was allowed to remove her respirator. But Karen proved not to be respirator-dependent, and began breathing on her own. She remained in a PVS and was fed through artificial nutrition and hydration until she died of pneumonia more than 10 years later, in June 1985.

The Missouri Supreme Court maintained the right of privacy for competent patients in *Cruzan v. Director, Missouri Department of Health,* (1990). In January 1983, 25-year-old Nancy Cruzan had a car accident that left her with permanent and irreversible brain damage due to oxygen deprivation. Like Quinlan, she was dependent on artificial nutrition and hydration. The court, however, upheld Missouri's requirement for "clear and convincing evidence" when an incompetent patient's wishes on refusing life-sustaining treatment are in question. In 1990, some of Nancy's friends provided testimony that satisfied the evidentiary requirement, and on December 14, the artificial feeding tube was removed. She died two weeks later. In 1991, the U.S. Congress passed the Patient

Self-Determination Act, requiring facilities that receive Medicare and Medicaid funding to inform patients about their right to complete advance health care directives.

It is important to note that even patients with a nonterminal illness have a right to refuse life-sustaining treatment. In *Bouvia v. Superior Court* (1986), the California Court of Appeals ruled that Elizabeth Bouvia, a young woman with severe cerebral palsy but without life-threatening illness, had the right to refuse treatment with artificial nutrition.

Most of these cases are very complex, and the courts have usually sided with the family that insists on continued life support, as in the case of Helga Wanglie. In December 1989, she slipped on a rug, broke her hip, and was hospitalized. Ms. Wanglie, 86 years old, had numerous complications, including irreversible damage to her brain, and she had to be on a respirator. The health care team recommended withdrawal of the life support in *In re the Conservatorship of Helga M. Wanglie* (1993). The family was adamant, however, that withdrawal of the respirator was tantamount to playing God. Since God gave life, only God could take it. Ms. Wanglie's husband was appointed guardian in July 1991, and she died several days later from septicemia.

The American model of care that emphasizes individual self-determination is not without its critics. Communitarians object to liberal individualism because one's values, preferences, and desires are not autonomously chosen but are shaped in a social context. Furthermore, a good society must recognize its obligations to help others (Miller, 2004). Recently, several disability advocate groups, such as "Not Yet Dead," have protested against "right to die" groups, Kevorkian, and others, and have supported the continued treatment of patients like Terri Schiavo of Florida. A running court battle has ensued between Ms. Schiavo's husband versus her parents, and the governor regarding the removal of her feeding tube. Ms. Schiavo has been in a persistent vegetative state since 1990.

The next section surveys various cultural viewpoints on nonbeneficial treatment.

CULTURAL PERSPECTIVES

In Israel, the main ethical issue is not patient autonomy but beneficence. Jewish tradition rejects shortening of life even though life may seem meaningless. Similarly, in Japan, the principle of autonomy is not as applicable as in the West. Buddhism teaches that the egoistic self should be suppressed. The dominant culture lends itself more toward medical paternalism. In China, quality of life is primary. However, things get cloudy when cases involve the elderly, owing to the Chinese practice of filial piety (Berger, 1998). In India, suffering may be considered due to karma; nevertheless, many favor omission of treatment so as not to prolong the dying process. A 1986 national survey in Italy showed that between beneficence and autonomy, the ratio was 50-50. British law allows consent only by the patient or a legally designated representative to withdraw life-sustaining treatment, while in Switzerland consent may be given by an independent physician who is not involved in the situation. In Spain and Portugal, physicians usually make decisions about terminal care (Nyman & Sprung, 1997). People in the Third World may take a more fatalistic approach because of the scarcity of high technology and because death is so much a part of everyday existence. Central African tribes make decisions based on the good of the society rather than the individual.

Dr. Richard Payne, former chief of the pain and palliative care unit at Memorial Sloan-Kettering Cancer Center in New York, an African American, says, "When death is inevitable and imminent, blacks are twice as likely as whites to request life-sustaining treatments." A few years ago, a group of African-American clergy in Houston asked him, "How can you ask us to trust an institution that one generation ago would not let us in the door?" (Payne, 2000). Murray (1992) observes that among African Americans, instead of the primacy of individual autonomy, the main values have been security/survival, power/self-determination, truth-telling, and justice. Another distinction is that while African-American ethos is more holistic, inclusive, and communalistic, Euro-American ethos is more particularistic, exclusive, and individualistic (Murray, 1992). With their history of slavery, segregation, and human experimentation (e.g., the

Tuskegee syphilis study) some African Americans worry that their race and/or socioeconomic status will make them more "disposable" and that palliative care is a code word for "no care" or "less care." Every procedure is suspect: from informed consents to do-not-resuscitate (DNR) orders to organ donation to advance health care directives.

Many Asians and Latinos residing in the United States generally prefer that "everything be done." An extended care facility study in Northern California conducted over a period of five years found that the "odds ratio of a feeding tube in place at death in the Hispanic and Asian/Pacific Islanders was 5.2 times as likely as in the non-Hispanic Caucasian group . . . . This was statistically significant with a p-value of < 0.0005" (Fowkes, 1998, p. 52). Those who support continued artificial nutrition and hydration argue that the treatment benefits patients who are disoriented and have electrolyte imbalance, and provides comfort to the family and caregiver. Besides, food has the symbolic meaning associated with faithfulness, love, nurture, and care. Hospice professionals, however, maintain that fluid overload can lead to ascites and peripheral edema and increase fistula drainage and complications such as infection and aspiration. Positive outcomes of withholding artificial nutrition and hydration include decreased bouts of vomiting and fewer choking and drowning sensations. It also appears that less artificial feeding may increase the body's ability to produce a natural analgesia.

Truth-telling

In North America, withholding the diagnosis from the patient may be a ground for legal action. However, several groups, including Chinese, East Indian, Filipino, Hmong, Iranian, Korean, Latino, Russian, and Vietnamese, usually prefer that the family spokesperson be informed first about the poor prognosis before it is disclosed to the patient. Often the purported reason is that the patient would just "give up." The Deontological Code of the Italian Medical Society stipulates that a serious or lethal prognosis can be hidden from the patient, but not from the family (Surbone & Flanagin, 1992). Compared to northern Europeans, physicians in southern and eastern Europe generally think that it is best to inform the family of the diagnosis before disclosing it to the patient (Thomsen & Wulff, 1993).

Navajo tribes may find discussions of negative information harmful, thereby making it difficult to provide full disclosure of a grim prognosis. In fact, Carrese and Rhodes (1995) question whether advance care planning is beneficial or harmful among members of the Navajo nation. They conclude that advance directives are "ethically troublesome and warrant reevaluation" (pp. 826–829). Lori Arviso Alvord, M.D., the first Navajo woman surgeon, suggests an indirect approach using a third party, such as, "Suppose someone from your tribe had an incurable illness, how should the tribe handle the situation?" (Alvord, personal communication, February 11, 2002). This approach avoids direct transactions such as, "Do you want CPR if your heart stops?"

Active Euthanasia

The High Court in Japan permits euthanasia, and not just the removal or withdrawal of nonbeneficial treatment. The Court requires the following:

(1) The patient's situation should be regarded as incurable with no hope of recovery, and death should be imminent; (2) The patient must be suffering from unbearable and severe pain that cannot be relieved; (3) The act of killing should be undertaken with the intention of alleviating the patient's pain; (4) The act should be done only if the patient himself or herself makes an explicit request; (5) The euthanasia should be carried out by a physician, although if that is not possible, special situations will be admitted for receiving some other person's assistance; and (6) The euthanasia must be carried out using ethically acceptable methods (Nagoya High Court, 1962, p. 674).

On April 1, 2002, Holland became perhaps the most liberal country in the world regarding euthanasia (CNN, 2002). Although the practice had gone on for nearly 30 years, it is now codified into law. Physicians are required to offer euthanasia in a medically appropriate manner, with voluntary consent, with the conclusion that there is no reasonable alternative, and after consulting with at least one other physician. Patients must sign a written statement and there must be agreement that the pain or suffering is lasting and unbearable, as found in Section 293(2) of the Dutch Criminal Code. There is no prohibition against administering euthanasia to a nonresident. France and Belgium will probably follow suit. Given Holland's legal stance on euthanasia, it is unlikely that nonbeneficial medical treatment would be required over the patient or family's objection.

In the sixth year of Oregon's Death with Dignity Act, the state reports that while there has been an increase in physician-assisted suicide (PAS), it remains small in comparison to the average 31,000 Oregon deaths every year. The major reasons patients chose PAS were concerns about "losing autonomy, a decreasing ability to participate in activities that make life enjoyable and loss of dignity" (Oregon Death with Dignity, 2004).

RELIGIOUS PERSPECTIVES

The Greek word *kairos* means seasonal or opportune time, as in a time to be born, and a time to die. In contrast to *chronos*, from which we derive chronology, or linear time (Greek lexicon, 2004), a *kairotic* perception of death can be viewed as choosing the right or opportune moment.

Muslim

Most Muslims believe that God chooses the time of death and that death is a return to God, which is most welcomed (Crowe, personal communication, August 11, 2004). When treatment carries no prospect of cure, it ceases to be mandatory. Heroic measures and interventions that merely prolong the dying process may be discontinued, but no action should be taken to bring about death. Muslims believe that if an affordable medical treatment is available, it must be administered to the patient without adding unusual pain and suffering (Death and Dying: Islamic View, 2004). More specifically, maintaining a terminal patient on artificial life support for a prolonged period in a vegetative state "is not encouraged" (Metropolitan Chicago Healthcare Council, 2004). A final detail is the preference for remaining "conscious" at the hour of death to declare the oneness of God. Hence, overmedication even for pain management is usually avoided. Affliction and pain are viewed as a test of faith and true resignation to the Creator. If a terminally ill patient terminates his or her life, this is a sin and the individual is excluded from inheriting a place in Paradise. If a person wishes to die, Anas ibn Malik the Prophet suggested (s)he say the following: "O Allah! Keep me alive as long as life is better for me and let me die if death is better for me" (Ebrahim, 2001).

Like other religious traditions, however, there are those who equate disconnecting life support systems as tantamount to active euthanasia. Rispler-Chaim views death and dying in fatalistic terms and regards an incurable illness as a test of God. As such, the experience should be borne without complaint, protest, or doubt. She maintains that the only recourse, therefore, is to endure suffering relying totally in God's power (Rispler-Chaim, 1993).

Nevertheless, an individual lives or dies in accordance with the will of Allah. The Qu'ran does warn against taking any human being's life, because it is sacred. The physician is under an obligation do what is best for the terminal patient. Generally, nonbeneficial treatment may be discontinued, but no action should be taken to actively bring about death. Confirmation of brain stem death would warrant discontinuation of a respirator, based upon the Islamic legal principle of "la darar wa la dirar/no harm and no harassment."

Jewish

Orthodox Jewish culture affirms the sanctity of life principle and holds that life is a precious gift that carries with it the burden of responsibility. Essentially, traditional Jews (Orthodox and Conservative) contend that the body belongs to God and that all life, regardless of its quality or duration, is of infinite value. Preservation of life (*pikuach nefesh*) is a fundamental responsibility. While most support the patient knowing his or her terminal diagnosis, some prohibit disclosure on the grounds that it may increase the individual's suffering and shorten life. Among Orthodox Jews, authorities agree that once a respirator has been started, it should not be stopped, even if the patient is brain dead. In principle, even passive euthanasia is forbidden, and all medical intervention must be used to prolong life. However, some believe that in special cases, it may be permissible to refuse further active treatment (e.g., surgery) when the risk-benefit ratio is not in the patient's favor (Feldman, 1986). While death is never looked at as "good," Jewish tradition says that a fast death after the age of 80 is a good death (Talmud, Moed Katan 28A).

Suicide is forbidden by Jewish law except in rare circumstances of martyrdom. For instance, during the Holocaust, a small number of European Jews chose to commit suicide rather than be forced to inform the whereabouts of other Jews. Unlike the Orthodox Jews who emphasize determining God's will, Conservative and Reform Jews are more likely to stress self-determination. Rabbi Elliot Dorff, a Conservative Jew, distinguishes between sustaining life and prolonging the dying process. "In our setting, this means that if the patient is dying of a terminal disease, we may relinquish aggressive medical treatment, even if it is effective in prolonging vital organs. We then may, and probably should, concentrate instead on relieving pain" (Dorff, 1998, p. 204). Furthermore, he rightly identifies artificial nutrition and hydration as medication or treatment, and hence, that they can be withdrawn if they are not beneficial. As with the case of the wise handmaiden mentioned earlier, Jewish sources teach that obstacles that delay the normal process of dying such as the "sound of chopping wood," and even medicines may be removed. Normal food and liquid should be offered by mouth as appropriate. For patients with PVS and advanced dementia, medical interventions may be stopped only after a reasonable amount of time has been allowed to determine whether the treatment is not medically indicated. Dorff advocates the use of pain management and hospice care and cautions about making hasty decisions, particularly toward vulnerable populations such as those with disabilities (Dorff, 1998).

Christian

PROTESTANT

Most of the Protestant churches, including Adventists, Baptists, Christian Scientists, Episcopalians, Mennonites, Methodists, Pentecostals, and Presbyterians, oppose euthanasia. Proponents of euthanasia, however, argue that ascertaining between deontological (duty), consequential (result), aim, and motive may provide some clarity as to whether euthanasia is ever morally permissible or even obligatory (Meilaender, 1998). Lebacqz (1998) makes a case that in certain circumstances when a terminally ill patient has intractable pain, active euthanasia may be morally justifiable. But she quickly adds that it should not become social policy.

Rev. Kelvin Calloway, an African Methodist Episcopalian minister, recommends integrating religious language with advance care planning. "It is vital to reframe constructs and talk about health care directives as *partnering with God in alleviating unnecessary suffering . . .* it is part of the church's prophetic, nurturing, and caring ministry fulfilling its mission as a voice for the voiceless" (Calloway, personal communication, October 12, 2002). Jehovah's Witnesses carry an Advance Medical Directive/Release requesting no blood transfusions and a release of liability for health care providers. Christian Scientists find that reality exists solely in the mind and regard prayer as the proper treatment for suffering. Thus, seeking medical care is contrary to their faith. Still, a note of caution is warranted whenever any group (religious or otherwise) overrules individual decision making (Fowkes, 1998, p. 57).

ROMAN CATHOLIC

The National Conference of Catholic Bishops (1995) specified the following directives:

57. A person may forgo extraordinary or disproportionate means of preserving life. Disproportionate means are those that in the patient's judgment do not offer a reasonable hope of benefit or entail an excessive burden, or impose excessive expense on the family or the community.
58. There should be a presumption in favor of providing nutrition and hydration to all patients, including patients who require medically assisted nutrition and hydration, as long as this is of sufficient benefit to outweigh the burdens involved to the patient.
60. Euthanasia is an action or omission that of itself or by intention causes death in order to alleviate suffering . . . . Dying patients who request euthanasia should receive loving care, psychological and spiritual support, and appropriate remedies for pain and other symptoms so that they can live with dignity until the time of natural death.

The term "extraordinary" pertains to all medicines, treatments, and operations that cannot be obtained or used without excessive expense, pain, or other inconvenience, or that if used would not offer a reasonable hope of benefit. The prominent Roman Catholic ethicist, Richard McCormick, S.J., states that withdrawal of artificial nutrition and hydration to terminally ill patients is *not killing* but allowing to die (McCormick, 1997).

In any case, the Bishops stress that allowing a terminal patient to die solely for the purpose of relieving suffering is morally equivalent to direct killing and thus constitutes a grave moral evil. Interestingly, despite the caveat providing for balancing the burdens and the benefits, Pope John Paul II recently commented that removing feeding tubes from those who are in vegetative states is immoral and tantamount to "euthanasia by omission" (The Guardian/Associated Press, 2004).

Hindu

Hindus respect all forms of life and generally oppose euthanasia. *Ahimsa,* a central feature of their culture, essentially means nonviolence. According to the *Caraka Samhita* (a classical text on medicine and religion), physicians were not to treat incurable diseases (Young, 2004).

A "good death" is one in which the dying person is in full possession of his or her mental and physical faculties and is fully cognizant of what is about to be experienced. A Hindu should participate in setting the proper stage for his or her own death. There is time to assume the proper frame of mind for what is to come and to take adequate leave of family and friends. The belief in *karma* tends to take on a fatalistic overtone. This, plus the scarcity of resources in India, prohibits an all-out effort to rescue the dying (Brannigan & Boss, 2001). Death that is sudden and quick, (e.g., heart attack or stroke) is not fortunate because the deceased did not have time to prepare. Even worse is a violent or accidental death, from which a ghost may return to afflict the living. Death preferably should come at home, or at one of the sacred Hindu pilgrimage sites like the Ganges River banks with one's spouse, children, and grandchildren.

Generally, physicians need to apply sensitivity in disclosing a terminal diagnosis unless specifically requested by the patient. Negative thoughts should not be imposed to create bad *karma* and hasten death. Nevertheless, a person who senses that death is approaching informs family members and refuses further nourishment. Holy texts or devotional songs help fix the mind of the dying person upon the Divine. Then, at a moment chosen, the dying person takes a final breath. Such a death is symbolically equated with a marriage party (Young, 2004).

A "self-willed death" on the other hand, is one where people who are old, but not terminally ill, "may virtually wait till death arrives, refusing to take any food or drink" (Menski, 1996). Other forms of "self-willed death" may include burying oneself alive and meditating, or jumping over a cliff or under the wheels of a temple cart. A "self-willed death" is distinguished from suicide (a spontaneous and irrational act). One that was heroic (to avoid capture or torture) or religious (properly performed and done due to an infirmity) is viewed as honorable. Moreover, fasting to death, in cases of terminal illness or debilitating old age, may be seen as analogous to requesting withholding or withdrawal of life-sustaining treatments with its voluntary nature (Young, 2004). Weiss describes the terms "reasoned suicide" or "religious suicide" of ascetics, pilgrims, and widows who performed the *sati* (the act of throwing themselves on the funeral pyre of their husbands) in terms of cultural values and not in terms of mental health. To be sure, Hindu beliefs regarding death and dying need to be understood in the context of rebirth and individual salvation (Weiss, 2004).

Buddhist

For 45 years following his enlightenment, the Buddha practiced medicine. The *Dhammapada* (sacred text containing the sayings of the Buddha) says that existence is a result of the mind. Thus, treating the illness of the mind, rather than healing the illness of the body, is the central concern of medicine. *Dukkha* (suffering) is caused by the illness of one's own mind. While illness, aging, and death are natural phenomena, they become suffering only when one perceives them through *tanha* (self-centeredness or craving). When *tanha* is dominant, one's actions become more unskillful and suffering increases. Buddhists say that one can change this by increasing knowledge. Fear, in particular fear of death, is an unhealthy state of mind that should be cured by treating *tanha*. If one's mind is sufficiently adept, one lives in peace and happiness, overcoming fear in spite of an incurable illness or death. Thus, the event of dying can be experienced with equanimity—a lack of sadness, disappointment, frustration, or other negative emotion. The meditation practice of mindfulness is an important daily practice for the Buddhist (Shoyo, 1994).

Since the universe is fundamentally impermanent, Buddhist ethics "strongly advocate comforting the terminally ill rather than trying to extend life through any means available" (Deal, 2004). A physician is given latitude to act in the manner that is consistent with the patient's best interests, but that does not necessarily afford autonomy. Telling patients the details of their terminal condition may not be appropriate from a Buddhist perspective. This is particularly true if the physician believes that it will harm the patient's psychological well-being. The physician is to make a decision out of compassion, the most important Buddhist virtue, and wisdom. It may be necessary for the protection of others to have full disclosure (e.g., a diagnosis of AIDS); however, the timing and manner of speaking must be carefully regarded.

A variation of a Buddhist perspective can be observed regionally. In Thailand for instance, sanctity of life is maintained and "self-willed death" is not encouraged even in cases of pain and suffering. In Japan and China, however, "self-willed death" and euthanasia are popular owing to the influence of the warrior circles (Young, 2004).

During the dying process, the goal is to maintain awareness without judgment. Chanting, meditation, and reading the *Book of the Dead* are observed, preferably with one's family and spiritual teacher. Clarity of thought is important in securing a favorable rebirth. Death is, therefore viewed as the quintessential moment, a welcomed release from life which is neither feared nor desired (Young, 2004).

TIPS FOR HEALTH CARE PROVIDERS/PROFESSIONALS:

1) Ask culturally sensitive questions, such as the following:
   - Can you tell me what you know about your illness? What do you think caused it?
   - Some people really do not want to be told what is wrong with them, but would rather their families be told instead. What do you prefer?
   - If this condition turns out to be something serious, would you want to know?
   - Would you like me to tell you the full details of your condition? If not, is there somebody else you would like me to talk to?

- Do you want me to go over the test results now and explain exactly what I think is wrong?

- Whom should I talk to about these issues?

More suggestions are found in the "Communicating Bad News" module of the EPEC Project (Emanuel et al., 2003b).

2) Use language that the patient and family understand:
   - Explain using 7th to 8th grade language what life-sustaining treatment are (e.g., CPR, respirator, nasogastric tube) and what they do, including the risks, benefits, and alternatives.

   - Some facilities use the term "allow natural death" (AND) instead of DNR.

   - In certain cases, the expression "forced feeding" might be appropriate, especially if the patient has not consented (or is not able to consent) to artificial nutrition and hydration.

   - Instead of saying "We've done everything we can . . . ," try, "We want to provide you the *best care possible* . . . during your stay here . . . we have excellent doctors who can help manage your pain, our nurses are trained in providing comfort care . . . we have social workers who can facilitate communicating with your family/loved ones . . . our spiritual care can provide spiritual resources . . . our library can provide educational tools and internet access . . . we have patient advocates," etc.

   - DO NOT ask: "Do you want us to do *everything*?" The patient/family will most likely say yes. Saying no would be tantamount to "signing a death warrant," and may trigger guilt and fear of abandonment. Instead, it is better to provide likely scenarios and options.

   - When speaking to patients who do not speak English, use the facility's interpreter's services instead of a member of the patient's family. The latter may tend to screen information to protect the patient.

3) Arrange interdisciplinary family conferences and utilize allied health services.

4) Be aware that some Muslim, Hindu, and Buddhist patients may prefer to avoid terminal/palliative sedation.

5) Consult with the Bioethics Committee in dealing with ethical dilemmas.

6) Be proactive by completing and promoting the value of advance health care directives. ■

■　　■　　■

Remembering Seth Webb Beyer, 15-year-old only child of
ElizaBeth and Tom Beyer, who died in hospice care on August 13, 2004.

Noel Tiano, ThD, BC, is the director of the Nevada Center for Ethics and Health Policy at the University of Nevada, Reno. He has a doctorate in theology and a graduate certificate in health care ethics, and is a board certified chaplain with the Association of Professional Chaplains, Inc. Dr. Tiano has been a pastor, chaplain, hospice volunteer, and is a minister of the United Church of Christ. In 2000, he served as project manager of the Community-State Partnership to improve care at the end of life in Nevada, funded by the Robert Wood Johnson Foundation. He was born and raised in the Philippines, and now resides with his family in Nevada.

ElizaBeth Webb Beyer, RN, MS, JD, is a registered nurse and attorney who practices primarily in medical malpractice and personal injury. She also acts as an arbitrator. As a nurse, her areas of practice included intensive care, hospice, and oncology. Currently, she is a rabbinic student at the Academy for Jewish Religion.

REFERENCES

American Medical Association. (1999). Medical futility in end-of-life care. *JAMA, 281*(10). 937–941.

Bay Area Network of Ethics Committees Nonbeneficial Treatment Working Group (1999). Nonbeneficial or futile medical treatment: Conflict resolution guidelines for the San Francisco Bay Area. *Western Journal of Medicine, 170*(5), 287–290.

Berger, J. (1998). Culture and ethnicity in clinical care. *Archives of Internal Medicine, 158*, 2085–2090.

Bouvia v. Superior Court, 225 Cal. Rptr. 287 (Cal. App. 1986)

Brannigan, M., & Boss, J. (2001). *Health care ethics in a diverse society.* Mountainview, CA: Mayfield Publishing Co.

Carrese, J.A. and Rhodes, L.A. (2004) *Western bioethics on a Navajo reservation. Benefit or harm?* JAMA *274*, 826-829.

CNN. (2002, April 1). Euthanasia now legal in Holland. Retrieved August 31, 2004, from http://www.cnn.com/2002/WORLD/europe/04/01/netherlands.euthanasia/

Cruzan v. Director, Missouri Department of Health, 110 S.Ct. 2851 (1990).

Deal, W. (2004). Bioethics in Buddhism. In S. Post (Ed.). *Encyclopedia of Bioethics* (3rd ed.) 1:337. New York: Macmillan Reference USA.

Death and Dying: Islamic View. Retrieved August 29, 2004, from http://filebox.vt.edu/org/islam/death.txt

Dorff, E. (1998). *Matters of life and death: A Jewish approach to modern medical ethics.* 176-220. Philadelphia: The Jewish Publication Society.

Ebrahim, A. (2001) *Organ transplantation, euthanasia, cloning and animal experimentation: an Islamic view.* Leicester, U.K.: Islamic Foundation.

Emanuel, L. L., von Gunten, C. F., Ferris, F. D., & Hauser, J. M. (Eds.). (2003a). Gaps in end of life care. *The education in palliative and end-of-life care (EPEC) curriculum.* Chicago: EPEC Project.

Emanuel, L. L., von Gunten, C. F., Ferris, F. D., & Hauser, J. M. (Eds.). (2003b). Communicating bad news. *The education in palliative and end-of-life care (EPEC) curriculum.* Chicago: EPEC Project.

Feldman, D. (1986). *Health and medicine in the Jewish tradition.* New York: Crossroad Publishing Co.

Fowkes, W. C. (1998). *Prolonged death: An American tragedy.* Long Beach, CA: Archstone Foundation.

Greek lexicon. (2004). Retrieved August 30, 2004, from http://encyclopedia.thefreedictionary.com

In re Griswold v. Connecticut, 381 US 479 (1965).

In re Quinlan, 70 NJ 10 , 355 A2d 647 (1976)

In re the Conservatorship of Helga M. Wanglie, No. PX-91-283, District Probate Division, 4th Judicial district of the County of Hennepin, State of Minnesota (1993).

Lebacqz, K. (1998). Reflection. In S. Lammers & A. Verhey (Eds.), *On moral medicine* (2nd ed.) (p. 667). Grand Rapids, MI: William B. Eerdmans Publishing Co.

McCormick, R. (1997). Vive la difference! Killing and allowing to die. *America, 177*(18), 6–12.

Meilaender, G. (1998). Euthanasia and Christian vision. In S. Lammers & A. Verhey (Eds.). *On moral medicine* (2nd ed.) (pp. 655-658). Grand Rapids, MI: William B. Eerdmans Publishing Co.

Menski, W. (1996). Hinduism. In P. Morgan & C. Lawton (Eds.). *Ethical issues in six religious traditions, 33.* George Square, Edinburgh: Edinburgh University Press, Ltd.

Metropolitan Chicago Healthcare Council. *Guidelines for health care providers interacting with Muslim patients and their families.* Retrieved August 29, 2004, from http://www.ispi-usa.org/currentarticles/muslimprotocol.html

Miller, B. (2004). Autonomy. In S. Post (Ed.), *Encyclopedia of Bioethics* (3rd ed.) (Vol. 1, pp. 246 – 251). New York: Macmillan Reference USA.

Murray, R. (1992). Minority perspectives on biomedical ethics. In E. Pellegrino, P. Mazzarella, & P. Corsi (Eds.), *Transcultural dimensions in medical ethics* (pp. 37-38). Frederick, MD: University Publishing Group.

Nagoya High Court. (1962, December 9). *Collected criminal cases at High Court.* 15, 674.

National Conference of Catholic Bishops. (1995). *Ethical and religious directives for Catholic health care services.* Washington, DC: UCC, Inc.

Nyman, D., & Sprung, C. (1997). International perspectives on ethics in critical care. *Critical care clinics, 13*(2), 409–415.

Oregon Death with Dignity. (2004, March 9). Sixth year report. DHS news release. Retrieved August 31, 2004, from http://www.dhs.state.or.us/news/2004news/2004-0309a.html

Payne, R. (2000, February 15). OUCH!; At the End of Life, Color Still Divides. *The Washington Post,* p. Z 13.

Rispler-Chaim, V. (1993). *Islamic medical ethics in the twentieth century* (pp. 94-99). Leiden, The Netherlands: E.J. Brill.

Roe v. Wade, 410 US 113 (1973).

Shoyo, T. (1994). Methodology of Buddhist biomedical ethics. In P. Camenisch (Ed.), *Religious Methods and Resources in Bioethics, 45.* Netherlands: Kluwer Academic Publishers.

Surbone, A., & Flanagin, A. (1992). Truth telling to the patient. *JAMA, 268*(13), 1661–1662.

Thomsen, O., & Wulff, H. (1993). What do gastroenterologists in Europe tell cancer patients? *Lancet, 341*(8843), 473–476.

The Guardian/Associated Press. (2004, March 4). Pope calls removing feeding tubes immoral. *Catholic News.* Retrieved May 3, 2004, from http://www.cathnews.com/news/403/122.html

Weiss, M. (2004). Bioethics in Hinduism. In S. Post (Ed.). *Encyclopedia of Bioethics* (3rd ed.) (Vol. 2, pp. 1148). New York: Macmillan Reference USA.

Young K. (1994). Hindu Bioethics. In P. Camenisch (Ed.), *Religious methods and resources in bioethics* (pp. 20-21). Netherlands: Kluwer Academic Publishers.

Young, K. (2004). Eastern thought. In S. Post (Ed.). *Encyclopedia of Bioethics* (3rd ed.) (Vol. 2, pp. 560–570). New York: Macmillan Reference USA.

Youngner, S. (2004). Medical futility. In S. Post (Ed.). *Encyclopedia of Bioethics* (3rd ed.) (Vol. 3, pp. 1718 – 1721). New York: Macmillan Reference USA.

"Please don't tell her."
Family Opposition to
Breaking Bad News

San Diego Hospice & Palliative Care

San Diego Hospice and Palliative care admitted a 62-year-old Hispanic woman to one of our inpatient units from a nearby acute care hospital. The patient had lived in the San Diego area for 35 years and was a United States citizen. She was Spanish speaking, raised Catholic, and was a full-time homemaker raising six children who were now young adults. Two of her six children spoke English fairly well. Many of her extended family lived in Mexico.

Several months before admission, she developed severe weakness and fatigue secondary to anemia. Since she did not have health insurance, she went to Tijuana several times to seek medical treatment. In Tijuana she received blood transfusions, but no workup for her anemia.

Eventually she developed persistent epistaxis, nausea, and severe back pain. She was then taken to a San Diego emergency room. At this acute care hospital, she was found to be severely anemic and was admitted. Workup of her pain with imaging studies showed many lytic lesions. A diagnosis of multiple myeloma was made, and oncology was consulted. The oncologist felt that the prognosis was grim and documented that "the social situation will make management a problem." He did not speak Spanish and therefore deferred to the primary admitting doctor, who also did not speak Spanish, to discuss her options. The primary doctor spoke with the patient's family, who did not want to tell their mom that she was going to die. The patient was not offered treatment for her illness and was not told her diagnosis. The family decided to sign their mother into hospice and transfer her to one of our inpatient units to get better symptom control. Is it ethical to follow the lead of the family, who knows the patient best, and not tell the patient her diagnosis?

In our inpatient unit, with an interpreter, we negotiated with the patient's family that we would ask the patient what she wanted to know about her illness. She informed us that she wanted to know everything about her illness and what her options were for treatment. The news of her diagnosis was shared with her, and an oncologist was consulted to see her in our unit. He felt that her life could be significantly prolonged and symptoms better controlled with low-toxicity chemotherapy. After receiving blood transfusions and after her symptoms were well controlled, she decided to start chemotherapy. Upon discharge, she had applied for Medicaid and continued to receive services through hospice. It is hoped that she will have a good response to chemotherapy and will not need hospice services until sometime in the future.

DISCUSSION

- Is it absolutely necessary to tell patients everything about their illness, or is it reasonable to find out how much they really want to know?

- In light of the cultural context, could we assume that she would defer to her family?

- If patients state that they do not want to know, are we obligated to obtain their consent for someone else to make decisions for them?

- To what degree does the lack of funding and the language barrier affect a patient's ability to get proper care?

- What does this case say about the dilemma of inappropriate referrals to hospice? In a climate where hospice referrals are often late, how can you give appropriate feedback to the referring physician? ∎

Gary Buckholz, MD, is a fellow at the Center for Palliative Studies, San Diego Hospice & Palliative Care.

CHAPTER 4

Ethics, End-of-Life Care, and the Law: Overview

Alan Meisel and Bruce Jennings

INTRODUCTION

The ethical and legal problems that arise in making decisions about starting, continuing, and stopping medical treatment are complex and are shaped by many factors. Among these factors are our legal traditions; the traditions of ethics in medicine and in moral philosophy more generally; and cultural, and social and religious values, which are quite diverse in the United States and may vary subtly from one state or region of the country to the next. Finally, a very significant factor has been the influence of medical technology. Most of the cases and dilemmas that have shaped the law on end-of-life care have involved patients whose lives could be prolonged by new medical treatments and technologies, but whose health, functioning, quality of life, and even conscious awareness itself could not be restored. At an earlier time, medical technology only permitted physicians to stand by and comfort while such patients moved toward a "natural" death. Today, decisions on whether or not to forgo "artificial" life-sustaining interventions must be made more intentionally, openly, and with appropriate deliberation, consultation, and accountability.

The main challenge facing the law of end-of-life care is to avoid the twin wrongs of burdensome overtreatment and neglectful undertreatment. The law is charged (a) to protect the interests and well-being of vulnerable individuals, near death, who are not in a position to protect themselves; and (b) to safeguard the rights of individuals to determine the course of their own medical care, to be free from unwanted and burdensome medical treatment, and to preserve the dignity and integrity of their person and body.

It is also important to remember that the law is not the only resource we have in coping with dilemmas of caregiving near the end of life. Like all societal problems that are susceptible to legal resolution, dilemmas that arise in trying to determine the right thing to do in the treatment of patients near the end of life are also susceptible to resolution by structures and procedures other than those created by law. This situation gives rise to a dilemma about when to use legal procedures and when to act extralegally.

This chapter will discuss these dilemmas, focusing on the interplay between the law and medical practice—that is, the way the development of medical practice has affected the development of the law, and the way legal rules and norms have affected medical practice at the end of life.

The Development of a Legal Framework on Decisions Near the End of Life, 1976–1990

Although, as will be discussed below, there are important legal rulings dating back to the early part of the 20th century on a patient's right to give or withhold consent to medical treatment, the law of end-of-life care began in the mid-1970s with the case of Karen Ann Quinlan in New Jersey (*In re Quinlan*, 1976). Following a mishap that cut off the oxygen supply to her brain for a prolonged period of time, Ms. Quinlan, a woman in her early 20s, suffered irreversible damage to the brain's neo-cortex and fell into a state of permanent unconsciousness now known as permanent (or persistent) vegetative state (PVS). Her life was sustained for just over a year on a ventilator, with artificial nutrition and hydration and other forms of medical and nursing care. Her family came to the conclusion that being kept alive artificially was not morally required, was not in Ms. Quinlan's best interests, and was not what she herself would have wanted done. Because her physicians refused to honor their wishes, the Quinlan family sought judicial relief, and in a landmark decision in 1976 the New Jersey

Supreme Court ruled that as her legal guardian, Mr. Quinlan, had the authority to have the ventilator withdrawn. The legal basis for this decision was Ms. Quinlan's constitutional right to privacy, which, in the aftermath of the United States Supreme Court ruling in the abortion case *Roe v. Wade*, was taken to mean that competent individuals had a right to control their own medical decisions. The fact that Ms. Quinlan was unconscious and unable to decide for herself did not mean that she forfeited these rights, the New Jersey Supreme Court held. It only meant that these rights would have to be exercised by someone else—in this case her father. This was the first time that an individual's right to refuse life-sustaining medical treatment was affirmed by an American appellate-level court.

But it would not be the last. In the mid-1980s a remarkably similar case unfolded in Missouri involving a young woman named Nancy Beth Cruzan who also fell into PVS after a devastating anoxic brain injury (*Cruzan v. Harmon*, 1988). There were important and interesting differences between the Quinlan and the Cruzan cases, however. Quinlan's parents wanted the ventilator removed; they never raised the issue of artificial nutrition and hydration. After the removal of Ms. Quinlan's ventilator she did not die, as everyone expected, but began to breathe on her own. (In PVS, the brain stem, which controls breathing and other involuntary life functions, is not damaged.) With feeding tubes and other care, she lived for another 10 years before she finally died of an infection, having never regained consciousness or any discernible awareness at all.

In the Cruzan case, Ms. Cruzan was not on a ventilator, and it was artificial nutrition and hydration that the family wanted withdrawn. Unlike its counterpart in New Jersey a decade earlier, the Missouri Supreme Court ruled that that guardians did not have the authority to terminate life-sustaining medical treatment on the basis of indirect or hypothetical reasoning about what the patient's wishes would have been. Instead, if surrogates are to make such treatment decisions, they must be based on clear and convincing evidence of what the patient wanted. If there is no clear and convincing evidence of a patient's wishes, the guardian is obligated to act in the patient's best interests, and for the Missouri Supreme Court, this meant the continuation of life and of medical life support. In coming to this conclusion, the Missouri court noted that it was disagreeing not only with the Quinlan court in New Jersey but with similar rulings in more than a dozen other states. Only in New York had the highest court also held that clear and convincing evidence was required in cases involving surrogate decision making (*In re Westchester County Medical Ctr.*, 1988).

The Cruzan family sought review of the ruling by the United States Supreme Court which held that U.S. Constitution confers a right ("liberty interest") to refuse medical treatment, even life-prolonging medical treatment (including artificial nutrition and hydration). However, it also held that states did not violate this constitutional right by requiring clear and convincing evidence of the patient's wishes when the patient lacked decision-making capacity (*Cruzan v. Director, Missouri Dep't. of Health*, 1990). The case was sent back to Missouri for retrial to determine if the clear and convincing evidence standard had been met. After additional testimony, the trial court ruled that the standard had been met and authorized Mr. Cruzan to withdraw the artificial nutrition and hydration from his daughter.

The Cruzan case marks the end of a period of legal consolidation because this was the first time that the U.S. Supreme Court had addressed end-of-life medical decision making in the light of the Constitution and established a right to refuse medical treatment. Today, well over 100 appellate level cases involving end-of-life treatment decisions have been decided in approximately half of the states. In addition to these court rulings, other legal instruments of public policy have been put into place, including many state statutes establishing mechanisms for advance directives (i.e., living wills and durable powers of attorney for health care), one federal statute (Patient Self-Determination Act, 1990) designed to promote the use of advance directives, and numerous administrative rulings together with guidelines and statements by medical, nursing, allied health, bar, and bioethics groups.

Taken together, this massive body of law and opinion constitutes a consensus on the elements of good medical decision making near the end of life. This consensus contains the following points (Meisel, 1993):

- Competent patients have a common law and a constitutional right to refuse medical treatment, even if that treatment is necessary to sustain life.

- Incompetent patients have the same rights as competent patients; however, the manner in which these rights are exercised is different.

- No right is absolute; it must be balanced against countervailing rights and interests.

- The decision-making process should generally occur in the clinical setting without recourse to the courts.

- In making decisions for incompetent patients, surrogate decision-makers should apply the following standards, in descending order of preference: subjective standard, substituted judgment, best interests.

- In ascertaining an incompetent patient's preferences (the subjective standard), the patient's advance directive provides "clear and convincing evidence."

- Artificial nutrition and hydration is a medical treatment and may be withheld or withdrawn under the same conditions as any other form of medical treatment.

- There is no ethical difference between withholding and withdrawing life-sustaining medical treatment.

- The right to refuse life-sustaining medical treatment does not depend on the patient's life expectancy or being "terminally ill."

- It is acceptable to provide pain medication sufficient to control a patient's pain even if that may foreseeably hasten the patient's death.

- Active euthanasia and assisted suicide are morally and legally distinct from forgoing life-sustaining treatment.

DECISION MAKING FOR PATIENTS WITH CAPACITY TO DECIDE: INFORMED CONSENT

American law governing medical decision making began to develop slowly at the end of the 19th century (*State v. Housekeeper*, 1889) and the beginning of the 20th century (*Pratt v. Davis*, 1906; *Schloendorff v. Soc'y. of New York Hosp*, 1914), entirely through the judicial process. The development progressed very slowly through the middle of the century. The emphasis in the early judicial decisions was almost entirely on the requirement of consent to treatment. Not until the second half of the 20th century did the emphasis begin to shift from obtaining consent to obtaining "consent worthy of the name" by providing patients with adequate information about treatment so that patients (and their consent) could be said to be "informed." Although the term "informed consent" was first used in a judicial case in 1957 (*Salgo v. Leland Stanford Jr. University Bd. of Trustees*, 1957), it was not until 1960 that the first true modern informed consent cases began to take shape (*Natanson v. Kline*, 1960).

The informed consent requirement implements the principle of autonomy (or self-determination) in the sphere of medical decision making by according individuals the right to decide whether to undergo or forgo medical treatment. As it has developed in the United States, originally through court decisions and later supplemented by legislation, informed consent requires first, that physicians provide patients with information about a proposed diagnostic or therapeutic procedure adequate to enable them to decide whether to undergo the treatment or not, and second, that physicians not administer such treatment unless patients consent to it. Informed consent, therefore, confers two separate but connected rights: the right to refuse medical treatment and the right to receive adequate information so that a patient can make an intelligent choice about whether to refuse or accept treatment.

Until the middle to late 1970s, informed consent and its corollary—the right to refuse treatment—usually arose in circumstances that were not life-and-death situations—and certainly not the kind of situations we now refer to as end-of-life decisions, in which the patient is terminally ill or permanently unconscious. In most of these earlier cases, the administration of treatment, if it were successful, would be likely to restore the patient to what was, for most people, a reasonably acceptable state of health. The development of so-called halfway medical technologies and treatments—treatments that could prolong life but not restore health—brought about a change in the archetypal medical decision-making situation.

As the law continued to develop, cases arose in which patients who were not terminally ill or permanently unconscious sought to refuse life-saving medical treatment (*Bouvia v. Superior Court*, 1986; *Satz v. Perlmutter*, 1978; *State v. McAfee*, 1989). Although the courts pay lip service to the existence of countervailing state interests, in practice in the case of competent individuals they rarely if ever give any weight to those interests. The net effect is that, in practice, the right of competent persons to refuse treatment is virtually absolute. Also noteworthy is the fact that these cases accept the notion that patients may decline treatment because their quality of life, as *they* judge it, is such that for them life is no longer worth living. However, before a refusal of treatment—whether the treatment is life-sustaining or otherwise—is considered legally valid, the patient must have made an informed decision after having received from the physician all information material to making such a decision (*McKay v. Bergstedt*, 1990).

Although the law rather clearly prescribes that treatment decisions for competent patients—whether at the end of life or otherwise—are to be made through a process of informed consent, the reality of clinical practice does not always conform to this model. Whether the deviations are the exception or the rule is difficult to say. Certainly we know that deviations occur, as evidenced by the lawsuits against doctors for failing to obtain informed consent.

DECISION MAKING FOR PATIENTS WITHOUT CAPACITY TO DECIDE

The previous discussion was premised on the assumption that the people refusing treatment had decision-making capacity.[1] Decision making in such situations is simple in comparison with decision making for people who lack decision-making capacity. In the former situation, informed consent is the mechanism for decision making. In theory, the doctor provides the patient with the necessary information, and the patient

---

[1] There is a great deal of confusion about the appropriate terminology. (Meisel and Cerminara, 2004 § 3.06). In the remainder of this chapter, we will frequently use the traditional legal terminology to refer to people who have decision-making capacity as "competent" and those who do not as "incompetent."

decides. As noted, however, in practice, there are a host of complexities.

Decision making for incompetent patients is problematic even at the conceptual level. Like decision making for competent patients, it starts from the assumption that the goal is to implement the patient's own values. When the patient possesses capacity, by definition the patient's decision embodies his or her values.

The threshold issue in all decision making about treatment is whether a patient possesses or lacks decision-making capacity. Despite the centrality of this issue, American law regarding the standards and procedures for determining the absence or presence of decision-making capacity is often ambiguous. However, some relatively simple rules probably govern the overwhelming majority of cases. First, people are presumed by law to be competent. This presumption—coupled with the fact that most people are competent—means that the issue of determining decision-making capacity rarely arises; there must be some factor to trigger an inquiry. At the other end of the spectrum of decisional capacity are patients who are unconscious. Such patients are clearly incompetent. There is no need to articulate standards for determining their capacity. In between, however, are a variety of different types of patients whose decision-making capacity is questionable. They include people with mental disabilities (including mental illness, mental retardation, and dementia) and those whose capacities are compromised by illness (for example, renal or hepatic toxicity) or by the treatment for the illness (for example, drug toxicity). The degree of incapacity may be highly variable; the incapacity may be permanent, or it may be transient.

Standards for Determining Decision-Making Capacity

The standards for determining decision-making capacity are not entirely clear in either law or clinical practice. Over the past two or three decades, a consensus in both law and clinical practice has begun to emerge about decision-making capacity, and thus a few things can be said with some degree of confidence about the standards for its determination. First, decision-making is "decision specific" (Buchanan & Brock, 1989). That is, a person may have the capacity to make certain kinds of decisions but not others. Thus, a patient who lacks the capacity to manage his or her financial affairs may possess the capacity to make other kinds of decisions. And a patient who lacks the capacity to make a decision about complex surgery may possess the capacity to make a decision about undergoing a computerized tomography (CT) scan.

Second, the essence of decision-making capacity is the ability to understand—specifically, the ability to understand information about the proposed treatment, including information about the treatment's risks, benefits, and alternatives. In other words, decision-making capacity entails the ability to understand the information that must be given to the patient to obtain the patient's informed consent (Meisel & Cerminara, 2004). However, more than cognitive understanding is required. The patient must also be able to "appreciate" the fact that this information relates to his or her very own situation. Sometimes patients whose mental faculties are impaired have the ability to understand information but not to understand that it entails possible consequences for their own well-being.

Who Decides?

Despite the centrality of the question of competence to medical decision making, there is very little law addressing the issue of who decides whether a patient is incompetent when competence is unclear. The long-standing practice is for the patient's attending physician to make a threshold determination. In hospital practice (and probably less frequently in nursing home practice), mechanisms may exist for the physician to obtain a consultation about such decisions—such as a psychiatric, psychological, legal, or ethics consultation. The hospital may also have procedures requiring or recommending that a judicial hearing be scheduled to make a legal determination of the patient's decision-making capacity. However, if the patient is being cared for at home, these institutional resources are less likely to be available for consultation. A judicial determination of incompetence is rarely if ever legally *required*.

If a determination is made—either in the clinical setting or judicially—that a patient lacks decision-making capacity, certain consequences follow. Most fundamentally, the patient is disenfranchised from making a decision about his or her medical treatment. When a patient is literally unable to make a decision, there is no practical consequence to this disenfranchisement. But in cases in which patients are able to communicate and voice decisions, the consequence is that the patient's decisions need not—and ordinarily should not—be followed. The second important consequence is that someone else must be designated to make decisions about medical treatment—and perhaps about related issues such as nursing home or hospice placement—for the patient.

A person who makes decisions for another is referred to in American law as a surrogate, and this is the term used to refer to a person who has the legal authority to make decisions for an incompetent patient. A surrogate may be designated in one of several ways.

Patient-Designated Surrogate. First, patients may designate a surrogate themselves before they lose decision-making capacity, through an advance directive. A patient-designated surrogate is referred to as a proxy, or in some states as an *agent.* Although the prevalence of patient-designated surrogates is increasing, it is still very low.

Judicially Designated Surrogate. Second, a surrogate may be appointed by a judge as part of the hearing in which a person is determined to lack decision-making capacity. This type of surrogate is usually referred to as a *guardian.* In the medical context, very few patients are subject to a judicial hearing to determine decision-making capacity either before or during hospitalization, and hence few patients have guardians.

Clinically Designated Surrogate. The most frequent way surrogates are designated is in the clinical setting. Here again, the law follows clinical practice. The long-standing clinical practice is for physicians to turn to patients' close family members to make decisions when physicians believe the patients lack decision-making capacity. This process is usually very informal. There may be little or no awareness on the part of physicians that they are determining that a patient lacks decision-making capacity and that the family should make decisions for him or her. To speak of making a *determination* of lack of decision-making capacity and the designation of a surrogate is probably to ascribe far more formality to and self-consciousness about the process than in fact usually exists. Be that as it may, judicial *decisions* have given their imprimatur to these closely related procedures of determination of incompetence and designation of a surrogate. Surrogates designated in this way are referred to as *common-law surrogates* or *clinically designated surrogates.*

Statutorily Designated Surrogates. Finally, in the past decade or two, many states have enacted legislation codifying this common-law process (Orentlicher, 1994). These laws, referred to as *family consent or surrogate decision making statutes*, contain a list of family members who are authorized to make medical decisions for a person who lacks decision-making capacity, who has not appointed a proxy, and for whom a guardian has not been appointed. The list also specifies the order in which these family members have authority to act. A surrogate designated pursuant to a statute of this kind is referred to as a *statutory surrogate*.

One of the most difficult issues in decision making for patients who lack decision-making capacity is how to make decisions when no close family members are available. Many so-called "unbefriended" patients now reside in nursing homes around the country, and probably a new generation of statutes will be needed to fit the special needs and circumstances their care presents (Karp & Wood, 2003).

In the case of all types of surrogates, various kinds of questions and disputes can arise as to the authority that each has. These matters should be dealt with first in the clinical setting by clinical personnel, but if they cannot be resolved and their consequences are significant enough, judicial guidance may be needed. However, in health care institutions there is a great aversion to taking end-of-life cases (indeed, any patient-oriented cases) to court for resolution. Consequently, when a disagreement about whether to continue or terminate treatment cannot be resolved in the health care institution, often the parties do not seek judicial resolution. They merely "agree to disagree," and treatment continues. In such cases, patients are often quite near death anyway, and they die in a relatively short time while treatment continues to be administered.

Standards for Surrogate Decision Making

The determination of who is to act as the patient's spokesperson is only the first difficulty in decision making. The second is how decisions by surrogates should be made. If the patient were competent, the physician would be required to obtain the patient's informed consent. Because the goal of decision making by surrogates is the same as decision making by competent patients—to promote autonomy by implementing the patient's will—when the patient is incompetent, the physician is still required to obtain informed consent, but from the surrogate rather than the patient.

If the patient were competent, the physician would be virtually bound by the patient's decisions, with a few exceptions. However, physicians are not necessarily and automatically bound by a surrogate's decision. Rather, the surrogate's decision must be in accord with the applicable standard for decision making for incompetent patients.

The goals of medical decision making are first and foremost to implement the patient's wishes and to protect the patient's autonomy and bodily integrity. This is the reason that there can be no treatment of a patient without informed consent; informed consent exists to protect the patient's autonomy. In the medical context, the patient's autonomy is the right to decide whether or not his or her bodily integrity will be compromised by the administration of medical treatment. The goal of decision making by a surrogate is the same: to protect and promote the patient's right to decide. Thus, the surrogate's first role is to determine not what treatment is best for the patient but what the patient's wishes are about treatment.

This much is relatively well accepted in the law of most states. Where there is some disagreement, however, is about the degree of certainty with which the surrogate must know the patient's wishes. Courts and legislatures have developed a variety of standards to resolve this issue.

Subjective Standard

Some states require that the surrogate be virtually certain about the actual subjective wishes of the patient, so much so that the surrogate's role is no more than to serve as a conduit of those wishes to the physician or, if there is a judicial proceeding, to the court. For example, in New York, when the issue is whether to decline life-sustaining medical treatment, "the inquiry . . . is limited to ascertaining and then effectuating the patient's expressed wishes, [and thus, the] focus must always be on what the patient would say if asked today whether the treatment in issue should be terminated [because] no one should be denied essential medical care unless the evidence clearly and convincingly shows that the patient intended to decline the treatment under some particular circumstances" (O'Connor, 1988). Ideally, proof of the patient's wishes is made by a written document such as a durable power of attorney for health care or a living will. Nonetheless, oral evidence of the patient's wishes is acceptable as long as it was made under solemn circumstances—that is, it was not a casual remark—and it can be proved by clear and convincing evidence. This subjective standard is often referred to as the "clear and convincing evidence" standard, but that is an unfortunate use of terminology, for the ordinary legal use of the phrase "clear and convincing evidence" is to denote an evidentiary standard rather than a standard for surrogate decision making.

Substituted Judgment Standard

Most states, however, are not nearly as demanding as New York. Exemplifying the majority view, New Jersey applies the predominant "substituted judgment standard." Under this standard, the surrogate's role is still to determine the patient's wishes about treatment, but the patient's wishes need not be as clearly and firmly articulated as in New York. Indeed, the Pennsylvania Supreme Court appears to have concluded that simply because a surrogate was the patient's mother, she would know what he would have wanted even though he had never expressed any views on the subject (*In re* Fiori, 1996).

Best Interests Standard

Finally, a small number of state courts have concluded that in the absence of clear knowledge or any knowledge of what the patient wants or would have wanted, the surrogate is empowered to make a decision that the surrogate, in good faith, believes is in the best interests of the patient rather than one that effectuates the patient's own wishes (*In re Conroy*, 1985; *Rasmussen v. Fleming*, 1987).

Futility

If the surrogate, in compliance with the appropriate standard for decision making, declines to consent to treatment or requests that treatment be withdrawn, the physician is bound to honor the surrogate's decision. However, if the facts are reversed—if the physician recommends that treatment be withheld or withdrawn and the surrogate wishes treatment to be administered—the law is unclear on what should be done. These so-called futility cases—cases in which the attending physician believes that further treatment is futile but the surrogate demands that it be continued—generated a tremendous debate in American medical and legal journals during the 1990s but resulted in very little litigation and very little informal consensus. The standard operating procedure in most health care institutions seems to be to accede to the surrogate's demands for treatment if the surrogate cannot be convinced to accept the physician's recommendation to forgo it. As a practical matter, it is likely that after the physician accedes to the surrogate's demands, surrogates themselves often come to see the futility of continued treatment and ultimately agree to its termination.

Advance Directives

Advance directives are now well accepted as a means of decision making for patients who lack decision-making capacity. As a practical matter, advance directives can sometimes provide the kind of evidence that surrogates need to convince physicians—and a judge, should a case go to court—of the patient's desires about treatment. The two kinds of advance directives serve related, but somewhat different, purposes.

Living Wills. The more traditional form of advance directive is a living will. This is a written document that gives instructions about what kind of medical treatment a person wants, or more likely does not want, if the person is terminally ill or permanently unconscious and unable to make decisions for himself or herself.

Health Care Power of Attorney. The other form of advance directive is a power of attorney—usually referred to in the medical decision-making context as a health care power of attorney, medical power of attorney, or proxy directive. In this kind of document, a patient designates a surrogate if the patient is unable to make his or her own medical decisions.

In principle, advance directives are simple; in practice, they are not always so. The problem with living wills is that they often do not contemplate the precise circumstances about which a decision needs to be made, or they are too vague to be given effect. In theory, a health care power of attorney is a more flexible and useful kind of advance directive because it gives the surrogate the authority to make decisions based on facts about the patient's condition as they actually are rather than as the patient anticipated—perhaps incorrectly—they might be.

However, in practice, the surrogate may make a decision that is significantly different from what others think is a wise course of action. For instance, a surrogate may insist that full treatment be administered even if it has an extremely small likelihood of being helpful to the patient. Another problem can be that a patient may have both a living will and a health care power of attorney, and the instructions in the living will may conflict with the decisions of the surrogate. Even if a living will is very specific and fits the situation, under most state laws the physician is not absolutely bound to follow it.

In the last quarter of the twentieth century, a consensus evolved in law, bioethics, and clinical practice about the appropriate standards and procedures for end-of-life decision making. All aspects of this consensus are based on the fundamental premise of the right to be free from unwanted interferences with bodily integrity. It is not limited to patients who can decide for themselves. Individuals who have lost decision-making capacity retain the right to have decisions about end-of-life medical treatment made for them, and they have the right to make the decision for themselves before losing decision making capacity through an advance directive. Whether or not patients have the right to compel the provision of medical treatment—as opposed to refusing unwanted treatment—that physicians believe to be futile is uncertain. Similarly, patients have the right only to have their deaths hastened by the withholding or withdrawing of medical treatment, but not by active intervention to hasten death such as a prescription of a lethal overdose of medication (with the exception of terminally ill patients in Oregon) or an injection of a lethal substance. ■

Alan Meisel is the Dickie, McCamey & Chilcote Professor of Bioethics, and Professor of Law at the University of Pittsburgh, and the director of its Center for Bioethics and Health Law. He is an authority on the law and ethics of medical decision-making in general and of end-of-life decision-making in particular. He is the primary author of the treatise, The Right to Die—The Law of End-of-Life Decisionmaking, *now in its third edition. He is also co-author of the first edition* Informed Consent: Legal Theory and Clinical Practice.

Professor Meisel served as Assistant Director for Legal Studies at the

President's Commission for the Study of Ethical Issues in Medicine in 1982, where he participated in the authorship of the Commission's studies on informed consent and on end-of-life decision making, and he also served on the Ethics Working Group of the White House Task Force on Health Care Reform in 1993.

Bruce Jennings is Senior Research Scholar at The Hastings Center, a bioethics research institute in Garrison, New York. Mr. Jennings has been with the Hastings Center since 1980 and served as its executive director from 1990 to 1999. A graduate of Yale University (BA) and Princeton University (MA), he has written widely on end-of-life care, long-term care, and health policy. He served on the Board of Directors of the National Hospice and Palliative Care Organization and the Hospice and Palliative Care Association of New York State. He has written or edited 18 books, including The Perversion of Autonomy: The Uses of Coercion and Constraints in a Liberal Society *(2nd ed. 2003; co-authored with Willard Gaylin). He is currently at work on a book on chronic illness, dementia, and long-term care policy.*

REFERENCES

Bouvia v. Superior Court (Glenchur), 225 Cal. Rptr. 297 (Ct. App. 3d 1986).

Buchanan, A., & Brock, D. (1989). *Deciding for others: The ethics of surrogate decision making.* New York: Cambridge University Press.

In re Conroy, 486 A.2d 1209 (N.J. 1985).

Cruzan v. Harmon, 760 S.W.2d 408 (Mo. 1988).

Cruzan v. Director, Missouri Dep't. of Health, 497 U.S. 261 (1990).

In re Fiori, 673 A.2d 905 (Pa. 1996).

Karp, N., & Wood, E. (2003). *Incapacitated and alone: Health care decision-making for the unbefriended elderly.* Washington, DC: American Bar Association.

McKay v. Bergstedt, 801 P.2d 617 (Nev. 1990).

Meisel, A. (1993). The legal consensus about forgoing life-sustaining treatment: Its status and its prospects. *Kennedy Institute of Ethics Journal, 2*, 309–345.

Meisel, A., & Cerminara, K. L. (2004). *The right to die: The law of end-of-life decision-making.* New York: Aspen.

Natanson v. Kline, 350 P.2d 1093 (Kan. 1960).

Orentlicher, D. (1994). The limits of legislation. *Maryland Law Review, 53*, 1255–1305.

Patient Self-Determination Act, 1990. Public Law No. 101-508, §§ 4206, 4751 (codified at 42 U.S.C.A. § 1395cc(f)(1), § 1396a(a)).

Pratt v. Davis, 79 N.E. 562 (Ill. 1906).

In re Quinlan, 355 A.2d 647 (N.J. 1976).

Rasmussen v. Fleming, 741 P.2d 674 (Ariz. 1987).

Salgo v. Leland Stanford Jr. University Bd. of Trustees, 317 P.2d 170 (Cal. App. 1957).

Satz v. Perlmutter, 362 So. 2d 160 (Fla. Dist. Ct. App. 1978).

Schloendorff v. Soc'y. of New York Hosp., 105 N.E. 92 (N.Y. 1914).

State v. Housekeeper, 16 A. 382 (Md. 1889).

State v. McAfee, 385 S.E.2d 651 (Ga. 1989).

In re Westchester County Medical Ctr. (O'Connor), 531 N.E.2d 607 (N.Y. 1988).

Current Ethical Issues in End-of-Life Care

All of the historical, ideological, cultural, and spiritual perspectives come into play as individuals and their families and caregivers cope with the ethical dilemmas posed at the end of life. The first chapter in this section, Jennings's "How Americans Want to Die—Grassroots Perspectives and Cultural Diversity" offers a bridge between this section and the preceding one. Jennings reviews the data emerging from surveys and community forums. A few conclusions are particularly noteworthy. One is how the nature of hospice care—effective palliation, holistic and family-centered care—has defined a public concept of the good death. As Jennings notes, the sense of the mission of hospice has broadly permeated our culture. A second finding is the recognition that end-of-life care is inherently complex and not served well by inflexible rules like those that limit hospice care to individuals in the last half-year of life, make too rigid a divide between palliative and curative care, or insist that effective end-of-life care can take place only in one setting, such as the home or hospital. Jennings speculates on why this consensus crosses cultural and religious traditions.

Teahan offers a case that underlines the ethical dilemmas posed by medical futility. This case illustrates the division between palliative and curative care, and leads to larger questions about the degree that individual choice needs to be accommodated to the larger social issue of the effective use of limited resources.

This case serves as an introduction to Lamers's chapter on autonomy, consent and advance directives. Lamers both reviews the rich history of these concepts and offers thoughtful recommendations as to how medical practice can enhance the viability of patient autonomy, consent, and the use of advance directives. There is here, perhaps, another ethical issue that will emerge in the future. Contemporary Western cultures give great value to patient autonomy and informed consent. Other cultures may have different perspectives. For example, many Native American cultures believe in the power of spoken language—that by naming a possibility such as the chance that an operation may lead to negative outcomes, one calls those outcomes into greater probability. Perhaps as these perspectives emerge in the future they will be employed in more culturally nuanced ways—truth–offering rather than truth–telling. The point is that informed consent entails the right to choose *not* to be informed.

Hammes and Briggs follow with a very practical chapter on the ways to initiate, facilitate, and honor end-of-life conversations. The authors reinforce the need to listen carefully to patients, to recognize the contexts of conversations, and to gently challenge patients to clarify their wishes.

Buckholz follows with an all-too-common case illustrating the deleterious effects of family conflict in end-of-life care. What can one ethically do when families or families and patients disagree about care? This case study serves to introduce Beckwith's chapter which examines this very issue. Beckwith reinforces the role of information, goal setting, and careful listening and the value of probing and clarifying family dynamics in resolving family disagreements. She also offers other innovative approaches including the role of expressive therapies and spiritual care in addressing these conflicts. These recommendations truly define the value of holistic hospice care.

Jennings follows with a chapter on the ethics of surrogate decision making. In many ways this chapter continues the discussion of patient autonomy, advance directives, and the role of family. Jennings's contribution is that he goes beyond the theory of surrogate decision making to ask probing questions: How realistic is it to expect that the surrogate can simply follow the wishes of the patient in an ever-changing context? How practical is it to believe that surrogates can set aside their own hopes, emotions, and beliefs? Jennings also takes note of the role of health care agencies in assisting the surrogate—especially (but not exclusively) in the cases where the patient is isolated and the surrogate is a stranger.

How far can we take autonomy? What occurs when the core value of autonomy clashes with other core values such as the sanctity of life? Should an individual decide to end his or her life? Suicide at the end-of-life is now emerging from a long taboo—generating legal battles throughout the Western world. Attig was given an extensive mandate—to review the rationality of suicide, and to discuss the ethical dimensions of physician-assisted suicide and developments in Oregon and the Netherlands where assisted suicide now has legal sanction. His conclusion is subtly different from that of many hospice providers. He concludes that suicide can be a rational act in a limited number of circumstances, especially when effective hospice and palliative care are not available. His analysis supports not so much a right to die as a right to decide. Many individuals in the hospice field, including those in the Hospice Foundation of America, believe that flexible and accessible hospice care may obviate the desire to end one's life. Interestingly again, the pace of technology may outrun the law. The conflict over physician-assisted suicide may become moot as the availability of information over the Internet may render the role of the physician superfluous in this respect.

The Pasinski case concludes this section. Here we see the conflict of how the many roles of hospice can intersect and even conflict. Hospice, as Pasinski reaffirms, is more than a system of care. It is a community resource. How does one deal with prior information—in this case, an earlier consultation over a patient contemplating suicide? How does one balance individual autonomy and professional confidentiality with the team and patient-centered philosophies that lie at the heart of hospice care? The case reminds us of how theory translates into the daily realities of end-of-life care. ■

CHAPTER 5

How Americans Want to Die— Grassroots Values and Cultural Diversity

Bruce Jennings

It is often said that America is a culture that denies death, and so we do in many ways. Yet we are also fascinated by the dilemmas that high-technology medicine has created for us, and we have a dim but growing awareness of the staggering social problems that loom in the graying of the baby boom generation. A concern with end-of-life care grew into a potent social movement in the 1990s and has not much abated in the opening years of the new century (Webb, 1997).

The 1990s saw the United States Supreme Court's first landmark ruling on end-of-life care in the Cruzan case, in which it affirmed the constitutional right to refuse life-sustaining medical treatment. This decision was quickly followed by the passage of the federal Patient Self-Determination Act and durable power of attorney for health care statutes in many states, all stressing the importance of considering one's preferences about end-of-life care in advance. Public education efforts to encourage the use of advance directives sprang up throughout the country.

In the mid-90s, a major study of treatment of patients in the last few months of their lives documented the alarming extent to which aggressive life-prolonging measures were still being used in situations where they were medically futile or were unwanted by the patients, or both (SUPPORT Principal Investigators, 1995). Even concerted efforts to improve communication between physicians and dying patients did not stem the technological momentum of end-of-life care in the country's major medical centers. Moreover, a large proportion of families reported post mortem that the patient had spent the last two or three days of life in severe, unrelieved pain.

Losing control of care at the end of life, of becoming dependent on machines, of being an emotional and financial burden to one's family, and of suffering owing to inadequate treatment of pain and other symptoms—all these fears and more led to a growing grassroots movement in the late 1990s to legalize physician-assisted suicide (PAS). The movement was dramatized by the public defiance of Dr. Jack Kevorkian, who assisted more than 100 persons in ending their lives and after three separate trials was finally sent to prison; by the debate over the Oregon referendum that legalized PAS for the first time in the United States; and by the Federal Appeals Court rulings in the Second and Ninth Circuits that temporarily struck down existing state laws against PAS before those appellate rulings were overturned by the U.S. Supreme Court in the summer of 1997 (Jennings, 1999).

In the past decade, several groups have mounted a less contentious educational and institutional change effort to improve end-of-life care and to address the concerns of the general public. Of course, the hospice movement has a history dating back to the 1970s, but interest in hospice and use of hospice services accelerated in the 1990s; in 2003 an estimated 750,000 patients had hospice care for some period of time before their deaths, but the average length of stay in hospice programs dropped from more than 50 days in the mid-1990s to close to 40 days in the late 1990s (Jennings, Ryndes, D'Onofrio, & Baily, 2003). Efforts by hospitals and community groups to educate consumers concerning the use of advance directives were also widespread during this period.

Within the health care professions, growing attention is being paid to improving the standard of practice in pain management and palliative care. Specialists in this area have long argued that medical education and the general skill and knowledge level within medicine are not sufficient to meet patient needs, and that there is systematic and persistent undertreatment of pain in the mainstream American health care system. New curricula for medical and nursing education are being developed and implemented, and a recent Institute of Medicine study (Field & Cassel, 1997) contains what may now be regarded as a consensus among experts in the area concerning what needs to be done.

IN SEARCH OF CORE VALUES NEAR THE END OF LIFE

This chapter is based on a review of the findings of grassroots civic dialogues, town meetings, and focus group projects conducted by various community health decision groups around the country. The methods used to organize these discussions are quite diverse. Even so, there is a remarkable degree of convergence in the values and attitudes expressed by participants. At the very least, the overlapping consensus of these studies suggests a potential core of end-of-life values in America. This core of values requires further description, refinement, and critical analysis.

I shall highlight information from three types of studies: telephone surveys, focus group studies, and community forum projects. The first two use random sampling techniques to recruit participants. The third uses advance advertising, word of mouth, and special invitations to recruit participants. The survey is rigidly scripted and structured, usually containing simple answers based on a standard scale. Focus groups have guiding questions and probes but are more open to spontaneous communication from participants. They may allow for interpersonal dialogue. Analysis is often done on transcribed audio tapes. Community forums have the least structure and the most give and take among participants. Content analysis is usually based on observer notes, although audio tape transcripts are sometimes created and used too.

TELEPHONE SURVEYS

Large-scale professional surveys have for many years confirmed that Americans are concerned about the circumstances of dying and the end-of-life care they and their loved ones are likely to receive. Fear of loss of personal control, of being a burden, of being abandoned, and of suffering from unrelieved pain stand out among the most common worries.

In 1996 the Gallup Organization conducted a telephone survey of more than 1,000 adults nationwide for the National Hospice Organization. Six out of ten respondents (61%) said that they had given some thought to preparing for the possible death of a family member or loved one. Seventy-five percent had experienced the death of a family member or close friend in the past 5 years, and one half of those said the death in question was the result of a terminal illness. About a third were involved in some form of caregiving to the person who died. A slight majority (57%) believed that society has grown more concerned with the needs of the dying, while 34% believed society has become more indifferent. Almost everyone (89%) felt that it is the family's responsibility to care for the dying, but nearly half (46%) also felt that it is the government's responsibility to meet the needs of the dying, with most of that burden going to the state government rather than to the local or federal government (Gallup Organization, 1996).

Some attitudes revealed in this survey seem inconsistent with the workings of the health care system. Nine out of ten adults would prefer to be cared for at home if they were terminally ill; at the same time, 62% say that if they were terminally ill they would continue to seek curative treatment (70% of those age 18 to 34 and 55% of those age 55 and older responded yes to that question). At the opposite end of the spectrum, 35% said that if they were terminally ill they would ask their doctor to end their life.

Finally, this survey asked respondents to name their greatest fear associated with death. The most frequent answer (40%) was "being a burden to family and friends." Next highest (14%) was being in pain. Losing control over one's care and losing one's dignity were next most frequently mentioned, at 8% each.

FOCUS GROUP STUDIES

Another widely used methodology among grassroots groups is the focus group study. Here random techniques (or targeted approaches) are used to select potential participants, who are then invited to take part in usually a 60- to 90-minute session, directed by a trained focus group leader who has prepared trigger questions in advance. Ideally, the facilitator guides the group but does not dominate or direct it in such a way as to predetermine the outcome. Participants may be paid a nominal sum to attend, and assistance with transportation and day care may be arranged so that no one gender or socioeconomic group is systematically excluded.

Unlike telephone surveys, to which responses are immediate and there is very little conversation or interaction between the respondent and the person conducting the survey, focus groups offer the opportunity for a reasonably extended period of civic conversation among strangers who listen and respond to one another's concerns in a face-to-face setting. It is not uncommon for participants in focus groups to gain information and new ideas during the process, as well as to give their perspectives and share their personal stories.

One of the largest and most carefully designed focus group studies to date on end-of-life care attitudes and beliefs is The Quest to Die with Dignity study conducted by American Health Decisions (1997). This study involved 385 participants in 36 focus groups held in 32 cities across the country. Like others, the Quest study found much overlapping consensus across ethnic and religious diversity, and a core set of attitudes and concerns emerged.

Americans are wary of the technological environment of the modern hospital as a place to die. They fear loss of control over what treatments they receive, and they prefer to die at home, or in a more intimate setting in the presence of family and friends. They do not believe that the current organization of the health care system is conducive to their image of ideal end-of-life care. They feel that it is overly oriented toward curing illness and prolonging life, and too driven by cost factors to serve the special needs of the dying.

The Quest study also revealed a growing sense of distrust and a rift between patients and physicians. People are no longer as confident as they once were that the doctor has their best interests at heart. They do not even necessarily see the doctor as a prime partner in advance care planning, although many participants seemed to change their mind about that as the focus group discussion went on and they came to see the complexity of the decision-making processes.

In line with the Gallup survey, the Quest study found a widespread desire not to be a burden on one's family. Here people understood the notion of "burden" broadly; they included economic, emotional, and physical burden in their thinking about this issue. They also feared losing control of what happens to them, living in unrelieved pain, and abandonment.

By and large, demographic factors such as age, religion, region, or ethnicity made little difference to the content of the focus group discussions in the Quest project. Ethnicity made some difference in the following ways:

- White and Asian participants were more likely to trust the health care system and more willing to terminate life support than were African American, Native American, or Hispanic participants.

- African American participants were more suspicious of quality-of-life language than other groups.

Among the recommendations drawn from the Quest study are the following:

- Reestablish trust in the doctor-patient relationship.

- Develop a new approach to advance care planning and advance directives; current forms and requirements are not helpful.

- Improve pain relief and palliative care.

- Expand hospice-type services.

- Empower families to make end-of-life care decisions and support them in providing care to a dying loved one.

- Provide stronger incentives to encourage people to fill out advance directives and take other steps to guard against unwanted and inappropriate treatments.

An important finding from the Quest study, and from a closely related follow-up study conducted by Georgia Health Decisions (1997), is that ordinary people want much more information than they now feel they have to assist them in making end-of-life decisions. As the Vermont project discussed below also found, they want specific, useful information that will help them find the right services and cope with difficult caregiving tasks or decisions.

People are isolated from full engagement with the topic of end-of-life care by several factors: (1) their own avoidance of the topic, (2) professional and legalistic language that is unfamiliar, (3) advance directive documents that are not user-friendly, (4) lack of information about the types of decisions they may be called upon to make, and (5) distrust of the health care system and alienation from their physicians.

People will talk, and want very much to talk, about end-of-life issues if they are given the appropriate setting and opportunity. More civic spaces or forum opportunities must be created in numerous venues in their everyday lives to enlist them in reform efforts for end-of-life care. They need access to knowledgeable professionals who can answer specific questions regarding advance planning and questions that will come up during the time when important health care decisions need to be made. More written information should be made available that is accessible and engaging. However, mass distribution of unsolicited materials is not believed to be effective. Strategic planning is needed to devise the right way and the right time to introduce ordinary people to educational and informational materials. End-of-life projects need to find the right teachable moment for reaching the public.

COMMUNITY FORUM PROJECTS

The most important recent project on grassroots values and end-of-life care to employ the community forum approach is the Journey's End project undertaken in 1996–97 by the Vermont Ethics Network (1997). In this project, 42 community forums were held throughout the state of Vermont with a total of 388 participants. The forums lasted from 1 to 2 hours, and attendance ranged from 3 to 50. Demographic characteristics on the participants were gathered from questionnaires distributed at the forums. A total of 172 questionnaires were collected and tabulated. The participants were overwhelmingly female (78%), healthy (only 16% said they had significant health problems), middle aged (70% were between the ages of 40 and 70), and fairly sophisticated about health care (78% had some experience with hospice, 40% had both a living will and a durable power of attorney for health care, and 88% had an established relationship with a primary care physician).

From an analysis of the discussions at the 42 community forums, nine concerns emerged, which were largely consonant with the findings of the other research I have surveyed. The Vermont concerns were communication with caregivers, decision making about treatment, controlling pain and other symptoms, the needs of families and friends, concerns about the availability and organization of care resources, the place where one dies, personal relationships in caregiving at the end of life, spiritual needs, and public policy issues.

The SUPPORT study discovered that improving communication between physicians and patients and families in the medical center setting did not affect physician behavior or the pattern of treatment the patient received (SUPPORT Principal Investigators, 1995). Nonetheless, at the grassroots level a belief remains that improving communication will change care for the better and enhance the experience of the dying process for all concerned. People want to know what to expect; even bad news is preferable to uncertainty, wondering, and guessing. Families want detailed "nuts-and-bolts" information about how to cope with patient needs and foreseeable crises. Patients do not appreciate physician avoidance of the subject of death and dying; frankness and candor are prized over false hope or silence.

The discussions in Vermont found some of the concern about remaining in control of one's own treatment and care that other surveys have found, but it also found a significant number of people who would defer, when the time comes, to the best judgments of their families and physicians.

Pain control and palliative care were central preoccupations in the discussions, although those who had been closely involved with end-of-life care recently did not report many serious complaints with the care their loved ones had received. While perhaps satisfied with the care they had observed firsthand, they were nonetheless aware of, and concerned about, the notion that physicians generally are not adequately trained in palliative care and that many people throughout the country suffer needlessly.

Most of the participants had direct caregiving experience with someone who was dying, and central to their discussions were the problems they had encountered in that role. They spoke of needing more information and of wanting to be "empowered" to be better care providers. Assistance in overcoming internal family conflicts and counseling regarding bereavement were high priorities for Vermonters.

Like the other survey and focus group studies, the Vermont project found that flexibility, multidisciplinary comprehensiveness, and continuity of care are very important to families. These factors give patients and families a sense of security and predictability about the services they will receive.

Where one dies is every bit as much on the minds of the citizens of Vermont as it is elsewhere. Compared with the national figures, the actual pattern there is slightly tilted toward out-of-hospital deaths: 45% of Vermonters die in the hospital, 24% at home, and 23% in nursing homes. But the discussion forums in the Vermont project, as is frequently the case with this type of civic meeting, went beyond the first-line question that the survey studies get at. Instead of simply revealing where people would prefer to die, this discussion probed what people believe is needed in each setting in order for their values at the end of life to be well served.

This discussion tells us that people do not believe that they can experience a good dying only at home—an inference often drawn from survey data. Instead, they believe that they can experience a good dying in various settings, but that each setting presents its own challenges and problems—the home no less than the hospital or the nursing home. To be sure, hospitals, with their cold, impersonal environment and their daunting and confusing round of activities, may pose the most difficult challenges. But they can be made more understandable with the proper orientation, and they can be made more hospitable to family and friends and less rigid in certain rules, such as visiting hours, opportunities for family to participate in caregiving to some extent, and the like. In the home, the key is providing the necessary professional and technical support to family caregivers when the going gets rough. In each setting, the goals identified in the Vermont discussions were the same: first, to provide the necessary medical services; second, to provide the relationships and the contact that allow for "living while dying."

Another significant facet of the Vermont findings was the emphasis that people, even those who were not overtly "religious," placed on the spiritual dimension of dying (O'Connell, 1994). It was clear that the availability of clergy for support and counseling was valued, but spirituality was also perceived as something that goes on between the dying person and family and friends. It has to do with the growth, enlightenment, or depth of feeling that can redound to the benefit of the survivors as much as, or more than, to the benefit of the dying person. It is interesting to note that people tend to associate the concept of hospice more with spiritual care and the care of the family and survivors, and not only (or even primarily) with direct care of the patient (Gallup Organization, 1996; see also Health Communication Research Institute, 1996). At the moment, hospice is unique in the health care system in assuming responsibility for family well-being and for continuing its service provision for at least 1 year following the death of the patient. Apparently that sense of hospice's broad mission is filtering down to the awareness of the general public.

At the policy level, the discussions in Vermont identified a wide range of problems and obstacles to the kind of care that is most valued at the end of life. A rigid and unrealistic split between good palliative care and continued curative care was one problem mentioned. Another was limiting hospice to those with less than 6 months to live. Another concern was the feeling that managed care would give low priority to the humanitarian aspects of end-of-life care. Finally, more resources should be made available, Vermonters argued, to allow respite periods for family caregivers, since the unremitting ordeal of that "36-hour day" can be exceedingly destructive.

RELIGIOUS AND CULTURAL DIVERSITY

The findings growing out of telephone surveys, focus groups, and community forums reviewed above show a remarkable convergence of views across religious and ethnic traditions. Yet there is every reason to think that end-of-life care should be at least as diverse and controversial in the views and values it elicits as any other major social issue; indeed, one might even expect it to be more culturally sensitive than other issues.

What are we to make of this seeming paradox? One possible explanation, of course, is that minority cultural perspectives are underrepresented and underarticulated in studies and projects of the type considered here. No doubt there is something to that, and participant self-selection in all these studies was certainly biased in favor of individuals who were willing to talk openly about death and dying. On the other hand, at least the telephone surveys and focus groups did try to randomize and control participation in such a way as to reflect social diversity.

A second possible explanation is that even when minority viewpoints are present in the discussions, there is something about the group dynamics of these civic spaces that inhibits the voicing of radically divergent perspectives. In order to express a feeling about death and dying, one may need to discuss one's religious experience or relationship with God in a very personal way, and it may feel awkward or unseemly to do so outside the company of one's fellow believers. Other forms of cultural difference may also be difficult to express in what feels like a highly secular and Western setting. More homogeneous groupings, led by community leaders who are better known and more trusted by the participants, may be required to open up different points of view effectively.

One final speculation: Religious and cultural traditions give individuals a language with which to comprehend and communicate their experience, a lens through which to perceive themselves and the world, and a repertoire of meanings and symbols with which to organize their experiences and make them cohere into some kind of whole (Cohen et al., 2000; Marty & Vaux, 1982). These traditions vary greatly on the surface, so to speak, but perhaps at a deeper level they tend to converge on some similar themes or "core values." The subjects of death, dying, pain, suffering, care, dignity, and peace at the end of life may in fact lead to that terrain where our diverse humanness recedes and our common humanity comes to the fore. That, too, may be some of what we are hearing in these studies.

In any case, cultural diversity poses several dilemmas and challenges for patients, families, and health care professionals. A growing body of literature is demonstrating the ways in which culture shapes patients' experiences and expectations regarding health care—from the way pain is experienced or articulated, to the preeminent role of the family in decision-making, to the meanings of death and dying (Carrese & Rhodes, 1995; Fins, 1995; Galanti, 1991; Gostin, 1995).

One point of tension between patients or families and caregivers concerns truth-telling (Orona, Koenig, & Davis, 1994; Thomasma, 1994).

Health care providers recognize a duty to respect patient autonomy, particularly by openly disclosing information to patients and encouraging their participation in treatment decision making—especially by ensuring that their consent to a treatment plan is voluntary and informed. Yet family members may not want a patient to be told "bad news" and may insist that caregivers withhold information. Such requests are not necessarily unreasonable once providers understand a patient's cultural background, but they remain troubling in the face of competing professional obligations.

Similarly, cultural influences on the expression of pain may influence the treatment patients receive. When patients do not articulate their pain in ways that the dominant culture expects or deems appropriate, caregivers may erroneously assume that it does not exist. Moreover, as Annette Dula (1994) has emphasized, the experience of unequal power and discrimination that African Americans often feel in health care institutions influences how they interact with caregivers.

One of the most important lessons to be learned from the proliferating literature on "cross-cultural" health care, however, is not about the potential pitfalls of working with patients from particular cultural or ethnic traditions, but the need to appreciate the ways in which culture, ethnicity, race, and a host of other factors powerfully but almost invisibly shape the interactions of patients and caregivers (Blackhall, Murphy, Frank, Michel, & Azen, 1995).

While it is important to appreciate the ways religious traditions shape patients' understandings of the end of life and expectations regarding care, it is equally important for caregivers to remember that no faith or cultural tradition is monolithic (Michel, 1994). One danger in becoming more sensitive to religious, ethnic, or cultural difference in end-of-life care is a kind of reverse stereotyping and losing sight of the individual patient within well-meaning cultural generalizations (Koenig & Gates-Williams, 1995).

Will the effort to reform and substantially improve end-of-life care in American succeed? More well-meaning people have probably worked harder on this problem during the past thirty years than on any other sector or problem in our health care system. There can be no gainsaying the fact that we have come a long way from the time when there was no hospice care for those who "failed" cancer treatment and when doctors often lied to patients about their terminal diagnosis. But it is equally evident that we still have a long way to go and much work to do. Putting so much of the burden on the patient and family through an emphasis on advance planning and advance directives is perhaps something that needs to be rethought. So does the tendency to turn physicians into mere technical experts or body mechanics instead of acknowledging and reinforcing their proper role as professionals and as moral agents in the decision-making process of end-of-life care. To resist medical paternalism is one thing, to undermine professionalism in medicine is quite another. Finally, we certainly need to stop driving a wedge between life-prolonging treatment and hospice and palliative care so that we force individuals and families to make a tragic choice they are unprepared and unwilling to make.

I believe that we can continue to make progress, correct any false starts, and make mid-course corrections as needed. My optimism on this score stems from the fact that amidst our diversity as a society, amidst our dynamic mosaic—which is not a melting pot and need not be— we finally do have a bedrock conception of the human good, including dying well, upon which we can anchor our end-of-life care practices and policies. That good does not consist merely of longevity or of choice, but of the freedom to choose relationships that are intrinsically valuable in their own right: compassion and caring; fidelity and witness; solidarity and reconciliation. ■

Bruce Jennings is Senior Research Scholar at The Hastings Center, a bioethics research institute in Garrison, New York. Mr. Jennings has been with the Hastings Center since 1980 and served as its executive director from 1990 to 1999. A graduate of Yale University (BA) and Princeton University (MA), he has written widely on end-of-life care, long-term care, and health policy. He served on the Board of Directors of the National Hospice and Palliative Care Organization and the Hospice and Palliative Care Association of New York State. He has written or edited 18 books, including The Perversion of Autonomy: The Uses of Coercion and Constraints in a Liberal Society *(2nd ed. 2003; co-authored with Willard Gaylin). He is currently at work on a book on chronic illness, dementia, and long-term care policy.*

REFERENCES

American Health Decisions (1997). *The quest to die with dignity.* Appleton, WI: Author. [May be ordered from AHD c/o The Hastings Center, Garrison, NY 10524.]

Blackhall, L. J., Murphy, S. T., Frank, G., Michel, V., & Azen, S. (1995). Ethnicity and attitudes toward patient autonomy. *JAMA, 274*(10), 820–825.

Carrese, J. A., & Rhodes, L. A. (1995). Western bioethics on the Navajo reservation. *JAMA, 274*(10), 826–829.

Cohen, C. B., Heller, J. C., Jennings, B., Morgan, E. F. M., Scott, D. A., Sedgwick, T., & Smith, D. H. (2000). *Faithful living, faithful dying: Anglican reflections on end of life care.* Allentown, PA: Morehouse Press.

Dula, A. (1994). African American suspicion of the healthcare system is justified: What do we do about it? *Cambridge Quarterly of Healthcare Ethics, 3*(3), 347–357.

Field, M. J., & Cassel, C. K. (Eds.) (1997). *Approaching death: Improving care at the end of life.* Washington, DC: National Academy Press.

Fins, J. F. (1995). Across the divide: Religious objections to brain death. *Journal of Religion and Health, 34*(1), 33–39.

Galanti, G-A. (1991). *Caring for patients from different cultures: Case studies from American hospitals.* Philadelphia: University of Pennsylvania Press.

Gallup Organization. (1996). *Knowledge and attitudes related to hospice care.* Arlington, VA: National Hospice Organization, 1996.

Gostin, L. O. (1995). Informed consent, cultural sensitivity, and respect for persons (editorial). *JAMA, 274*(10), 844–845.

Health Communication Research Institute. (1996). *Telephone survey on end of life decision-making.* Sacramento, CA: Sacramento Healthcare Decisions.

Jennings, B. (1999). The liberal neutrality of living and dying. *Journal of Contemporary Health Law and Policy, 16*(1), 97–126.

Jennings, B., Ryndes, T., D'Onofrio, C., & Baily, M. A. (2003). *Access to hospice care: Expanding boundaries, overcoming barriers.*

Hastings Center Report Special Supplement 33(2), S11–12.

Koenig, B. A., & Gates-Williams, J. (1995). Understanding cultural difference in caring for dying patients. *Western Journal of Medicine, 163*(3), 244–249.

Marty, M. E., & Vaux, K. L. (1982). *Health, medicine and the faith traditions: An inquiry into religion and medicine.* Philadelphia: Fortress Press.

Michel, V. (1994). Factoring ethnic and racial differences into bioethics decision making. *Generations, xviii*(4), 23–26.

O'Connell, L. J. (1994). The role of religion in health-related decision making for elderly patients. *Generations, xviii*(4), 27–30.

Orona, C. J., Koenig, B. A., & Davis, A. J. (1994). Cultural aspects of nondisclosure. *Cambridge Quarterly of Healthcare Ethics, 3*(3) 338–346.

SUPPORT Principal Investigators (1995). A controlled trial to improve care for seriously ill hospitalized patients: The study to understand prognoses and preferences for outcomes and risks of treatments (SUPPORT). *JAMA, 274,* 1591–1598.

Thomasma, D. C. (1994). Telling the truth to patients: A clinic ethics exploration. *Cambridge Quarterly of Healthcare Ethics, 3*(3) 375–382.

Tyler, Beverly. (1997) *Georgian's views on health care decisions at the end-of-life.* Atlanta, Georgia Health Decisions.

Vermont Ethics Network. (1997). *Vermont voices on care of the dying.* Montpelier, VT: Author.

Webb, M. (1997). *The good death: The new American search to reshape the end of life.* New York: Bantam.

Patient Autonomy, Beneficence, Medical Futility, and the Hospice Health Care Provider

Hospice of Palm Beach County

Paul was a 55-year-old male with extensive medical history, although information received remained inconsistent and sketchy. Paul had a history of hepatitis C and of testicular carcinoma, which was successfully treated. In his late 40s, Paul suffered a stroke and developed hemiparesis with resulting seizure disorder. He had a history of deep vein thrombosis (DVT) and numerous episodes of aspiration pneumonia, and difficulty with feeding tube with evisceration and enterocutaneous fistula[1]. He also had a history of oliguria[2] with acute chronic renal failure and cardiac arrest. His hospice diagnosis was "septicemia with aspiration pneumonia complicated by wound dehiscence with evisceration of abdominal contents."

During previous admissions to the hospital where Hospice of Palm Beach County has an inpatient unit, there was an understanding from staff that Paul had voiced that he had wanted "everything done, and did not want hospice." However, during these hospital admissions, Paul had signed a "Do Not Resuscitate" order (DNR). Three months prior to hospice

---

[1] enterocutaneous fistula: a pathological passage or connection from the intestines boring outwards towards the skin with drainage of intestinal content

[2] oliguria: decreased urine output, usually due to renal disease

admission, he had been admitted to a hospital from a local skilled nursing facility for aspiration pneumonia. During this lengthy hospital stay, a psychiatric consult was ordered because Paul had expressed suicidal ideas. Paul's mother, acting as his health care surrogate, had reported to the psychiatrist at the time that Paul "did not have previous history of suicide and that he had a strong will to live, and wished to continue fighting." Findings at that time were that Paul did not demonstrate suicidal intentions, and that his insight and judgment were limited. Thought processes were intact, however.

Paul's condition deteriorated in the ensuing months. Throughout this time, primary physicians made several referrals to Hospice of Palm Beach County. When our admissions' nurses met with family members, however, they were not ready to transition to the hospice palliative philosophy. Paul's mother wanted to make sure that his siblings were on board with her decision for hospice. She also wanted to make sure that she had "pursued everything possible medically" before "going to hospice." Eventually, with the support of her other children, Paul's mother admitted him to our care. He was unconscious, minimally responsive and nonverbal at the time of admission. Questions quickly came to the forefront between the health care providers from both hospital and hospice teams as to whether Paul's wishes had been followed (to exhaust all medical interventions) versus admission to the hospice program. Although there were no written health care surrogacy papers, through proxy, Paul's mother had decision-making ability.

Had Paul been adequately informed when he was conscious of the seriousness of his condition, would he have still chosen curative versus palliative care through hospice? Paul had a short length of stay, and died four days later. The case was sent to the Ethics Committee for review.

DISCUSSION:

- What are the challenges when working within a system that exists essentially on the opposite continuum of yours (hospital versus hospice)? What are the needs for education of the hospital staff and how do you bridge these differences to the greater good of the patient and his/her needs and those of the family?

- What are the obstacles in assuring sound biopsychosocial decisions were made in a timely manner by hospice staff, thus avoiding extending patient or family members' emotional pain in decision-making role?

- Were issues of medical futility versus curative treatment fully understood by the patient and family? How did this information (or lack of) impact care?

- How did issues of documentation of the patient's previous hospital stays and documentation of his wishes impact and/or delay hospice admission and patient/family being able to receive our support and intervention sooner?

- Did personal values shared by hospital or hospice staff on the issues of patient rights, specifically autonomy and beneficence, impede early intervention or support? Did this identify a need for further education on these issues? Should the case have been brought to the Ethics Committee earlier?

Ethical dilemmas often arise because a patient or family has not been heard accurately, or there is some misinformation or misinterpretation of the information given. This particular situation gave Hospice of Palm Beach County an opportunity to review our own organizational values and protocols, and to identify opportunities for education and growth, as we continue to provide end-of-life care to families in our community. It also provided an opportunity for further education with the health care community and brought to the forefront, once again, the need for written advance directives. Most importantly, we were able to recommit to the reality of what we who work in hospice always have known—that our families always challenge us to new levels of caring and dedication. ■

Maria Teahan, ACSW, LCSW, CTS, is Supportive Care Manager of Hospice of Palm Beach County, Florida. She submitted this case study on behalf of Hospice of Palm Beach County Ethics Committee.

■ CHAPTER 6 ■

Autonomy, Consent, and Advance Directives

William M. Lamers, Jr.

> *... a century and more ago, there was no human expectation whatsoever that medicine could significantly extend individual life or effectively combat the infirmities of old age.*
> —Callahan (1987)

New medical techniques and treatments can save and often extend the lives of persons who, in the past, undoubtedly would have died. While this has generally been good news, the ability to extend life causes some to fear that they may be kept alive despite their desire to be allowed to die a "normal" death. For some, the availability of rescue procedures and life support techniques has been a blessing; for others, it poses a threat. The prospect of living on in a vegetative state, supported by mechanical devices, unable to make decisions about what happens, is a forbidding one. Some say they would not want to be kept alive if it meant there was no "quality" to living. Others are concerned that the cost of prolonged life support will deplete family savings. Some argue that people in a persistent vegetative state are functionally dead. A number of popular movements have arisen, centered on the "right to die." The difficult-to-define slogan, "death with dignity," caught the public fancy. Many varieties of a legal document entitled "living will" arose in different parts of the country. The resulting public involvement, combined with conflicting pressures within the medical establishment, contributed to the development of the bioethics movement (Kieffer, 1979).

Bioethicists continuously grapple with dilemmas on several levels related to technology, the law, definitions of life and death, priorities for utilizing limited resources, coercion versus consent, and conflicts between personal rights and the good of society. Today, ethical issues regarding the end of life have a profound impact on society and technology. This chapter deals with three interrelated concepts in bioethics. We will examine their origins and the debate surrounding them and discuss some of their implications in law and clinical practice.

Autonomy is a fundamental concept in the law that proclaims the right of individuals to act on their own, to make decisions, to determine their fate.

Consent is a legal term indicating an agreement regarding something to be done. It is an act of reason following upon deliberation. Consent offers an alternative to submission. Consent is one of the derivatives of autonomy.

Advance directive is a legal document, usually consisting of two elements: a living will and a durable power of attorney for health care. Advance directives are based on the concept of autonomy. They ensure continuity of decisions made while an individual is competent in the event of later loss of decisional ability.

Autonomy affirms the right to make decisions; consent describes the process of making decisions; advance directives ensure continuity of decisions across time. The bioethics movement resulted not only from unanticipated progress in medical science that affected matters of dying and death; it also reflected dramatic changes in the doctor-patient relationship that stemmed from a number of different factors.

Early in the last century, doctors tended to make unilateral treatment decisions on the basis not only of their superior knowledge of disease (sapiential authority) but also of the elevated nature of their calling (moral authority) and their presumed right to control based on God-given grace (charismatic authority). The doctor in earlier times was one of the four robed professions (priest, lawyer, professor, doctor) that claimed special authority derived directly from God. Assumptions on the part of both patient and doctor that derived from this tradition gave rise to the practice of "benevolent paternalism." Doctors were more likely to speak with one another about diagnosis, prognosis, and treatment options than to discuss them with the patient. At the same time, many patients relinquished treatment decisions completely to their doctors.

Following World War II, the highly publicized trials of Nazi war criminals, including doctors, alerted many to the violations of human rights in medical experimentation on unwilling human subjects (Annas, 1992). One important outcome of the trials was the development of ethical standards for medical research and treatment. Concern about violation of human rights during wartime stimulated interest in the rights of human subjects during medical research programs. When it was revealed that 22 seriously ill patients had been injected with live cancer cells at one of America's leading research institutions, the medical community began to seek new standards to protect patients' rights and to curtail the abuse of patients (Lerner, 2004).

The consumer movement in the United States set in motion the questioning of most areas of human activity, from automobile safety to the processing of foodstuffs, the efficacy and safety of drugs, and the ranking of hospitals and colleges. The power of informed consumers began to have an impact on providers of care as well as on producers of goods.

While consumers were becoming better informed and sometimes organized, medical technology made it possible to remove functioning internal organs from persons presumed dead and transplant them into the body of another person who could not live long without the vital organs. The moral, legal, and ethical ramifications of this dramatic possibility forced a reexamination and redefinition of both life and death (Beecher, 1966).

Other medical techniques, instrumentation, and procedures not only made it possible to resuscitate persons who otherwise would have died, but transformed the demography of dying. At the onset of the 20th century, the majority of all deaths in any year occurred in children under 15 years of age. By the end of the century, most deaths in any year occurred in persons over 65 years of age. People were now living almost twice as long as their grandparents. Diseases that once inevitably caused death could be successfully treated. However, extended duration of life was not always accompanied by elevated quality of life. The specter of spending endless days and months in an institution caused people to think about their own inevitable death.

The situation was further complicated by the rising cost of increasingly complex health care; the threat of lawsuits for undertreating patients that led to unwanted, protracted, and expensive care; and the shift of locus of care from the home to the hospital, with most care provided by health care professionals to the exclusion of family caregivers.

The care of seriously ill and infirm elderly persons has also suffered under the rubric of "institutional care" (i.e., providing care by the numbers and according to hospital policy rather than in accord with patient/family wishes). Shared responsibility among several disciplines, "standing orders," and placing hospital policy and tradition above patient preference all have contributed to the difficulty of providing excellent care for seriously ill persons even in some of the most noted hospitals in the country. The SUPPORT (Study to Understand Prognoses and Preferences for Outcomes and Risks of Treatment) Study (1995) was designed "to improve end-of-life decision making and to reduce the frequency of mechanically supported, painful and prolonged process of dying" (p. 1591). The result of the phase 1 observation clearly documented problems in communication, the frequency of aggressive treatment, and the characteristics of death in these hospitals. For example, only 47% of physicians knew when their patients wished to avoid cardiopulmonary resuscitation. Forty-six percent of do not resuscitate (DNR) orders were written within the last 2 days of life, and family members reported that 50% of conscious patients who died in the hospital experienced moderate to severe pain more than half the time.

Calland (1972), a physician with progressive renal failure, previously observed the same problems from his vantage point as a patient in a major teaching hospital:

To many patients, the point that is most important is the quality of life. I believe strongly that the patient should have a doctor who is interested in the art of medicine—namely, the *care* of the patient—so that he (the patient) may return to a more "normal" life, whatever that means to him, not what it means to the doctor (p. 324).

The value-laden concept "quality of life" gradually replaced the more difficult-to-define phrase "death with dignity." The imagery inherent in both phrases was used to bolster arguments that arose out of advancing technical ability to resuscitate persons presumed dead and to prolong life in the absence of conscious brain function. Advances in science and technology led to new techniques and procedures that had implications beyond the envelope of written law. The U.S. Constitution, which guaranteed, among other things, the right to life, could not at the same time allow clinicians to end a life that was sustained, even by "artificial" means. The landmark Quinlan, Cruzan, and Schiavo legal cases highlight the evolving resolution of great dissonance between the law and clinical practice. This chapter is intended as a guide to the issues.

AUTONOMY

Regard for the rule and regard for the person are widely separated and often irreconcilable interests. The law, or the rule, knows no friends, cherishes no affectionate solicitude for the human soul, and offers no consolation to the individual. For it, the individual is a mere abstraction, and the community or the state the true and only reality.
—Dixon (1935)

The rule of law deals with the general population, considered as a whole. Law addresses the many, not the individual, whose needs may differ from the norm. The law is reluctant to allow exceptions to the rule. There is a tension between the rights of the individual and the good of society, as expressed in the rule of law.

The legal concept of autonomy originated in ancient Greece, where it described the capacity of a state or country to declare its right to self-determination. The concept of autonomy applies to individuals as well as to states. Within a democracy, autonomy has become synonymous with the basic rights of the individual. Autonomous persons can choose, within certain limits, what they wish to do or not do. Autonomous is equivalent to independent, and refers to the state or quality of being self-governing. The concept of personal autonomy implies self-determination, moral independence, and self-directing freedom.

Because it declares the right of an individual to act on his or her own behalf, autonomy is basic to health care decisions. People need not submit to treatment; they can knowingly consent to or refuse treatment. The American Medical Association (1996) emphasized the importance of autonomy in its revised Code of Ethics: "Physicians have an obligation to relieve pain and suffering and to promote the dignity and autonomy of dying patients in their care."

In its broad sense, autonomy deals with the physical, social, psychological, and spiritual dimensions of the individual. Autonomy helps to define how the individual relates to and functions as a member of society. Autonomy, therefore, serves to counterbalance the anonymity of the individual under the rule of law. Respect for the individual as unique is fundamental to the decisional ability of the individual in a democracy. Autonomy makes it possible to declare, "I am an individual with self-determination. I know what I want and what I do not want. I can make choices about what happens to me and I expect my choices to be respected."

Autonomy is a fundamental right that enables us to be treated as individuals rather than as numbers or part of a collective. Autonomy makes us "real." Autonomy makes it possible for us to speak out, affirms our right to choose what happens to us, and allows us to be represented as persons of interest; persons with needs, a past, a present, and a future. The concept of autonomy empowers us to make informed treatment decisions that are consistent with our culture, our values, and our belief systems.

In health care, caregivers sometimes disregard patient wishes as irrelevant. Though legally valid, advance directives are not always respected (Lo & Steinbrook, 2004). The decision of the treating physician or the tradition of the institution may be the determining factor. The rationale for disregarding patient wishes and decisions is justified on the basis that "The patient could not have foreseen the present circumstances," or "We know what is best for this patient," or "This is the way it has always been done here."

CONSENT

> *To count as moral at all, an action must stem from*
> *a free choice; autonomy is an underlying requirement.*
> —Callahan and Dunstan (1988)

Webster's (1994) defines consent as "compliance in or approval of what is done or proposed by another" and "agreement as to action or opinion." A legal dictionary defines consent as "A concurrence of wills; an agreement as to something to be done. An act of reason accompanied with deliberation, the mind weighing, as in a balance, the good or evil on each side" (Kling, 1970, p. 111).

In simplest medical-legal terms, consent is an act that gives permission for a specific therapy, treatment, or procedure to be performed. All procedures entail a risk/benefit ratio. The potential benefits and the attendant risks must be made clear to the patient or to the person responsible for the decision to treat or not treat. Ideally, consent is not a singular event, but an ongoing process that involves clear communication between patient and physician. In the health care field, consent is a complex interaction with serious legal implications. To perform a procedure or treatment on a patient in the absence of consent constitutes abuse and subjects the one who performs the procedure to charges of abuse or assault. Consent to perform procedures on patients who lack the ability to provide consent lies with a guardian appointed by the local court. Parental consent is required in order to treat children and juveniles.

Informing Patients

The initial responsibility for consent to a procedure or treatment program resides with the doctor, who must provide the patient (or proxy) with information concerning the need for the procedure or treatment, the anticipated outcome, benefits, risks, possible side effects, timing, and cost. Questions raised by the patient or proxy should be respected and answered. There is still considerable room for improvement in the matter of doctors providing patients with the information they need to make informed decisions. One study (Lamont & Christakis, 2001) asked doctors if they would give a candid survival estimate to terminally ill cancer patients. Less than 40% said that they would. According to Lo and Steinbrook (2004), many legal requirements and restrictions relating to advance directives are complicated and counterproductive. They suggest it might be better if patients discussed their end-of-life care wishes with their physician rather than completing a formal, legal document.

The field of cancer research has been criticized by some for taking advantage of the vulnerability of patients who are asked to participate in medical trials of yet unproven therapies. Agrawal and Emanuel (2003) contend that some phase 1 oncology studies have been criticized for "poor quality informed consent" (p. 1075). The major reasons for criticism are as follows:

- Deficiencies of disclosure—failure to provide sufficient detail to the patient about the nature of the research, potential complications, side effects, and risk/benefit ratio

- Deficiencies of understanding—inability of the patient to fully comprehend the nature of the proposed research

- Deficiencies of voluntariness—lack of freedom for the patient to make a decision without regard to feelings of indebtedness, gratitude, or dependence on the doctor

Deficiency of disclosure is still a serious problem in this country. Lamont and Christakis (2001) acknowledge that the physician's primary obligation to patients is to do no harm, yet they emphasize that while physicians may be trying to protect patients, not frankly disclosing the truth can hurt the patients more.

Generally, doctors are reluctant to use explicit words when discussing diagnosis and prognosis. For example, only 37% of Chicago-area doctors who referred patients to a cancer treatment program said they would give their best (prognostic) guess to a patient. Some doctors cite the ancient medical dictum, "Primum non nocere" ("In the first place, do no harm") as a rationale for not saying anything that might be upsetting to the patient. Twenty-three percent said they would not provide any estimate, and 40% said they would consciously give an incorrect estimate. Three-fourths of the latter group said they would knowingly describe a more positive scene than they really believed (Lamont & Christakis, 2001). Lamont and Christakis also claimed that two out of three patients may have to make crucial medical and personal decisions based on missing or unreliable information given from physicians.

Yet not all patients would agree. In his book about his own experiences as a patient with end-stage cancer during which he was involved as a subject in research studies, Alsop (1973) suggested that when doctors communicate with patients, they should tell "the truth and nothing but the truth . . . but not the whole truth."

Informed Consent

There are few subjects in law and bio-ethics that excite physicians to such an extent as does informed consent . . . . And the excitement extends from fear . . . anger . . . and hurt feelings to dismissive scorn.
—Capron (1988)

Informed consent is a voluntary decision made by a person with decisional capacity who is cognizant of all the relevant facts to allow performance of a medical procedure. It includes but is not limited to diagnosis, prognosis, side effects, possible outcome, risk/benefit ratio, hazards, and cost. The phrase "informed consent" implies that the person who grants consent is truly informed about the subject of consent and capable of making a decision based on the facts. Others, aware of the many pitfalls in obtaining consent, have referred to informed consent as "a felicitous misnomer" (R. Fulton, personal communication, Dec. 18, 2003). It is unlikely that the average patient can understand the details and implications of most of the procedures for which consent is sought these days. Some consent forms are excessively detailed; some are printed in very small type; others are presented to the patient as almost a *fait accompli*, especially in an emergency.

When confronted by a decision involving technical complexity, the patient must exercise a certain amount of "benevolent expectancy" based partly on trust in the doctor and the hope that all will proceed without misadventure. Many capable persons and some not so capable persons provide consent without fully understanding all that they should about what they are consenting to. Some choose not to know, not to read, or even not to listen to whatever explanation is provided.

Consent evolved out of earlier concepts that involved issues of trespass and bodily integrity. Much of the impetus for what we know as "consent" today derived from analysis of the abuse of human subjects in Nazi concentration camps. It was further augmented by the consumer movement and the realization that the demographics and economics of dying were undergoing dramatic change. Further, doctors were seen as having an advantage over patients. The law compensated by requiring more complete disclosure by doctors (Katz, 1984).

Beneficence, which once characterized the doctor-patient relationship, and benevolent paternalism ("Doctor knows best") had diminished the necessity of patient involvement in treatment decisions. Recognition of patient autonomy inevitably led to a greater awareness of the need to offer patients information about all aspects of treatments—even the option of no treatment.

To knowingly consent to a treatment or procedure, the patient must understand the problem, treatment alternatives, and possible outcomes (including side effects, cost, and timing) and also needs to know what might happen in the absence of treatment. The patient must trust that the doctor is providing accurate information. Yet not every patient wants full disclosure from the doctor. A Yale School of Medicine study revealed that 40 percent of the 205 terminally ill patients preferred not to discuss their prognosis. (Fried, Bradley, O'Leary, 2003).

The Yale study further stated that, "Although the doctors recalled providing a prognosis, sixty-nine percent of the patients said it was not discussed. And though the doctors remembered delivering news about life expectancy, eighty-nine percent said they did not receive it" (p. F4). Part of the problem is due to the veiled language, euphemisms, and vocabulary of the medical profession. Yet a large part is obviously due to patients' unwillingness to hear what the doctor is saying. My own experience working in a cancer center taught me that even when the doctor carefully chose unambiguous words and allowed time for questions and discussion, some patients could not or would not hear what was so plainly spoken.

Another aspect of consent to take into account is the matter of "implied consent." Most consent is explicit; it is a written legal agreement, signed and dated. Yet consent can also be implicit. The doctor can assume, rightly or wrongly, that statements made by the patient express the patient's choices. Implicit consent is not adequate. There is no record that all necessary facts were revealed, that the patient had an opportunity to discuss the issues and ask questions, nor is there any record of the decision to accept or reject recommended treatments or procedures.

Advances in medical science, technology, and the development of improved procedures for extending life have created, in advanced countries, a new cluster of dilemmas. On the one hand, the "medical research complex" has strong incentives to try new procedures and treatments that may result in extended life and perhaps cures for certain illnesses. Countering these incentives is the inviolable right of the individual to say "No" to treatments and procedures that are, for whatever reason, not desired at the time.

There is concern that cancer patients who have not responded to conventional treatment have experienced undue pressure to participate in research on unproven treatments. One approach used to recruit volunteers is to say that such research offers the outside chance of remission or recovery. Or patients may respond to an opportunity for altruistic behavior. A recent study (Agrawal & Emanuel, 2003) showed that abuse of the consent process was not a problem in recruiting patients for phase 1 cancer research studies.

ADVANCE DIRECTIVES

Advance directives are legal documents that indicate the type and extent of care and treatments an individual would want or not want should he or she become disabled and unable to make such decisions. Advance directives consist of two parts: a living will plus a durable power of attorney for health care.

Life-saving and life-extending treatments developed during the last century make it possible to resuscitate persons who otherwise might have died. Pneumonia, once known as "the old man's friend" and a common cause of death, is now routinely treated with antibiotics. The various treatments and therapies developed to treat cancer, heart disease, AIDS, and a number of other diseases have contributed to the longevity of the population. Improved nutrition coupled with public health measures have also dramatically altered the demographics of living and dying. In general, people in advanced societies live longer, healthier lives than did their grandparents. Yet life extension in itself is not without complications. We are aware of exceptional cases of persons in apparent vegetative states who were maintained on life support despite the requests of some family members to allow them to die a "natural" death (Lamers, 2003). The evolution of advance directives has taken a circuitous path following several landmark legal cases, especially those involving three young women: Karen Ann Quinlan, Nancy Cruzan, and Terry Schiavo. All of these cases reinforced the idea that while advance directives are helpful in difficult cases, they provide no guarantee of a harmonious or satisfying result.

Development

During the late 1960s, a variety of formal documents called living wills were developed to help formalize the wishes of people regarding care at the end of life should they be incapacitated. In 1973, the American Hospital Association published the "Patient's Bill of Rights," which declared that patients had the right to informed consent as well as the right to refuse treatment. The decision of the New Jersey Supreme Court in the Quinlan case (1976) established the primacy of patient wishes regarding care over the state's duty to preserve life. In the same year, California became the first state to legalize advance directive statutes. The following year, laws allowing refusal of treatment were enacted in Arkansas, Idaho, Nevada, New Mexico, North Carolina, Oregon, and Texas. By 1984, 22 states and the District of Columbia recognized the validity of advance directives. In 1990, the U.S. Supreme Court in the Cruzan decision established the right under the U.S. Constitution to refuse treatment. Later that same year, Congress passed the Patient Self-Determination Act (PSDA), the first federal act regarding advance directives. The legal ramifications of the Schiavo case in Florida are not yet fully known. At present, the role of Florida Governor Jeb Bush in helping to develop legislation that would affect a single patient (Schiavo) for a brief period of time to allow re-insertion of a feeding tube is under scrutiny by the state court.

Advance directives are a way of carrying personal health care decisions into the future. They come into play if persons are disabled and unable to make decisions about their medical care. People can describe what they want and do not want in the eventuality of later disability. They can appoint someone with legal authority to ensure adherence to their wishes. For some, advance directives may be a way to conserve assets, lest unwanted life-support treatments exhaust their savings or deprive survivors of assets. Also, a growing number of persons are more desirous of quality of life than duration of life. They would rather be allowed to die a "natural death" than be sustained by artificial means when they have little or no quality of life. Others do not want to subject their loved ones to the expense, emotional distress, and extended litigation that has characterized some notable cases of life extension.

Probably the most useful application of advance directives occurs when there is lack of family unanimity when one of their members is in a persistent vegetative state. For example, a California man, Robert Wendland (Ressner, 2001), crashed his pickup truck into a tree in September 1993. Following the accident he was brain damaged, unable to talk, walk, eat or drink, or in any way communicate his wishes. In 1995, his wife asked his doctors to remove his feeding tube, stating that he had told her before the crash that he would not want to be kept alive under these conditions. His mother and sister opposed this move, saying that he was minimally conscious but not comatose. In August 2001, the California Supreme Court ruled in favor of the mother and sister. The court noted that families have no right to discontinue life support for conscious patients who are not terminally ill and who have left no explicit instructions allowing them to do so or who have not formally delegated someone with durable power of attorney for health care (Nieves, 2001).

Misunderstandings

The legal language in advance directives coupled with the widespread reluctance to deal with matters of dying and death has led to a generalized resistance to completing these important documents. Resistance is further complicated by misunderstandings about the nature and function of advance directives. This resistance is discussed in papers that deal with common myths and misunderstandings about advance directives, one by an attorney, the other by physician-educators.

Warm and Weissman (2000) inform us that there are a number of common misunderstandings regarding power of attorney; some persons mistakenly believe that if they have developed power of attorney for financial matters, they also, by default, have developed power of attorney for health care. Another common misconception is that advance directive planning should wait until one is seriously ill. Warm and Weissman also say that some persons view advance directives as equivalent to a desire for no treatment. Also, some falsely suspect that naming a proxy for health care decisions is tantamount to losing control from that point forward. Others believe that a lawyer is needed to assist in the development of advance directives. This is not the case, though a lawyer who deals in the field of aging and/or health care can be quite helpful. States vary in their requirements for witnesses and the recording of documents by a notary public. In all states, health care providers are legally obligated to follow advance directives. However, the SUPPORT Study showed that only about half the physicians in that study knew what their patients wanted in the way of treatment at the end of life.

Many persons believe that advance directives are of value only for persons in the later stages of life. On the contrary, the Quinlan, Cruzan, and Schiavo cases teach us that it is wise for younger persons to indicate clearly their desires for care should they become unable to make health care decisions (Lamers, 2003).

Another mistaken assumption about advance directives is that persons can designate their doctor as their proxy in a Durable Power of Attorney (DPA) for Health Care document. This is not the case. No member of a person's health care team can serve as proxy for that person's DPA for Health Care.

The complexity of issues and questions surrounding advance directives led Sabatino (2001), a lawyer specializing in elder law, to develop a list of 10 common myths about advance directives. They include:

1) Everyone should have a living will.

2) Written advance directives are not legal in every state.

3) Just telling my doctor what I want is no longer legally effective.

4) An advance directive means "Don't treat."

5) When I name a proxy in my advance directive, I give up some control and flexibility.

6) I must use a prescribed advance directive from my state.

7) I need a lawyer to do an advance directive.

8) Doctors and other health care providers are not legally obligated to follow my advance directive.

9) If I do not have an advance directive, I can rely on my family to make my care decisions when I am unable to make my own decisions.

10) Advance directives are a legal tool for old people.

DISCUSSION

Autonomy, consent, and advance directives are interrelated. Current legal dilemmas emphasize the importance of even young persons developing advance directives. Persons who have not prepared advance directives and are later rendered permanently unconscious may cause a crisis for their families if there is disagreement over how to proceed with supportive care. Advocates of the right to life and those who advocate a "natural death" have been known to enter into prolonged disputes over treatment alternatives. The right to life and the right to die are emotionally charged subjects that have philosophical, moral, religious, and political dimensions. In Florida, as mentioned above, the state legislature and the governor have become embroiled in a family dispute over the level of care that should be provided to a patient who has been declared to be in a persistent vegetative state.

In the matter of *Satz vs. Perlmutter* (1980), the Florida Supreme Court deliberated on the question of providing or withholding life-saving measures. Its decision stated, among other things, that this issue "is not well suited for resolution in an adversary judicial proceeding. It is the type of issue . . . more suitably addressed in the legislative forum, where fact finding can be less confined and the viewpoints of all interested institutions . . . can be . . . synthesized."

In 1990, the U.S. Supreme Court set forth the principles involving the withdrawal of medical treatment for people without living wills who are no longer competent (Lamers, 2003).

The Schiavo case illustrates the strong confrontations that still occur when the issue of withdrawing life support from a disabled person is raised (Povar, 1990). One side characterized its stance as follows: "When courts apply law that threatens the lives of the vulnerable, legislatures have the authority to reform the law—and that includes saving people with disabilities from deliberate starvation" (Balch, 2003, p. 10). The other side, which disagreed with the intervention of Governor Bush, responded, "This abuse of power [by Governor Bush] should concern everyone. Based on this precedent, whenever the political pressure becomes too great to resist, meddling politicians can set aside court orders they disagree with and veto the difficult decisions made by patients or family members" (Simon, 2003, p. 10).

Recently, the Association of Attorneys General of the United States (Edmondson, 2003) has developed an initiative to facilitate the development and use of advance directives in all states. The stated objectives of this program are as follows:

1) Simplify and deemphasize mandatory forms/language in advance directives

2) Support/enhance the role of the proxy

3) Clarify proxy/surrogate authority in medical research settings

4) Ensure portability of advance directives across state lines

5) Recognize default surrogates

6) Support advance planning knowledge skills across all systems: in the community, the medical profession, and the government

The law is a viable patchwork approach to setting standards of behavior that allow us to function as a society (community) in spite of the significant differences that sometimes exist between individuals or groups with differing beliefs and opinions. The law is dynamic, not static. It is a repository of valuable historical content distilled out of centuries of experience. Each nation and, in the case of our country, each state, has its own set of laws. Each jurisdiction can interpret existing law as it sees fit, although there is one guiding principle called "precedence" which dictates that new decisions and interpretations should not stray significantly from the path of prior decisions. The doctrine of precedence keeps the law from swinging too abruptly from one pole to the other.

While autonomy and consent have a rich legal and social heritage, advance directives are a relatively new concept in health care and bioethics. We have not heard the last word about consent or about the complex ramifications of advance directives. Debate surrounding these vital issues will continue to escalate as health care pushes the envelope of moral and ethical considerations (Wrenn, Levinson, & Papadatou, 1996). ■

William Lamers is the Medical Consultant to the Hospice Foundation of America. He is a physician, psychiatrist, and one of the early hospice developers (Hospice of Marin) in the United States. He served on the Bioethics Committee of the Foothills Provincial Hospital in Calgary, Alberta, Canada from 1982–1985 as well as on the Bioethics Committee of the Los Angeles County Bar Association from 1986–1993.

Dr. Lamers has written and co-authored a number of books and papers on a variety of subjects in the fields of medicine, psychiatry, and hospice care. He has lectured widely in the United States and in many foreign countries. In 1982 he received an honorary doctorate of humane letters for his pioneering work in hospice development. He has been presented many awards for his work in end-of-life care.

REFERENCES

Agrawal, M., & Emanuel, E. (2003). Ethics of phase 1 oncology studies: Reexamining the arguments and data. *New England Journal of Medicine, 290*(8), 1075–1082.

Alsop, S. (1973). *A stay of execution: A sort of memoir.* New York: Lippincott.

American Hospital Association (1973). *Patient's bill of rights.* Chicago: Author.

American Medical Association. (1996). *Code of medical ethics: Section E-2.20: Withholding or withdrawing life-sustaining medical treatment.* Retrieved October 12, 2004, from http://www.ama-assn.org/ama/pub/category/8457.html

Annas, G. J. (1992). The changing landscape of human experimentation: Nuremberg, Helsinki, and beyond. *Health Matrix Cleveland, 2*(2), 119–140.

Balch, B. (2003, December). They must protect the vulnerable. *AARP Bulletin,* vol. 10.

Beecher, H. K. (1966). Ethics and clinical research. *New England Journal of Medicine, 274,* 1354–1360.

Callahan, D. (1987). *Setting limits: Medical goals in an aging society.* New York: Simon & Schuster, Inc.

Callahan, D., & Dunstan, G. R. (Eds.). (1988). *Biomedical ethics: An Anglo-American dialogue.* New York: Annals of the New York Academy of Sciences.

Calland, C. (1972). Iatrogenic problems in end-stage renal failure. *New England Journal of Medicine, 287*(7), 334–336.

Capron, A. (1988). Biomedical Ethics: An Anglo-American Dialogue. [*Annals of the New York Academy of Sciences, 530*], 38.

Dixon, W. M.. (1935). *The Gifford lectures.* London: Guilfoile and Son.

Edmondson, D. (2003). *Improving end-of-life care: The role of the attorneys general.* Washington, DC: National Association of Attorneys General.

Fried, T.R., Bradley, E., O'Leary, J. (2003). Journal of the American Geriatrics Society, 51 (10), 1398.

Katz, J. (2002). *The silent world of doctor and patient.* Baltimore: John Hopkins University Press

Kieffer, G. (1979). *Bioethics: A textbook of issues.* San Francisco: Addison-Wesley Publishing Company, Inc.

Kling, S. G. (1970). *The Legal Encyclopedia & Dictionary.* New York: Pocket Books.

Lamers, W. M. (2003). *The Encyclopedia of Death.* New York, MacMillan.

Lamont, E. B., & Christakis, N. A. (2001). Prognostic disclosures to patients with cancer near the end of life. *Annals of Internal Medicine, 134*(12), 1096–1105.

Lerner, B. H. (2004). Sins of omission—Cancer research without informed consent. *New England Journal of Medicine, 351*(7), 628–630.

Lo, B., & Steinbrook, R. (2004). Resuscitating advance directives. *Archives of Internal Medicine, 164,* 1501–1506.

Nieves, E. (2001, August 10). California justices limit families' right to end life support. *New York Times,* A10.

Povar. G. (1990). Withdrawing and withholding therapy: Putting ethics into practice. *Journal of Clinical Ethics, 1,* 50–56.

Ressner, J. (2001, March 26). When a coma isn't one. *Time,* 62.

Sabatino, C. P. (2001). *Commission on legal problems of the elderly: 10 legal myths about advance medical directives.* Retrieved October 20, 2004, from American Bar Association Web site: http://www.abanet.org/aging/myths.html

Florida Supreme Court. Satz vs. Perlmutter (1980).

Simon, H. L. (2003, December). Abuse of power should concern all. *AARP Bulletin,* 10.

SUPPORT Principal Investigators. (1995). A controlled study to improve care for seriously ill hospitalized patients. *JAMA, 274*(20), 1591–1598.

Warm, E., & Weissman, D. (2000). *Myths about advance directives.* Fast Fact and Concepts #12. End of Life Palliative Education Resource Center. Retrieved June 23, 2004, from http://www.eperc.mcw.edu

Wrenn, R. L., Levinson, D., & Papadatou, D. (1996). *End of life decisions: Guidelines for the health care provider.* Tucson, Arizona: The University of Arizona College of Medicine.

▪ CHAPTER 7 ▪

Initiating, Facilitating, and Honoring Conversations about Future Medical Care

Bernard J. Hammes and Linda A. Briggs

INTRODUCTION

This chapter concerns the process of planning for future health care rather than the technique of completing an advance directive document.[1] Since the terms "advance directive" and "advance care planning" can be used in many different ways or may be used with no specified meaning, it is first important to define them.

An "advance directive" is a *plan* for health care created for some uncertain future. Thus, an advance directive is different from a plan to have a specific future medical intervention, such as hip replacement. An advance directive is about something that may or will happen, although it is not known when or where. An advance directive may or may not be written. If written, it may be documented in many different ways. For example, it may be a legal document such as a power of attorney for health care, or it may be recorded less formally as an individual's letter or a physician's note.

---

[1] The content of this chapter is based on material presented in the *Respecting Choices® Facilitator's Manual* (Hammes & Briggs, 2002).

"Advance care planning" is a *process* of decision making about potential future health decisions. In the best of circumstances, this process requires (1) a good understanding of the medical issues and choices as well as relevant personal goals and values, (2) reflection on what choices best represent what is important to the person, and (3) a clear communication and interaction with others who are likely to be involved in those future decisions. Advance care planning optimally involves selecting another person to make decisions; defining that person's authority; describing how decisions should be made; indicating what values or goals are most important; providing specific instructions about what medical treatment a person does or does not want; and indicating what type of care and comfort may be important if the end of life is near.

It may be easy to conclude that advance care planning is either impossible or unhelpful. How can someone effectively plan for all future health care events? Fortunately, planning for everything is not necessary. What is necessary is to plan for future events when (1) it would be impossible for the person to make his or her own decisions, and (2) the medical condition is one where there could be significant differences among individuals about what interventions would or would not be wanted.

For example, we would not need to plan for a situation in which a conscious, competent person is brought to the hospital with an inflamed appendix. Here the person is able to make his or her own decisions, and the condition typically can be treated. We do need to plan for a situation in which there is a significant neurological injury from which the person will not recover. We need to explore at what loss of cognitive function the person would want to change the goals of medical treatment from attempting to prolong life to allowing death to occur. We do not need to plan for a situation in which efforts to resuscitate have failed. We do need to plan for a situation in which there is cardiac arrest, there is a low chance of survival, and the intensity and burden of treatment would be high.

It is also important to recognize that advance care planning is not a one-time process. Not only is it important for a healthy adult to initiate conversations as a component of routine medical care, but it is also important to keep the conversation alive throughout the continuum of care and lived experiences. Professionals should review plans on a regular basis.

Additionally, certain situations should trigger renewed conversations, such as the diagnosis of a life-limiting illness, frequent hospitalizations for declining physical condition, declining functional status, and, of course, whenever the person expresses an interest in learning more about options for future medical care.

THE SKILL OF ADVANCE CARE PLANNING

Given the focus in the United States on patients' legal rights to complete statutory advance directive documents (i.e., living wills and powers of attorney for health care), it is easy to understand why the focus of discussions and education has been on giving adults information about their legal rights, providing a statutory document, and assisting in the completion of this document. It is also easy to understand why adults who complete this process assume they have "taken care of the issue." When advance care planning, not merely the completion of an advance directive, is the goal, the skills needed to initiate such conversations are much more complicated. There are several critical messages to convey about beginning this conversation, which aims to engage the person in this process and to plant the seeds of inquiry that will germinate with time and experience.

Message 1: Initiate this conversation in a way that both builds and enhances a therapeutic relationship. To accomplish this, reassure the person that having this conversation is part of quality, routine care. ("At some point I speak to *all* my patients about future medical care.") Everyone needs to plan for an unexpected event (e.g., a car accident), and if the person is no longer able to speak or make his or her own decisions, health professionals must turn to loved ones to carry this burden—an overwhelming responsibility at best. Remind the person that this conversation will help to ensure that health professionals and those close to this person always provide all the care and only the care the person would want if he or she could speak for himself or herself. Help the person realize that this planning is of benefit to him or her and to close friends or family. Additionally, reinforce the concept that this conversation will need to be continued over time and revisited as goals for medical care change, a health condition deteriorates, or new information is needed to explore additional treatment options.

When individuals feel this activity is part of routine care and when they can see that their values and perspectives are important to decision making, starting this conversation is easier and actually can build trust. And when they can appreciate that this is a dynamic process—that they can change their minds at any time—they will be more willing to engage in future conversations if needed.

Message 2: Take the time to explore the person's understanding, values, and experiences. Often, the advance care planning process proceeds too quickly to a decision phase (e.g., "What do you want if your heart stops?" or "Would you consider hospice care?" or "What do you want if you are in a coma?"). When persons are expected to make decisions too quickly, they can feel unprepared and may be left with the impression that the health professional's agenda is driving the conversation. They may also feel that they are being pressured to "give up" and forgo potentially life-prolonging medical treatment.

To begin this exploration, first assess the person's understanding of his or her state of health, perceptions of goals and values, and views of his or her close relationships. The key skill here is active listening. It is important to identify gaps in knowledge, fears, and misperceptions. All too often, health professionals see their primary role as providing information. While this certainly is a legitimate role, if individuals have beliefs that are different from the norm, if they have fears that are unidentified or questions that go unanswered, the information the health professional provides may effect little or no change. In order to help individuals plan, it is important first to understand their perspectives and provide information as it relates to these perspectives.

In this process it is often necessary to explore statements, ask questions, and clarify beliefs. What one individual means by "Don't keep me hooked up to machines" may be quite different from what another means. The health professional must not assume understanding without first clarifying the individual's meaning. In this process, often the person planning first becomes fully aware of his or her own assumptions, beliefs, or fears. The point here is to learn from the individual and to assist him or her to actively reflect on personal perspectives, feelings, and concerns.

Doing so may help individuals gain new understanding of their illness and their values and goals.

One of the questions that is helpful to ask, especially if a patient has a serious illness, is, "What does it mean for you to live well at this point in your life?" (Hammes, Bottner, & Lapham, 1998). This is a primary question about goals and values. It is also a question about the person with an illness rather than a question about a disease and its treatment. Such a question can help persons explore their goals independently of a disease model or framework.

Exploring past experiences and allowing individuals to tell their own story is a valuable advance care planning skill. What did they learn from these experiences? What would they want differently for themselves? Responses can provide powerful insights for the professional who is attempting to guide patient-centered decision making.

Message 3: Assist the individual to understand the specific decisions related to his or her own state of health. Once the time has been taken to build a trusting relationship and explore values, beliefs, and experiences, the stage is set to move into more specific decisions. However, advance care planning is not a "one-size-fits-all" process, with a script that can be delivered to every person. Depending on the person's state of health or illness, the specific decisions that need to be considered will be different (Teno & Lynn, 1996). Healthy adults, for example, have fewer things to plan for than adults with a life-threatening illness. Healthy adults can understand the potential reality of a sudden car accident that would leave them unable to make decisions. They are less likely to see the value in talking about what they would want if they had cancer or end-stage heart failure. They are more likely to engage in a conversation about goals and values when they can imagine themselves unaware and unlikely to recover from a sudden accident or unexpected illness. Would they prefer to have life-sustaining interventions continued in such a state of health, or would they prefer to forgo such interventions?

A person with a specific life-limiting illness, however, is living the realities of progressive decline in functional ability. The decisions that are required are more pressing. For example, a patient with end-stage heart failure needs to decide if cardiopulmonary resuscitation (CPR) should be attempted and if intubation and mechanical ventilation is acceptable if lung failure occurs, among other critical decisions. And the patient will need information on the benefits and burdens of these options in order to make a truly informed decision.

It is unethical to initiate a conversation about a CPR decision and simply say "It is your decision to make." The professional must have the skill to provide accurate information and to assist the person in weighing the benefits and burdens in accord with personal values.

Often, the specific decisions presented to individuals focus only on what treatments they do not want in certain circumstances. For some individuals, especially those with life-limiting illnesses, it is equally important to focus on what they do want in terms of end-of-life care. For example, the meaning of comfort care, emotional care, and environmental options should be explored. When the conversation includes an emphasis on the variety of nonmedical interventions and choices that can be considered, new opportunities for advance care planning interventions arise, and new avenues of hope open for individuals to control their own end-of-life experience.

Message 4: Assist in the selection and preparation of a surrogate decision-maker. Perhaps one of the most important planning decisions is who should make decisions and how decisions should be made. Too often, a person is named as a surrogate without careful consideration or even a minimal discussion. It is especially important to determine if the person "nominated" as the surrogate decision maker (i.e., health care agent) is willing, is comfortable with the instructions provided, and can serve as a good decision maker when faced with complex and stressful decisions. It is particularly crucial to actually explore the qualifications and responsibilities of being a good health care agent, proxy, or representative with both the person selecting and the person being selected.

Health Professionals' Role in Advance Care Planning

Whose role is it to initiate and facilitate advance care planning? It may seem obvious that the answer to this question is the physician. When advance care planning is narrowly conceived of as giving medical information and making treatment decisions, this seems a plausible answer. But advance care planning is much more than establishing a medical treatment plan.

Clearly, physicians can and do have a central role in advance care planning. They play a key role in initiating and motivating patients to plan; in reviewing, completing, and revising plans; and ultimately in interpreting and implementing plans.

However, other qualified health professionals have contributions to offer in facilitating the advance care planning process. Depending upon a patient's degree and type of illness, a social worker, nurse, chaplain, nurse practitioner, or physician assistant trained to facilitate discussions about future medical care can and should be quite involved in the planning process. These health professionals have multiple opportunities to improve a patient's understanding of future medical issues and to help clarify a patient's goals and values. In some respects, they might be in a better position to assist patients. Their responsibilities might be better designed to provide time to accomplish this type of work, they may have better skills at exploring a patient's understanding and goals, it might be a better use of resources, and patients may feel more willing to discuss their concerns with someone who has less authority over their treatment.

Ideally, advance care planning would be seen as a team effort in which clear roles and responsibilities are established. For example, using a set of preestablished criteria, a medical assistant may identify that a patient would benefit if advance care planning were introduced. She then puts educational materials in the patient's admission packet and invites the patient to review the material. When the physician interacts with the patient in an exam room and sees the educational materials, she can introduce the topic and encourage the patient to begin the process of advance care planning. The physician can ask the patient to further review the educational materials and refer the patient to an advance care planning facilitator. The physician then would have an opportunity, at a later visit, to review and clarify any plan the patient has made.

Adopting a team approach to initiating and facilitating conversations about future medical care has multiple advantages for an organization as well as its surrounding community. When a variety of professionals are educated in the skills of communication and providing information about advance care planning, they not only are able to plant seeds early and in different venues, but they are also able to make referrals to one another when the needs of the individual require more expertise. Often, professionals express concern over initiating such conversations for fear of time constraints, questions they cannot answer, or lack of comfort dealing with emotional responses. With a team approach, one professional does not have to "do it all." Professionals who learn to rely on the skills of colleagues also offer new opportunities for patients.

It must be acknowledged, however, that few professionals have had any formal training in the types of communication skills that these sensitive conversations may require. This lack of preparation and skill development is a major barrier to initiating conversations about future medical care. Professionals must be offered the opportunities to learn these skills and be supported by their colleagues to implement and improve them.

ADVANCE CARE PLANNING OR AN ADVANCE DIRECTIVE IS NOT ENOUGH

While the focus of this chapter has been on the skill of advance care planning, it is very important to note that even with the best of planning, patient care is not improved unless the plan is clearly documented, is available, and is translated into orders when needed. In short, unless advance care planning is part of a larger system of eliciting and honoring patient preferences, this planning may make no difference in how patients receive care at the end of life.

Unfortunately, much of the concept of advance care planning has been driven by efforts to complete statutory documents, by the requirements of the Patient Self-Determination Act, and by "social wisdom." The statutory documents, especially the living will, typically focus on "terminal conditions" and on specific neurological diagnoses such as persistent vegetative state. These documents are generally unhelpful because they are either too vague or too narrow. In addition, they are not helpful because the goal is completion of the document, rather than actual understanding, reflection, and discussion. They give neither family nor health professionals a clear idea of what the injured or sick person intended. The Patient Self-Determination Act focuses on giving information about legal rights to refuse treatment and on how to complete statutory documents. The social wisdom suggests that a person who signs an advance directive document has taken care of the problem of decision making at the end of life (Prendergast, 2001).

What is needed is a system in which health care professionals develop ways to document patient preferences and instructions that flow from a good process of discussion and are not constrained by some legislative formula. The documented plan needs to be clear and complete for all the "stakeholders"—patient, family, and health professionals. The plan may be a legal document like a power of attorney for health care with specific, individualized instructions. But the written plan may also be updated with a physician's or advance care planning facilitator's note or a more specialized treatment plan form. What should be most important is not the appearance of the document, but the existence of a written plan that reflects the patient's preferences and clearly helps health professionals provide the right care in the future. From a social policy perspective, it sometimes seems we have been more worried that advance directives would be used to "do in" patients than about whether the written plan reflects a patient's choices and is honored.

Once a written plan is created, we also need to make sure that it is available to those providing health care and medical treatment to the patient at any time. This has been a challenge in most health care organizations and communities. It is important that health professionals begin to see these elicited patient preferences as crucial information in the delivery of treatment. It is just as important, for example, as knowing that a patient has an allergy to a medication.

There are efforts to store this information in community-wide, statewide, or national advance directive "banks." Some communities have sought to make arrangements among health care facilities to acquire, store, and transfer documents as part of medical record systems. At this point, there is no clear evidence as to which systems are most effective. Perhaps there will be different systems for different places. If the goal is both to make the advance directive available and to update plans as part of the routine of health care, then there seems to be a clear need to keep the patient's advance directive closely connected to the patient's medical record.

The last part of the system is to make sure that the patient's preferences are translated into physician orders. This means both that when a person is admitted to a hospital, nursing home, or hospice, the orders that are written reflect the patient's preference if the patient cannot make decisions, *and* that there is a system to respect these preferences out in the community. The most tested and proven system for creating and transferring orders in a community is Physician Orders for Life-Sustaining Treatment (POLST).[2] Currently, in the United States, the POLST form is being used state-wide in four states and in a region of four other states. Research suggests that when a patient's preferences can be translated into medical orders recognized by other health professionals and emergency personnel, these preferences will be honored (Tolle, Tilden, Nelson, & Dunn, 1998).

Finally, to make sure that such a system is effective, it is necessary to manage the system and to apply basic principles of continuous quality improvement (Lynn et al., 2002). A system like this cannot function without oversight. It is essential to determine whether the processes in fact work and whether the desired outcomes are in fact being achieved.

---

[2] For more information about POLST, see www.POLST.org

CONCLUSION

Medical decision making when a patient is incapacitated and seriously ill is always challenging. Good advance care planning provides the opportunity to ensure that the patient's perspective can be incorporated into care and treatment plans. For such planning to be effective, health professionals need to have the skills to initiate and to facilitate planning with patients at all stages of health and illness. They also need to work in a system that values this process, provides opportunities to learn necessary advance care planning skills, and ensures that plans are well documented, available when needed, and formulated into orders. Any gap in this system represents poor care or medical errors (Lynn & Goldstein, 2003). Until this larger vision of advance care planning is embraced and becomes part of the routine of health care, advance directives will largely be pieces of paper that have little impact on decisions. When we have effective systems of advance care planning, we will see an increase in planning, plans being available to health professionals, and patient preferences being reflected in decisions (Hammes & Rooney, 1998; Molloy et al., 2000). It is only when such advance care planning systems are in place that our care of patients at the end of life will have a chance to be more humane. ■

Bernard "Bud" Hammes, PhD, is an ethics consultant and director of Medical Humanities, Gundersen Lutheran Medical Foundation. Dr. Hammes' doctorate is in philosophy. He has provided ethics education and consultation and advance care planning education to the medical staff, house staff, medical students, nurses, social workers, and chaplains since 1984. His work has focused primarily on improving end-of-life care at Gundersen Lutheran Health System and in the La Crosse, Wisconsin, community. He is the chair of both the institutional ethics committee and institutional review board and has led the development of two successful, award-winning advance care planning programs: "If I Only Knew . . . " and Respecting Choices®. In addition, he has published 25 articles and book chapters about end-of-life issues.

Linda Briggs, RN, MSN, MA, is an ethics consultant and assistant director of "Respecting Choices" at Gundersen Lutheran Medical Foundation. With 25 years of nursing experience as a critical care staff nurse, nurse manager, clinical nurse specialist, and educator, Ms. Briggs brings extensive insight to clinical and educational perspectives related to health care ethics. She received her master of science in bioethics and has published her thesis, "A Competency Based Educational Curriculum for Ethics Committee Members," and is co-author of Respecting Choices® Advance Care Planning Manual for Facilitators. She provides education and consultation to individuals and organizations interested in implementing the nationally recognized Respecting Choices® Advance Care Planning Program. In her role as an ethics consultant, she facilitates the development of several ethics committees in Wisconsin.

REFERENCES

Hammes, B. J., & Briggs, L. A. (2002). *Respecting Choices® Facilitator's Manual.* La Crosse, WI: Gundersen Lutheran Medical Foundation.

Hammes, B. J., Bottner, W., & Lapham, C. (1998). Expanding frames . . . opening choices: Reconsidering conversation about medical care when cure is not possible. *Illness, Crisis, & Loss, 6,* 352–356.

Hammes, B. J., & Rooney, B. L. (1998). Death and end-of-life planning in one midwestern community. *Archives of Internal Medicine, 158,* 383–390.

Lynn, J., & Goldstein, N. E. (2003). Advance care planning for fatal, chronic illness: Avoiding commonplace errors and unwanted suffering. *Annals of Internal Medicine, 138,* 812–818.

Lynn, J., Nolan, K., Kabcenell, A., Weissman, D., Milne, C., & Berwick, D. M. End-of-Life Care Consensus Panel (2002). Reforming care for persons near the end of life: The promise of quality improvement. *Annals of Internal Medicine, 137,* 117–122.

Molloy, D. W., Guyatt, G. H., Russo, R., Goeree, R., O'Brien, B. J., Bedard, M., Willan, A., Watson, J. W., Patterson, C., Harrison, C., Standish, T., Strang, D., Darzins, P. J., Smith, S., Dubois, S. (2000). Systematic implementation of an advance directive program in nursing homes: A randomized controlled trial. *JAMA, 283,* 1437–1444.

Prendergast, T. J. (2001). Advance care planning: Pitfalls, progress, promise. *Critical Care Medicine, 29*(Suppl.), N34–N39.

Teno, J. M., & Lynn, J. (1996). Putting advance-care planning into action. *Journal of Clinical Ethics, 7,* 205–213.

Tolle, S. W., Tilden, B. P., Nelson, C. A., & Dunn, P. M. (1998). A prospective study of efficacy of the physician order form for life-sustaining treatment. *Journal of the American Geriatrics Society, 46,* 1097–1102.

The Withdrawal of Ventilator Support at Home

San Diego Hospice & Palliative Care

San Diego Hospice was asked to evaluate a patient in a long-term care ventilator facility for transport home and withdrawal of ventilator support. The patient was an 81-year old retired fighter pilot who had a wife with advanced dementia and two daughters. Five weeks before consultation he had a central nervous system event during or shortly after a coronary artery bypass surgery, with subsequent quadriplegia and complete ventilator dependence. The patient could not talk, but had decision-making capacity and could answer by nodding yes or no. There was palpable tension between his two daughters, but they agreed hospice would be useful in helping get their father home. His older daughter was his health care surrogate in the event that her dad could not make decisions. Despite the tension and anger between his two daughters, the older would often yield to her sister in order to keep the peace.

Our evaluation involved several team/family meetings as well as two interdisciplinary group (IDG) meetings. During the IDG meetings, the whole patient assessment was reviewed, other therapeutic interventions were considered, and teams (admissions, home care, crisis [continuous] care, pharmacy, transport services, bereavement care) were coordinated. Ethical principles of beneficence, nonmaleficence, justice, and autonomy were integrated into the process. Principles guiding practice, such as patient/family agreement, sustained or durable decisions, truth-telling, continuity of care, informed consent, and safety of the patient, family, and staff, were also integrated into the process.

Initially, the patient had some ambivalence about ventilator withdrawal, but at a third family meeting his decision was clear. He wanted to be transported home the next day, spend an hour or two saying good-bye to loved ones, and then be withdrawn from the ventilator. His plan of care was changed to help him achieve this goal. After an enormous amount of interdisciplinary time and effort was provided to support the patient's wishes, the plan had to be changed. It became clear that the younger daughter intended to get her father home but was not ready for him to die. The transport service was worried about the situation when this daughter said she would pay them extra to keep him alive as long as possible. The hospice team felt that the plan was not safe for the patient or the hospice staff secondary to likely interference from one or both of the daughters during withdrawal of ventilator support. Team members felt the daughters would not allow us to physically disconnect him. In addition, we were not able to care for him at home on the ventilator indefinitely without the transport service, which agreed to provide the ventilator.

After the team decided that we could not help him get home, his daughters did not want us to be involved with their dad's care. However, the patient's respiratory support was withdrawn the very next day without hospice involvement, and he died at the ventilator facility. Evidently the younger daughter allowed this to happen, but we do not know if her feelings concerning her father's decision really changed. The facility apparently felt comfortable performing the procedure in its controlled environment. Since the facility did not have a contract with hospice, the patient was never admitted to hospice. After learning of his death, the team developed a plan to offer the patient's family bereavement services.

DISCUSSION

- Patient and family disagreement: Are there cases in which health care providers cannot fully support a patient's goal? Should hospice have accepted the safety risks and moved forward with the plan of care?

- Durable request: When the patient's goals are ambiguous for a period of time, is a durable or sustained request required for withdrawal of therapies? What period of time is reasonable?

- Justice: Are patients who are in a hospital without a hospice contract able to take full advantage of a federal entitlement to hospice care? Can hospices be more involved with patients on ventilators? How can health care providers best care and advocate for these patients?

- Distributive justice: Should cost be considered in these cases? If we look at death as a medical event, focusing only on efficiency and cost, we might not offer home ventilator withdrawal. On the other hand, this option allows patients to experience death as a more dignified human event. ■

Gary Buckholz, MD, is a fellow at the Center for Palliative Studies, San Diego Hospice & Palliative Care.

■ CHAPTER 8 ■

When Families Disagree: Family Conflict and Decisions

Samira K. Beckwith

A society will be judged on how it treats those in the dawn of life, those in the twilight of life, and those in the shadow of life.
—Senator Hubert Humphrey

In the hospice community, we speak of cherishing the end of life as much as we cherish its beginning. Admittedly, it's a concept that appears to run counter to modern culture. Yet only a few generations ago, when death was a more conspicuous part of life, the thinking was different. Families were the primary providers of care for loved ones at the end of life. Life often ended where it began—at home. Like birth, death was a family affair. Today, birth is a widely celebrated event, with expectant fathers and their video cameras in the delivery room. However, we tend to distance ourselves from the natural death of a loved one, who is more likely to die in a care facility than at home. Despite the growth of the hospice movement in the United States in the past 30 years, more than 50% of Americans die in hospitals and long-term care facilities.

We know how to embrace birth, but our culture seems to have forgotten how to accept death. As a result, the dying process of a loved one is often a very difficult family experience that can test even the closest relationships. Family caregivers provide more than 80% of all home care services, yet they receive no formal training or support in their roles. Like birth, death requires preparation, education, and support, as well as special attention to the needs of the family. Through hospice, we are leading the way in preparing families for the issues, concerns, and conflicts at the end of life.

Life today is much different from life a hundred years ago. In 1900, the average life expectancy was only 50 years and the infant mortality rate was very high. Thanks to improved sanitation, antibiotics, immunization programs, new therapies, and amazing technological advances, Americans can now expect to live into their 70s and 80s. The field of medicine has become infinitely more complex. One interesting result is that many people now feel as though death is optional or avoidable.

Health care's increasingly complex system has its own unique language and culture. It can be confusing for the most experienced, and often there are no clear or obvious answers. In this environment, patients and family members must not only try to make sense of it all, they must make difficult decisions based on the information they receive.

From the physicians' perspective, the core principles of medical ethics are "beneficence" and "nonmaleficence." Beneficence refers to their efforts to "benefit the sick," while nonmaleficence means to "do no harm" in the process. Physicians are trained to cure and may be troubled by the thought of a medical "failure." Many people think the health care system is not set up to deal with dying because it is designed to cure the sick. Patients and families obligated to choose a physician from a list imposed by a managed care plan may have no sense of connection or trust. Adding to the physician's conflict are more and more modern-world legal and ethical issues. According to a study reported in *JAMA* (2000), "one of the most difficult situations physicians face is how to handle conflicts with families over forgoing life-sustaining treatment. Physicians may feel their competence or judgment is not trusted and turn to legal or ethics consultants for help with what they feel is a wrong decision by the patient or the patient's proxy decision maker. Families may feel isolated, misunderstood, or abandoned and begin to doubt the healthcare team's commitment to the patient's well-being. As a result, there can be tension and disagreement between physician and family, adding to the family's stress" (Goold, Williams, & Arnold, pp. 909-914).

According to some families, initially there must be a good communication link to the physician. Unfortunately, in one study, nearly one-quarter of family members surveyed believed that neither the patient nor the family was part of the discussion about end-of-life decisions (Hanson, Danis, & Garret, 1997). Good communication with patients early in the clinical course whenever possible assists in reducing conflicts. A nonconfrontational, sympathetic, and compassionate approach to family members and legal surrogates facing the immediate death of their loved ones leads to the best possible outcome. It is the duty of the physician and the health care providers to assure the patient and the family that they will not abandon the patient. Effective communication is the key to solving almost all ethical dilemmas when caring for the dying ... patient (Krishna & Raffin, 1998).

CAUSES OF CONFLICT

Adding to families' difficulties is the increasing complexity of family life itself. Today's families may be spread out across the country, with no shared hometown. There are more children from previous marriages and new types of relationships. More and more legal issues confront physicians and families today. Furthermore, given that most people do not want to discuss the end of life until they must, it is no wonder that making any decisions on behalf of a dying loved one has become so overwhelming. Making decisions such as whether to maintain life support is difficult enough for an individual. The difficulty can readily be compounded when decisions must be made by "committee," or family.

An approaching death often produces conflicts, as loved ones must come together to make decisions in a highly stressful setting that they have never before experienced. To understand the root causes of family disagreement, one must look at the individuals within the family. In some cases, the only thing that family members may have in common is DNA. Their belief systems, interests, lifestyles, experiences, and codes of ethics may all be different. Even in close-knit families, each person remains an individual with a unique perspective. Patient and family members react to the stress of illness in different ways. They process their emotions and thoughts at different speeds. Various family members have different perspectives, perhaps feeling guilty, or trying to make decisions without fully understanding the complete context of the situation. Like victims and witnesses at the scene of an accident, each family member may see things completely differently, depending on their emotional state, their relationships with other family members, their age, and other factors. Further, everyone deals differently with his or her emotions. Family members may fall back on their own lifelong mechanisms for coping, such as avoidance or control. Emotional expression can depend on the temperament of the individual, family heritage, and gender.

UNIVERSAL ISSUES

Even with the best input and support from medical professionals, family members may find themselves at odds over virtually any issue associated with the care of a loved one. A hospice counselor worked with a mother and daughter who never came to an agreement on the husband/father's funeral arrangements. The counselor soon determined that the mother and daughter had spent a lifetime disagreeing on most everything.

In the case of one dying father, siblings complained to their counselor that their sister, the appointed trustee, refused to share information with them about the father's estate, the funeral arrangements, or any other matters. On behalf of the siblings, the counselor tried to talk with her, but she refused. The siblings all indicated that the sister had always been this way—she had no close family relationships. In fact, she hadn't even been around their father in 10 years.

Families may argue over where the patient should die. While many patients may express the desire to die in the comfort and familiarity of their own home, some family members do not want those kinds of memories. A spouse or sibling may want the patient moved to a hospice house or nursing home.

Family members often disagree on how to care for the surviving spouse. The adult children may argue over where the mother should live. A married couple, working full time in another city, may want the mother to move in with them, while other brothers and sisters may also try to persuade her to move in with them.

Perhaps the most common issue is settlement of the estate, which has been an issue as long as there have been estates.

Further, the more mundane aspects of daily living must also be addressed. Who will pay the bills? Who will feed the pets? Who will do the grocery shopping? Who will get the prescription medications filled? Who will do the chores around the house? In some cases, there is argument over which siblings are perceived as not doing their fair share. Those who are able to provide daily, hands-on assistance may resent family members who live farther away and aren't available to help. The reality that most hospice patients are older and seriously ill, yet are cared for by younger family members, produces difficult reversals in generational hierarchies. The daughter or daughter-in-law, who typically becomes a caregiver for her or her husband's parent, must adjust to new patterns. Long-standing unresolved conflicts may reappear under these stressful conditions and may lead to power struggles and other dysfunctional expressions.

Regardless of family dynamics and issues, it is well documented that most couples and families simply do not want to discuss death. But at the point where there is no avoiding the subject, patients often cannot participate in the conversation because they are too ill or sedated. Decision making falls to the surrogate or to unprepared family members, in consultation with the medical team, at perhaps the most emotionally difficult moment in their lives. Decisions of such import are emotionally stressful and are often a source of disagreement. Failure to resolve such disagreements may create conflict that compromises patient care, engenders guilt among family members, and creates dissatisfaction for health care professionals. However, the potential for strained communications is mitigated if clinicians provide timely clinical and prognostic information and offer the patient and family aggressive symptom control, a comfortable setting, and continuous psychosocial support. Effective communication includes sharing the burden of decision making with other family members. This shift from individual responsibility to patient-focused consensus often permits the family to understand, perhaps reluctantly and with great sadness, that intensive caring may involve letting go of life-sustaining interventions (Prendergast & Puntillo, 2002).

In the experience of one hospice caregiver, the best means of circumventing these problems are early referral to hospice and advance directives. Ideally, the patient should be admitted while still competent and capable of making and communicating decisions, and at that point, the patient's preferences should already be documented. This relieves the family of the stress of making decisions based on guesses and assumptions, and leaves less room for debate.

THE CASE FOR ADVANCE DIRECTIVES

The highly publicized Schiavo case has resulted in years of legal battles among family members. The patient's husband, Michael Schiavo, maintains that the feeding tube sustaining his wife Terri should be removed so that she can be allowed to die after years in a persistent vegetative state following a heart attack. Meanwhile, Terri's parents continue to hold hope that she will recover. Michael claims that Terri would not want to be kept alive in this circumstance, although there is no confirming documentation.

In part because of the Schiavo case, there is growing interest in advance directives as a means of enabling families to avoid disputes over end-of-life care and to help patients protect their wishes and rights. "Advance directives" is a general term referring to an individual's instructions about future medical care in the event that the person becomes unable to communicate. Every state now has standards for how these documents should be prepared. A federal statute enacted in 1990 requires hospitals and other health care agencies to provide patients with general information about how their end-of-life issues can be handled. Many hospices, including Hope, have begun informational campaigns to raise community awareness about advance directives.

In matters of personal health, every competent adult has the legal right to choose or refuse medical treatment. However, when people are no longer able to make these decisions because of a mental or physical condition such as Alzheimer's disease, they are considered incapacitated. Advance directives can authorize the physician to provide, withhold, or withdraw life-prolonging procedures. They can also designate another individual to make medical decisions on the patient's behalf if necessary, and they can designate anatomical donations after death.

Some people make advance directives when they are diagnosed with a life-threatening illness. Others do it while they are in good health, sometimes as part of estate planning.

Advance directives should be considered equally important to patient and family. However, completed forms or checklists of desires and preferences cannot fully meet anyone's needs. It is not enough to have the individual's words on paper. It would be quite unrealistic to expect all possible decisions to be covered in black and white. Decisions may have to be made that cannot be guided by written statements. Therefore, it is imperative to know the real person from the inside, to know how he or she would think and feel in a given situation. In other words, open, ongoing communication among family members and medical professionals is key.

With or without advance directives and open communication, though, conflict can arise. The decision to withhold or withdraw life-sustaining treatment is now regularly considered at the end of life. Families are usually supportive advocates and concerned surrogate decision makers for patients, although they may also counter the wishes of the patient and disagree with the treatment team. Understanding the range of factors that can influence family responses helps in working with families at this critical juncture in an illness, and must include internal and external factors confronting the individual members and the family as a whole (Rothchild, 1994).

In a case cited by Jackson, Wilde, and Williams (2003), many physicians view family members as allies useful in resolving conflict between patient wishes and professional judgment, although they also find family members in conflict with one another when determining the course of care, even to the point of being directly opposed to the patient's stated wishes. In their case, an elderly woman who was admitted because of complications resulting from a bowel obstruction made very clear that she did not want surgery and requested no cardiopulmonary resuscitation. The medical team had conducted extensive counseling with the family, and the family was aware of her aversion to medical treatment. However, as her condition deteriorated during her hospital stay, some family members expressed a desire to pursue surgery. The disagreement became violent, resulting in arrests and threats of litigation. This presented an ethical dilemma for the medical team. Should they continue to honor the wishes of the patient, in spite of some of the family members? Should they reduce the patient's sedation, on the chance she would be able to restate her wishes? Should they consult with a surgeon, or transfer the patient to another medical team or even another institution? Or, as a last resort, should they call for a meeting of the hospital's ethics committee? They opted to bring in a consulting surgeon, who explained that, given the patient's condition and the risks of surgery at that point, along with the patient's own wishes, he would not operate. The family members finally agreed to palliative intervention only.

To further complicate the advance directive process and potentially add to the pressure on families, some patients have indicated that they want their family's wishes to take precedence over their own previously stated wishes, in the belief that the family will do what is best (Sehgal, Galbraith, Chesney, Schoenfeld, & Lo, 1992). Patients may also assume that the family will be in a position to make decisions for them even if they have not prepared an advance directive. This is not always true. Depending on state law, the family may not be allowed to make decisions about life-sustaining treatments. Even in the states that do permit family decision making, treatment may continue if there is conflict among family members.

Although advance directives may not be fully adequate in some instances, they do offer an opportunity for open, healthy discussion among family members. Many hospices are now becoming more proactive in introducing families to advance directive planning.

HOSPICE CAN HELP

Hospice is at a unique point in the care of patient and family. Disagreements and emotional attitudes may have begun to form among family members during the hospital or nursing home stay or in years past, but when it is time for end-of-life care, they may feel the need for final resolution.

Moreover, hospice has an ethical responsibility to assist. For hospice philosophy always has emphasized that the *family itself* is the unit of care. This infers a responsibility to assist the family even as they disagree, to reach, if possible (and sometimes it may not be possible), a solution that does not render the family further asunder.

To best help the family, the hospice worker must continuously assess the family dynamics. When asked how they are feeling, hospice patients may express that they are feeling alone—even though family members are ever-present. How can this be? Family members may spend a great deal of time discussing the dying family member among themselves, excluding the dying loved one from the conversation. They may be gathered on one side of the room, speaking in whispers, while on the other side of the room, their loved one is alert and aware of the environment and the circumstances. Hospice workers have witnessed heated arguments within earshot of the patient. To rectify this situation, the social worker or chaplain may encourage them to include the dying family member in their conversations. They may ask the patient, "Is it okay if your family asks you questions about how you're really doing, and asks your opinion on how to handle things for you?" Often the patient will say yes. Asking the patient for ideas and opinions makes his or her wishes known. This can give assurance that real human needs will be mutually understood and met by the family.

When family differences reach an impasse, there may be an opportunity for the professional caregiver to assist in an ethical, nonjudgmental way. Assertive, aggressive members of conflicted families may assume power over the patient's care and conceal information. Less assertive family members may withhold their opinions. A member of the hospice care team may point out what he or she is observing, and ask each person to articulate their feelings in a group setting. At that point, the "talker" in the family is obliged to listen, and the passive listener has the floor. This can replace emotion with clearer thinking and promote more effective coping strategies. Open, ongoing communication within the family can help to alleviate the patient's anxiety and depression.

All appropriate family members should be involved in the decision-making process with the physician and health care team. The same information should be given consistently to all adult family members. Reassuring a patient while giving bad news to his or her spouse or other family members will result in conflict.

The more information given, the greater the sense of control for the patient and family. Giving the patient and family an opportunity to maintain control restores a sense of hope, although the objects of the hope may change. Assistance with the cognitive aspects is one of several basic needs of the family of the dying patient, in order to make well-informed decisions, to have peace of mind, and to avoid conflict. Meeting the needs of the family reduces conflicts. These needs include being with the patient, helping the patient, knowing that the patient is comfortable, and being informed of the patient's condition. When these needs are met, family members will be in a much better position to find harmony, to cope, and to let go of a loved one.

Assisting the family in setting goals for care can reduce conflicts. Family members may request futile treatments as a means of conveying that (1) the loss of the patient is tantamount to losing part of themselves, (2) the patient should not be abandoned or devalued in any way, or (3) the patient is owed special obligations by virtue of the special relationship in which the family and the patient stand (Sehgal et al., 1992). Jecker and Schneiderman (1995) maintain that families can best express these important messages by caring for patients, rather than by making requests for futile interventions. Likewise, when life-sustaining measures are futile, health providers can best fulfill their professional obligations by ensuring patients' dignity and comfort, rather than by applying futile interventions. We can assist family members by helping them to identify what they *can* do to assist their loved one.

To aid patients and families in setting realistic goals and expectations, and to guide decision making, several versions of a patient's, or dying person's, bill of rights have been created. The bills recognize the patients' rights to make decisions regarding their treatment, care, and well-being and contain a number of common components, including the right to be comfortable and free of pain, the right to know the truth, the right to make and participate in decisions about care, and the right to express feelings and emotions.

Ironically, in comforting the patient and family by honoring their rights and meeting their needs, including the right to know the truth, the right to participate in decisions, and the right to be informed, we confront them with potentially uncomfortable choices about life and death. The goal of health care workers is not to take an active role in making choices or resolving family disagreements, but to promote the best interests of patient and family throughout the dying process while upholding respect for the patient's and family's values.

Aiding the family and assisting in the resolution of conflict at the end of life is rarely an easy task for hospice counselors, who may be faced with their own ethical dilemmas. Obligated to protect the client, the counselor may not be able to share personal information with other family members—not unlike a priest hearing a confession. In one instance, a family member told a counselor that the client could become "dangerous." Should the counselor take action or not? Ethical ramifications accompany either choice. If the counselor believes the client is in danger, professional ethics and some state laws require the counselor to take action to protect the client. The counselor is even permitted to violate confidentiality in order to ensure the welfare of the client. However, in doing so, the counselor risks violating the client's right to autonomy and self-direction. One way out of an ethical dilemma such as this is for the counselor to encourage the family member who has knowledge of the problem to take charge of the situation and report to the appropriate authorities. The counselor is then free to remain a staunch advocate for the client.

In hospice care, counseling and therapy can play an important role in conflict resolution before death.

Expressive therapy can be one way to put a family at ease. In one instance, while creating a video about Hope Hospice, we filmed a distraught family that had begun to work together on a collage to celebrate the life of the husband/father, who was actively dying. Each family member was selecting photos and pictures clipped from magazines, sharing memories as they worked. On the tape, you can actually see smiles begin to appear on their faces. The atmosphere became visibly relaxed as they collaborated. Such a review of things enjoyed and loved, such as people, places, events, and experiences, can bring genuine comfort and relief to patient and family.

Spiritual support may be helpful for some family members, but this requires thorough exploration from the outset of care and could prove to be problematic. In the study reported by Abbott, Sago, Breen, Abernathy, and Tulsky (2001), 48% of family members spontaneously mentioned faith or spirituality as a significant and reassuring aspect of their hospital stay. However, when family members are of different faiths or when some are nonbelievers, the provision of spiritual care as a means of comforting and unifying the family can become complex. It is not the responsibility of health care providers to resolve religious differences, but rather to assess and provide spiritual support as desired by the patient and family. In a study of members of 48 families of patients previously hospitalized in the intensive care unit (ICU) who had been considered for withdrawal or withholding of life-sustaining treatment, many of the families perceived conflict during end-of-life treatment discussions in the ICU. Conflicts centered on communication and staff behavior. Families identified pastoral care and prior discussion of treatment preferences as sources of psychosocial support during these discussions. Families sought comfort in the identification and contact of a "doctor-in-charge."

While social workers, counselors, and chaplains aid patients and families with "anticipatory grief," they may at the same time serve as neutral arbiters of family disagreements. Somewhat surprisingly, one senior counselor claims a "75 to 80% success rate." However, this does not always mean that the conflict has been fully resolved. For example, it may mean helping an ostracized family member to live with the situation. It may mean helping family members to understand that a particular problem can never be worked out, and it's okay to let it go. Emotional support and counseling can help to unite the family members and give them confidence to assume the challenges of patient care. Caregivers need to reassure patients and their families that care, compassion, and concern will always be available to them and that they will not be abandoned.

When a loved one is dying, the challenge for family members is to find a sense of hope. Even in the face of disagreements, they may still encounter an opportunity to bond and reaffirm their love for one another as they share in the celebration of the life of the dying loved one. Family conflict and disagreement over end-of-life issues can actually be beneficial if they lead to honest, open discussion. However, some decisions may forever be questioned. Closure can be elusive. As the husband of a hospice patient told us, there can be no fairy-tale endings.

In our experience at hospice, we have found that families have two basic expectations for peace of mind: (1) In the curative stage, they need assurance that the medical team did everything possible to try to make the patient well again, and (2) in the palliative care stage, they need assurance that the hospice care team did everything possible to enable the patient to be completely comforted. Fulfilling these expectations can certainly help to circumvent conflict.

The end of life is not an easy time for families, but we can make it less difficult. I see hospice as a model for identifying and perfecting the best methods of helping people through these times. Hospices can easily and competently care for more patients and their families in need of good end-of-life care. By popular demand, birth has become an intimate family time that is a celebration of life. As a nation, we must recognize that no one is more vulnerable and in need of well-informed, harmonious family support than a person at the end of life.

Because of the demographic diversity in southwest Florida, Hope Hospice cares for people from throughout the United States, from every economic level, from an array of cultures and religious backgrounds. Our goal must be to establish best practices that provide communication throughout the experience and to identify them as soon as possible and begin interventions. Hospice can be a lab of the future, leading the way in successfully addressing family issues associated with the end of life. ■

Samira K. Beckwith, LCSW, CHE, is the President and CEO of Hope Hospice and Palliative Care in Fort Myers, Florida. She has played a leadership role in end-of-life care at local, state, and national levels for more than 20 years. She was recently appointed to Florida's Long-Term-Care Policy Advisory Council, and has been elected to serve on the Board of Directors for the National Hospice and Palliative Care Organization.

REFERENCES

Abbott, K. H., Sago, J. G., Breen, C. M., Abernathy, A. P., & Tulsky, J. A. (2001). Families looking back. *Critical Care Medicine 29*(1), pp. 197-201.

Hanson, L. C., Danis, M., & Garret, J. (1997). What is wrong with end-of-life care? *Journal of the American Geriatrics Society, 45*, 1339–1344.

Jackson, W. C., Wilde, J. O., & Williams, J. (2003). Using clinical empowerment to teach ethics and conflict management in antemortem care. *American Journal of Hospice Care, 20*(4), 274-278.

Jecker, N. S. & Schneiderman, L .J. (1995) When families request that everything be done. *Journal of Medicine and Philosophy 20*(2), 145-163.

Goold, S. J., Williams, W., & Arnold, R. (2000) Conflicts regarding decisions to limit treatment: a differential diagnosis 2000. *JAMA, 283*(7), 909–914.

Krishna, G., & Raffin, T. A. (1998). The dying thoracic patient. *Chest Surgery Clinics of North America, 8*(3), 723–739.

Prendergast, T. J., & Puntillo, K. A. (2002). Withdrawal of life support. *JAMA, 288*(21), 2732 -2740.

Rothchild, E. (1994). Family dynamics in end-of-life treatment decisions. *General Hospital Psychiatry, 16*(4), 251–258.

Sehgal, A., Galbraith, A., Chesney, M., Schoenfeld, P., & Lo, B. (1992). How strictly do dialysis patients want their advance directives followed? *JAMA, 267*(1), 59–63.

■ CHAPTER 9 ■

Ethical Dilemmas in Surrogate Decision Making

Bruce Jennings

Thirty years ago, medical ethics and the law faced a novel and very disturbing challenge. Can life-extending medical technology be deliberately withheld or withdrawn when the patient refuses to consent to those treatments or when they serve only to prolong the patient's dying?

There was a time when a physician was on solid ethical ground in doing "everything possible" to stave off death. An advancing "half-way technology" (Thomas, 1974) in medicine beginning roughly in the 1960s put an end to that. Not powerful enough to cure, to restore health, or to restore the person to activity or interaction that was meaningful to the patient, the technologies used with critically ill and dying patients were nonetheless powerful enough to sustain vital biological functions for a lengthy period. The extreme condition that would lead one reasonably to consider forgoing life-sustaining treatment could be due to permanent unconsciousness as a result of stroke or other severe brain injury, to advanced dementia, or to a number of other factors associated with systemic and multiple organ system failure.

The first challenge came in the landmark case of Karen Ann Quinlan in New Jersey, and the answer has evolved in more than 100 appellate level court rulings, culminating in the U.S. Supreme Court decision in the Cruzan case in 1990 (*Cruzan v. Director, Missouri Department of Health*,

1990), in advance directive statutes in all 50 states, and in scores of documents from medicine, nursing, the allied health professions, churches, government commissions, and academic experts in biomedical ethics.

From these sources, something like an ethical, legal, and professional consensus has taken shape. (See chapter 4 [Meisel and Jennings] of this volume and Meisel, 1993.) It is centered on the right of the individual patient to refuse any and all forms of medical treatment, including life-sustaining treatment. It is an individualistic and autonomy-respecting consensus. Since it places such a strong emphasis on the voice of the patient in the decision-making process, one of its main goals is to continue to be guided by that voice as much as possible, even when the patient has lost decision-making capacity and can no longer speak or decide for himself or herself. Hence the emphasis that has been placed on educating patients to fill out advance directives (living wills and durable powers of attorney for health care).

FAULTY DIAGNOSIS

Unfortunately, this consensus alone will not be enough to carry us through the new century. Ragged edges have appeared in the end-of-life care consensus, and they require us to reconsider its underlying philosophy as well as its practical implementation. This chapter focuses particularly on the theory and practice of surrogate decision making for persons who lack decision-making capacity. But before turning to that topic, let me review more generally the cluster of problems that surround it in end-of-life care today.

I believe some of the most serious shortcomings of the current legal-ethical-medical consensus on end of life care are the following:

The excessive rationalism of the consensus.

The consensus works best for those who plan ahead for their terminal illness. Most Americans find that exceedingly hard to do. The denial of death and the reluctance of individuals to engage in advance planning remain very strong in mainstream American culture. The number of people who prepare advance directives remains abysmally small. The consensus forces us to acknowledge our own mortality and the limits of what medicine can promise.

The excessive individualism of the consensus.

Patient autonomy is the cornerstone, both ethically and sociologically, of the way we have approached decisions near the end of life for the past three decades. The legacy of that emphasis has produced a movement in favor not just of the right to refuse medical treatment, but also of the right to medical assistance with suicide. The end of life is not the best time to wage battles on behalf of autonomy. Caring, family solidarity, mutual respect, love, and attentiveness to the dying person are the qualities most needed then. Our consensus has if anything been rather distrusting of families, and tends to make them morally invisible in the official dying process. They are empty conduits of the patient's wishes. Mothers and fathers, brothers and sisters, and relatives lose their names in bioethics and become "surrogates" or "proxies"—appropriately cold terms to denote an impersonal role.

The middle-class cultural bias of the consensus.

As already suggested by the rationalism and the individualism of the consensus, this framework for decision making at the end of life does not travel well across cultures and traditions within our increasingly pluralistic society. Durable powers of attorney for health care may be literally translated into many languages, but substantively they may often be incomprehensible. Is planning and decision making the only or the most appropriate response to the recognition that one is dying? Is everyone's first thought a concern to protect the family from being burdened? How does one respond to the suspicion, built up over a lifetime of experiencing discrimination, that advance directives are racist documents designed to limit resources offered to persons of color?

The misdiagnosis of the problem.

The consensus has been based on the belief that inappropriately aggressive and unwanted treatment at the end of life is fundamentally a problem of prognostic uncertainty and poor communication. And yet, as the SUPPORT study demonstrated, physician behavior is not altered significantly by addressing uncertainty and poor communication alone (SUPPORT Principal Investigators, 1995). These are elements of the physician-patient relationship seen as a personal interaction. The fundamental problem with end-of-life care, however, may be structural and institutional in nature. In the modern acute care hospital, virtually everything is oriented toward using life-sustaining equipment and techniques, not forgoing them. The informal culture of specialty medicine, the reward system, the institutional pressures faced by family members, the range of choices people in extremis are being asked to make—each of these factors and more make up a system that is remarkably resistant to change when confronted with an ideal, countercultural decision-making model, even one that is to some extent backed up by the force of law and professional ethics.

The solution to these problems is not yet clear. Perhaps a counter-vailing system—one oriented toward palliative and hospice care—needs to be created to give patients and families at least one real alternative (Jennings, Ryndes, D'Onofrio, & Baily, 2003). It is hard to see how anything short of this alternative system (which exists now in bits and pieces) will suffice. Until then, we will continue to urge individuals to prepare for death in advance, and we will continue to require them to make a series of agonizing microdecisions in order to stay on the right pathway toward death.

SURROGATE DECISION MAKING IN THEORY

The aim of this chapter is to reexamine the ethical rationale and justifica-tion of the role of health care agents or surrogate decision makers in end-of-life decision making. In the area of surrogate decision making many dilemmas abound, and there is a wide gap between legal and ethical theory, on the one hand, and clinical practice and everyday lived reality, on the other. Many efforts still need to be undertaken to reduce this gap, not the least of which is to improve the support hospitals give to individuals who are called upon to act as surrogates.

First, a word about terminology. When I use the word "surrogate," I intend to include both those authorized by a patient's durable power of attorney for health care (sometimes called "agents" or "proxies") and those family members or close friends ("surrogates") who are consulted by physicians in making decisions for patients who have lost decision-making capacity and who have not executed an advance directive. The legal author-ity of agents and surrogates is quite different; but they each perform a similar function in the decision-making process, and they each need appropriate institutional resources and supports if they are to perform this function well. There is no point in limiting the discussion to the issues confronting only officially designated agents (who remain relatively few in number) and omitting the more numerous group of surrogates who have not been made guardians by a court or have not been given a durable power of attorney for health care by the patient. Throughout this chapter, unless otherwise specified, the term "surrogate" includes both legally authorized agents and informally consulted family members, or close friends and long-established caregivers who may not share a kinship relation with the patient. Moreover, the discussion in this chapter is limited to surrogate decision making for adult patients. Pediatric decision making near the end of life is sufficiently different legally, ethically, and psychosocially that it is best left to a separate analysis.

The 1990s began with the United States Supreme Court's first landmark ruling on end-of-life care in the Cruzan case, in which it affirmed the constitutional right to refuse life-sustaining medical treatment. That same year the federal Patient Self-Determination Act (1990) was enacted, followed later in the decade by durable power of attorney for health care statutes in many states, all stressing the importance of considering individual preferences about end-of-life care in advance (Sabatino, 1999). Public education efforts to encourage the use of advance directives sprang up throughout the country.

At about the same time, the SUPPORT study provided rigorous documentation of the alarming extent to which aggressive life-prolonging measures were still being used in situations where they were either medically futile or unwanted by the patients, or both. Even concerted efforts to improve communication between physicians and dying patients did not stem the technological momentum of end-of-life care in the country's major medical centers (SUPPORT Principal Investigators, 1995; Teno et al., 1997).

Despite slow progress in prompting patients to use their rights under existing state law to execute advance directives, patient and professional education remains one of our principal tools to improve the ethical sensitivity of decision making near the end of life. These efforts should continue, but they also should be expanded in new directions and supplemented by closely related innovations. In recent years, national efforts to encourage and implement the use of advance directives in end-of-life medical care have concentrated on two main objectives.

The first objective has been to make individual patients aware of their options to execute advance directives under the law and to encourage them to do so in the context of good information and advance care planning within an ongoing physician-patient relationship.

The second objective has been to ensure that both health care agents authorized in durable powers of attorney for health care and other surrogate decision makers (such as family members) have information about the patient's medical condition and about the patient's prior wishes and values. Several state court decisions calling for clear and convincing evidence of the patient's wishes are examples of public policy instruments oriented toward these two objectives (*Cruzan v. Harmon*, 1988; *In re Eichner*, 1981; *In re Westchester County Medical Center*, 1988).

These two objectives have proved more difficult to fulfill than the end-of-life care reformers of the 1990s anticipated. Not only that, but it is also now becoming clear that in and of themselves, they are insufficient to produce ethically responsible and responsive surrogate decision making for critically and terminally ill patients who lose decision-making capacity. Future efforts to improve the quality of surrogate decision making need to focus on areas such as the following:

- First, we need to focus on the agent/surrogate rather than the patient and develop an intervention designed to be helpful after, as well as before, the patient has lost decision-making capacity. *Thus far we have focused almost exclusively on how to empower agents to make decisions; we now must also begin to address how to enable them to make good decisions.* Clearly it is very important to work with patients before they lose capacity to get advance directives in place; and it is no less important to encourage appropriate communication between the patient and the agent who is named. But it does little good to get durable powers of attorney for health care in place if we ignore the quality of the decision making that will follow the loss of capacity.

Agents are thought to be preferable to written treatment instructions (living wills) precisely because an individual on the scene has the flexibility to exercise judgment and to interpret the patient's wishes and values in light of specific (and sometimes rapidly changing) medical information about the patient's condition, treatment options, and prognosis (Lynn, 1991). Written instructions cannot have these qualities of flexibility and judgment. Living wills cannot interpret the patient's wishes and values and fit them to present circumstances and future prospects.

Agents and surrogates are expected to possess precisely these qualities and skills. Formally, the standards of surrogate decision making are as follows: First, do as directed in writing or orally by the patient. Second, if the patient's specific treatment preferences are not known, then make an inference from the knowledge you do have of the patient as to what the patient most likely would want under the circumstances. (This is often referred to as the "substituted judgment" standard.) Third, if not enough is known about the patient to make such an inference, then decide on the basis of what a hypothetical "reasonable person" would want under the circumstances, or in other words, do what is in the reasonable best interests of the patient. This is a judgment arrived at by weighing the benefits and burdens of a proposed medical treatment (Hastings Center, 1987; National Center for State Courts, 1993).

The fundamental point—often misunderstood in a clinical setting, by families, and at times even by judges and attorneys—is that these standards are *patient-centered.* They always require that the *patient's* preferences, if known or knowable, and the *patient's* interests be the touchstone of surrogate decision making. The surrogate is expressly forbidden to make the decision based on what the surrogate would want done. Surrogates must not project their own hopes, fears, emotions, and expectations or beliefs onto the patient.

However—and this is the rub—the fields of bioethics and the law have not often seriously asked how psychologically or existentially realistic such expectations are.[1] How realistic is it to expect the surrogate to empty himself or herself to the extent seemingly required by the standards?

---

[1] The significant court decision that discussed the complexities of surrogate decision making in the greatest detail was the *Conroy* case decided by the New Jersey Supreme Court, from which so much important jurisprudence in end-of-life law has come (*In re Conroy*, 1985). This decision has had relatively little impact on either the theory or the practice of surrogate decision making because it sets forth a conceptual structure that is so complex and has so many fine distinctions that it virtually collapses of its own weight.

Especially at a time of emotional turmoil and a struggle to understand the information (not always clear, not always even accurate) being given by health care professionals, the surrogate may be in the least auspicious position to be detached, rational, and patient-centered. Clinically, the most problematic and common situation arises not, as in the classic court cases, when the physicians are pressing for aggressive life-sustaining treatment and the surrogate is resisting, but when the surrogate (or other family members) is demanding all possible treatments against the advice and judgment of the physicians. Even more interesting from an ethical point of view are those situations (I suspect they are more frequent than we know) in which the surrogate knowingly disregards the wishes of the patient and opts for aggressive life-sustaining treatment (the placement of a Percutaneous endoscopic gastrostomy [PEG] tube, for example) in response to the surrogate's own psychological needs. The central ethical reason why this departure from the patient-centered decision making is wrong is that it is the patient, not the surrogate, who will have to suffer the burdensome consequences of a mistaken decision (pain, suffering, indignity) and because disregarding a patient's known wishes in this fashion is a serious kind of ethical disrespect. And yet, the surrogate must bear the consequences of the decision making also, often for a long time. The surrogate must repair broken relationships with spouses or other family members who disagree long after the patient has died.

The wide gap between the theory of how surrogates are supposed to decide and the exceeding complexity and difficulty of the practice of surrogate decision making near the end of life shows itself in many ways. In terms of empirical research, it shows in some of the dubious performance often demonstrated by surrogates (Emanuel & Emanuel, 1992; Hare, Pratt, & Nelson, 1992; Pearlman, Uhlmann, & Jecker, 1998; Seckler, Meier, Mulvihill, & Paris, 1991; Schneider, 1998).

■ Second, we must acknowledge and insist upon the fact that hospitals and other health care facilities have an institutional and systemic responsibility to facilitate better surrogate decision making. This is not to say that individuals and families do not have a responsibility to prepare for these decisions on their own initiative, nor is it to say that community-based educational programs are not valuable or needed. Both patients and health care professionals have responsibilities in the end-of-life decision making process; both communities and health care institutions have responsibilities and a constructive role to play in this arena as well. For the most part, however, the institutional side of the equation has been relatively neglected (Dubler, 1995; Farber-Post, Blustein, & Dubler, 1999).

Tools are needed to assess current institutional practices in this regard and to improve them in the future. Health care professionals must become more knowledgeable about, and sensitive to, the special needs of surrogates and the special burdens of their role. An appropriate interdisciplinary response should be brought to bear on improving the quality of support that agents and surrogates receive, including medicine and nursing, but also ethics, pastoral counseling, social work, and other sources of expertise about the full range of cognitive and emotional work surrogate decision making entails.

- Third, we need to pay much more attention to understanding the organizational and environmental conditions in the health care setting that are most conducive to good decision making, and we need to develop protocols of education, counseling, and support aimed at enabling surrogates to engage in it.

- Finally, we must recognize that most, if not all, surrogates need more than information concerning the patient's medical condition and prior wishes and values. They need to articulate a context within which that information has meaning and validates their own past relationship with the patient and their own identity as loving, caring, responsible people faced with life-and-death decisions in the midst of shock, loss, grief, and possibly guilt (Collopy, 1999; Jennings, 1992).

Consider the following questions. What if no family members are available? Should "bonded" long-term care givers, if available, become the de facto surrogate decision makers, because they have had the relationship and the knowledge of the individual over a long period of time (Buchanan & Brock, 1989)? Or what if two potential surrogates disagree about what treatments ought to be undertaken? How does a person who has been close to and cared for the patient, whether a relative or not, stand in relation to a blood relative who has not been bonded or in contact with the patient, and who has not taken part in the patient's care? Should one be given priority over another? Does past caregiving "entitle" one to standing as surrogate?

Health care surrogacy is always, and especially in end-of-life decision making, both a cognitive and an affective task. (For many persons, this context or framework of meaning will relate to spiritual concerns and to the resources made available by a particular religion or faith tradition. The involvement of pastoral counseling and a more holistic approach to the experience of the surrogate are essential.) It involves complex medical information, moral and religious ideas, probabilistic judgments, and deep-seated emotions. While it should be primarily focused on the wishes, values, and best interests of the patient, there is no gainsaying the fact that the decisions a surrogate makes affect the surrogate himself or herself, and the entire family.

To see surrogacy as simply an information-processing task is to miss most of its human angst and drama. And yet that is the approach that many health care facilities have taken, implicitly or explicitly, by the resources they provide to agents and surrogates, by the nature and style of communication they offer, and by the low priority most of them give to multidisciplinary counseling and support.

THE UNBEFRIENDED PATIENT

In concluding this discussion, I want to focus on one particular area of surrogate decision making that poses the following ethically difficult dilemma: How shall we devise a system of "stranger surrogacy" when formal legal processes to appoint a guardian are too costly and too time-consuming, and yet decisions need to be made that require someone's consent on behalf of the incapacitated patient? This is the problem of the so-called unbefriended patient, which has only recently come to the forefront of serious attention in bioethics and end-of-life care (Karp & Wood, 2003).

The plight of isolated and unbefriended individuals in health care facilities is a source of concern to all those who care for them. Identifying this population and defining its special needs are complex problems.

Surely, the isolated and the unbefriended are among the most vulnerable persons in our health care system. With no one to advocate for them, they are at high risk of abuse and neglect or substandard care and attention.

The problem is virtually neglected in important works on end-of-life decision making.[2] One reason is that there seem to be few options from which to choose in these cases. The main recourse is to obtain a court-appointed guardian or judicial permission to make a particular treatment or nontreatment decision. Arizona, North Carolina, and Oregon have laws that permit physicians to make decisions for patients without surrogates (Miller, Coleman, & Cugliari, 1997). The existence of these laws raises concerns about physicians' personal and cultural values, their conflicts of interest, and the nature of their knowledge of and relationship with the patient, among other issues (Rai, Siegler, & Lantos, 1999). Another approach involves establishing public guardianship programs, in which isolated patients are assigned a stranger surrogate charged with acting in the patient's best interest. Another approach involves creating independent, quasi-judicial committees modeled on committees for isolated patients in mental health facilities (Sundram, 1988, discussing Article 80 of the New York Mental Hygiene Law). Still another approach, favored by the New York Task Force, would allow physicians to make decisions based on the best interests of the patient and then to have an internal ethics commit-tee review those decisions (New York State Task Force on Life and the Law, 1992, pp. 159–171).

No one really knows how many long-term care residents fall into the category of isolated and unbefriended persons (Miller, Coleman, & Cugliari, 1997, p. 369). The numbers involved depend on one's definition of the category. For the purposes of analysis and research, I believe a rather broad definition of "isolated" or "unbefriended" persons in long-term care should be used.[3] It will include (a) those who have no relative, guardian,

---

[2] "In the voluminous literature on bioethics, the special needs of [patients without surrogates] have received little attention"(Miller, Coleman, & Cugliari, 1997, p. 369). One of the first detailed treatments of the problem appeared in a report by the New York State Task Force on Life and the Law (1992). In a literature search I employed the following databases: bioethicsline, PubMed, Nexis, and NLM Gateway, as well as the National Reference Center for Bioethics literature at 1-800-MED-ETHX. Search words used were "unbefriended patients," "patients without surrogates," "nursing homes or legal guardians," "single person or vulnerable persons," and "absence of proxy."

[3] In this chapter I use these two terms interchangeably. For what may be the origin of the term "unbefriended," see Gillick (1995).

or responsible party named on the medical and administrative record; (b) those whose relative listed on the record cannot be contacted; and (c) those whose relative can be contacted but is known to be unresponsive or has refused to become involved in decision making concerning the patient. Where records of visitation exist and can be consulted, one might also include in the population patients who have not received a visitor during the past two years, regardless of whether the address of a living relative is known. Using this definition, I believe that a substantial number of long-term care residents are isolated and unbefriended (perhaps as high as 30% or more in some facilities in and around the New York City metropolitan area, for example).

Defining the special needs and vulnerabilities of this population is as difficult as determining their numbers. In the context of end-of-life care, unbefriended residents may be at risk of burdensome and perhaps unwanted aggressive life-sustaining treatment. This is particularly likely when the law inclines in that direction, as it does in states that require clear and convincing evidence of a patient's wishes before a decision to forgo life-sustaining treatment can be made. On the other hand, they may equally be at risk of discriminatory undertreatment because no one is there to serve as their advocate or to ensure accountability. Too readily, the isolated and unbefriended may be made candidates for withholding or withdrawing life-sustaining treatments in this era of cost containment and fiscal pressures (Meier, 1997).

Even if isolated and unbefriended persons have decision-making capacity, they are too often left without the options of choosing among treatment alternatives that the rest of society takes for granted. Communication with them may be more difficult. Ethnic or cultural background factors may be harder to clarify and accommodate responsibly. A history of mental illness or social marginality and powerlessness may influence their values, expectations, and preferences for health care. For example, at this time we are witnessing the graying of the homeless population, many of whom are beginning to enter long-term care facilities. Little is known about the way the life experience of prolonged homelessness or chronic mental illness affects a person's health care preferences and values.

For isolated and unbefriended patients who have lost decision-making capacity, the strong ethical and legal bias in favor of the subjective preference of the patient as the decision-making standard, and for relatives or bonded friends as candidates for surrogate, often means that literally no one is authorized to make major medical decisions for them. The prevailing standard of care then becomes one of waiting until a condition worsens to the point where an emergency can be declared and the emergency exemption to the informed consent requirement can be invoked. This is the opposite of good advance care planning and decision making.

The isolated and unbefriended population poses a number of challenges to the mainstream paradigm of ethical decision making. The assessment of decision-making capacity and the ethical significance of informed consent may be more complicated with isolated residents (Gillick, Berkman, & Cullen, 1999). Many cognitively impaired nursing home residents may nonetheless possess sufficient capacity to execute a health care proxy (Mezey, Teresi, Ramsey, Mitty, & Bobrowitz, 2000). However, advance planning concerning end-of-life decisions is more difficult and less routinely done in nursing homes than in some other settings (Bradley, Peiris, & Wetle, 1998). Without the assistance or corroboration of family members or friends, it may be difficult to resolve ambiguities in the values history or the expressed preferences of isolated individuals, even if their capacity is intact (Jecker, 1990). With individual preferences and values in doubt or inaccessible, is it appropriate to turn to some sort of community values and standards in end-of-life decision making?

When the isolated and unbefriended resident is determined to lack capacity, decision making in all settings becomes prone to disagreement and dispute. Long-term care facilities may feel more pressure to transfer such residents to the hospital when a condition becomes serious or life-threatening, and hospitals find such transfers particularly difficult to manage for lack of guidance from advance directives or surrogates (Saliba et al., 2000). Long-term care staff may be the only de facto family the individual has, but there is a conflict of interest inherent in such persons serving as surrogate decision makers.

In sum, the de facto standard of practice in decision making with isolated patients is reactive and abuses the intent of the emergency exemption to the informed consent requirement. A new standard of practice should be defined and promulgated to ensure timely, accountable, and respectful decision making. In general, an isolated and unbefriended person should be treated just the same way as a person accompanied by an involved and concerned family.

CONCLUSION

Not just where unbefriended patients are concerned, but in the entire arena of surrogate decision making, existing judicial opinions, statutes, and administrative regulations affecting long-term care facilities sometimes hinder innovation and good decision making. Surrogates need more counseling and support, and new ways must be found to tap—and train—volunteers to stand in as surrogates when no more natural choice is available. Surrogate decision making can be abused, and vulnerable patients need to be protected. The decision-making process should be accountable. The best short-term strategy is to pursue a large number of small, incremental changes that allow physicians and the health care team to work and communicate more effectively with surrogates. In the longer term, legal change may be required and new structures may need to be created and funded. ■

Bruce Jennings is Senior Research Scholar at The Hastings Center, a bioethics research institute located in Garrison, New York. Mr. Jennings has been with The Hastings Center since 1980 and served as Executive Director of the Center from 1990 to 1999. A graduate of Yale University (BA) and Princeton University (MA), he has written widely on end-of-life care, long-term care, and health policy. He served on the Board of Directors of the National Hospice and Palliative Care Organization and the Hospice and Palliative Care Association of New York State. He has written or edited 18 books, including The Perversion of Autonomy: The Uses of Coercion and Constraints in a Liberal Society *(2nd ed. 2003; co-authored with Willard Gaylin). He is currently at work on a book on chronic illness, dementia, and long-term care policy.*

REFERENCES

Bradley, E. H., Peiris, V., & Wetle, T. (1998). Discussions about end-of-life care in nursing homes. *Journal of the American Geriatrics Society, 46,* 1235–1241.

Buchanan, A. E., & Brock, D. W. (1989). *Deciding for others: The ethics of surrogate decisionmaking.* Cambridge, U.K.: Cambridge University Press.

Collopy, B. J. (1999). The moral underpinning of the proxy-provider relationship: Issues of trust and distrust. *Journal of Law, Medicine and Ethics, 27,* 37–45.

In re Conroy (1985). 486 A.2d 1209 (N.J.).

Cruzan v. Director, Missouri Department of Health (1990). 497 U.S. 261.

Cruzan v. Harmon (1988). 760 S.W.2d 408 (Mo.).

Dubler, N. N. (1995). The doctor-proxy relationship: The neglected connection. *Kennedy Institute of Ethics Journal, 5*(4), 289–306.

Emanuel, E., & Emanuel, L. (1992). Proxy decisionmaking for incompetent patients: An ethical and empirical analysis. *JAMA, 267,* 2067–2071.

Farber-Post, L., Blustein, J., & Dubler, N. N. (1999). Introduction: The doctor-proxy relationship: An untapped resource. *Journal of Law, Medicine and Ethics, 27,* 5–12.

Gillick, M. R. (1995). Medical decision-making for the unbefriended nursing home resident. *Journal of Ethics, Law and Aging, 1*(2), 87–92.

Gillick, M., Berkman, S., & Cullen, L. (1999). A patient-centered approach to advance medical planning in the nursing home. *Journal of the American Geriatrics Society, 47,* 227–230.

Hare, J., Pratt, C., & Nelson, C. (1992). Agreement between patients and their self-selected surrogates on difficult medical decisions. *Archives of Internal Medicine, 152,* 1049–1054.

Hastings Center. (1987). *Guidelines on the termination of life-sustaining treatment and the care of the dying.* Bloomington, IN: Indiana University Press.

In re Eichner (1981). 438 N.Y.S.2d 266.

In re Westchester County Medical Center (O'Connor) (1988). 531 N.E.2d 607 (N.Y.).

Jecker, N. S. (1990). The role of intimate others in medical decision making. *The Gerontologist, 30,* 65–71.

Jennings, B. (1992). Last rights: Dying and the limits of self-sovereignty. *In Depth 2* (Fall), 103–118.

Jennings, B., Ryndes, T., D'Onofrio, C., & Baily, M. A. (2003). *Access to hospice care: Expanding boundaries, overcoming barriers,* Hastings Center Report (Special Suppl. 2), 33, S3–S59.

Karp, N., & Wood, E. (2003). *Incapacitated and alone: Health care decision-making for the unbefriended elderly.* Washington, DC: American Bar Association.

Lynn, J. (1991). Why I don't have a living will. *Law, Medicine and Health Care, 19,* 101–4.

Meier, D. E. (1997). Voiceless and vulnerable: Dementia patients without surrogates in an era of capitation. *Journal of the American Geriatrics Society, 45,* 375–377.

Meisel, A. (1993). The legal consensus about forgoing life-sustaining treatment: Its status and its prospects. *Kennedy Institute of Ethics Journal, 2,* 309–345.

Mezey, M., Teresi, J., Ramsey, G., Mitty, M., & Bobrowitz, T. (2000). Decision-making capacity to execute a health care proxy: Development and testing of guidelines. *Journal of the American Geriatrics Society, 48,* 179–187.

Miller, T. E., Coleman, C. H., & Cugliari, A. M. (1997). Treatment decisions for patients without surrogates: Rethinking policies for a vulnerable population. *Journal of the American Geriatrics Society, 45,* 369–374, at 369.

National Center for State Courts. (1993). *Guidelines for state court decision making in life-sustaining medical treatment cases* (2nd rev. ed.). Saint Paul, MN: West Publishing Company.

New York State Task Force on Life and the Law. (1992). *When others must choose.* Albany: New York Department of Health.

Patient Self-Determination Act (1990). Public Law No. 101-508, §§ 4206, 4751 (codified at 42 U.S.C.A. § 1395cc(f)(1), § 1396a(a)).

Pearlman, R. A., Uhlmann, R. F., & Jecker, N. S. (1988). Spousal understanding of patient quality of life: Implications for surrogate decisions. *Journal of Clinical Ethics, 3,* 114–121.

Rai, A., Siegler, M., & Lantos, J. (1999). The physician as a health care proxy. *Hastings Center Report, 29,* 14–19.

Sabatino, C. P. (1999). The legal and functional status of the medical proxy: Suggestions for statutory reform. *Journal of Law, Medicine and Ethics, 27,* 52–68.

Saliba, D., Kington, R., Buchanan, J., Bell, R., Wang, M., Lee, M., et al. (2000). Appropriateness of the decision to transfer nursing facility residents to the hospital. *Journal of the American Geriatrics Society, 48*(2),154-163.

Schneider, C. (1998). *The practice of autonomy: Patients, doctors, and medical decisions.* New York: Oxford University Press.

Seckler, A. B., Meier, D. E., Mulvihill, M., & Paris, B. E. (1991). Substituted judgment: How accurate are proxy predictions? *Annals of Internal Medicine, 115,* 92–98.

Sundram, C. J. (1988). Informed consent for major medical treatment of mentally disabled people: A new approach. *New England Journal of Medicine, 318,* 1368–1373.

SUPPORT Principal Investigators. (1995). A controlled trial to improve care for seriously ill hospitalized patients: The Study to understand prognoses and preferences for outcomes and risks of treatments (SUPPORT). *JAMA, 274,* 1591–1598.

Teno, J., Lynn, J., Wenger, N., Phillips, R. S., Murphy, D. P., Connors, A. F. Jr., et al. (1997). Advance directives for seriously ill hospitalized patients: Effectiveness with the patient self-determination act and the SUPPORT intervention. *Journal of the American Geriatrics Society, 45,* 500–507.

Thomas, L. (1974). *The lives of a cell.* New York: Bantam Books.

CHAPTER 10

Rational Suicide in Terminal Illness: The Ethics of Intervention and Assistance

Thomas Attig

In *Last Wish*, Betty Rollin (1985) tells the story of the death by suicide of her mother, Ida Rollin. A summary of Ida's life circumstances and her last hours will provide a beginning for a discussion of rational suicide in terminal illness.

Ida Rollin described herself as a happy woman. She was not religious, but feeling that she "had to thank someone," she "thanked God" for her "wonderful" child Betty and "son," Ed, as she called Betty's husband. Throughout her life she was intelligent and articulate, in full command of her faculties, and determined to decide for herself.

Two years before her death, Ida was diagnosed with ovarian cancer. She underwent an arduous round of chemotherapy that sapped her vitality. She spoke openly about wanting to end her life if she found it no longer worth living. When her cancer recurred, she reluctantly began a second round of chemotherapy. But it became clear to all, including her physician, that the effort was futile. The prognosis was that she would likely die over months, not weeks. The only hospice in New York City that offered home care services (in 1983) was overbooked. She found a "wonderful" home care nurse. Still, the treatments available to her provided only marginal comfort. She was weak and bedridden. She was in constant pain, relieved only by occasional sleep. She was profoundly nauseated. She could see no way in which her continued living would benefit either her or her children. In a pivotal conversation with Betty, Ida confides,

> "Every day is bad. Every day. I'm not saying it couldn't be worse. I know how some people suffer and still they cling to life. But to me this isn't life. Life is taking a walk, visiting my children, eating! Remember how I loved to eat? The thought of food makes me sick now." She closed her eyes. "Everything makes me sick now. This isn't life. If I had life, I'd want it. I don't want this." She looked up at me the same way she had before, in the same hard-eyed way.
>
> "Mother," I said, holding each word before letting it go, "is that what you really want—to die?"
>
> "Of course I want to die," she said. "Next to the happiness of my children, I want to die more than anything in the world" (Rollin, 1985, p. 150).

On the day of her death, Ida instructed Betty to bring a gift she had bought to a friend. She ate a light meal at midday. Before she left, the visiting nurse described Ida as "cheerful" in her medical chart. Ida called to give the night nurse the night off. She took an anti-nausea medication some time before taking fatal doses of two different sedatives, one to induce sleep quickly and the other for long-lasting effect. After dressing in a favorite nightgown, she tucked herself into bed, fell asleep, and never awakened. Ida's visiting nurse found her dead the next morning.

Stories like Ida's enable us to tune into the humanity and vulnerability of the dying and to appreciate the uniqueness of their life circumstances. Learning the stories of the terminally ill and their personal caregivers is essential for professionals and volunteers who care for them and support them in evaluating life options and making decisions at the end of life. Later we will learn more about Ida's story and the experiences, perspectives, and responsibilities of her family and professional caregivers.

SUICIDE AND HUMAN RESPONSIBILITY FOR DEATH

To sharpen focus on the ethics of suicide intervention and assisting suicide among the terminally ill, it is important to understand precisely how what Ida Rollin did is a suicide and not a death by some other means. Had she simply waited through the months that the doctor predicted it would take for her to die from her cancer, she would have died of natural causes. Instead, she completed a deliberate act of suicide, literally an act of self-killing. By definition, suicide is something persons do to themselves with the intention of bringing about their death. Suicide is inherently active and intended. Ida was momentarily passive in waiting for the pills to take their effect, but she was active in taking the pills. And she intended to die as a result of taking them.

By contrast, like some other terminally ill people, Ida might have accidentally taken a fatal dose while drowsy or half asleep; after misreading the label; forgetting that she had already taken a strong but prescribed dose; mistakenly believing that there was no hazard in taking so many; believing that she was taking another medicine she knew to be safe; or simply failing to heed warnings from her doctor or from the label. She might have fallen on a flight of stairs in the dark. She might have taken too large a mouthful of food and choked to death. In all such cases, something she did would have led to her death. But the crucial element of intention to die would have been missing. These would be accidental or negligent self-killings, not suicides. Ida would have been physically responsible, but not morally responsible for causing her death.

Had Ida refused life-prolonging medical treatment, such as the first round of chemotherapy, she would have had some responsibility for dying earlier than she did. She would have passively allowed death to come rather than taking active steps to bring it about. She might have anticipated the possibility of dying sooner but accepted that risk without intending it. More likely she would have intended to avoid unwanted side effects of the treatment. The cause on her death certificate would have been cancer or some other natural cause, not suicide.

We can also distinguish suicides from cases where deaths result entirely or in part from the actions or omissions of others. Ida could have died at the hands of another in any of the ways that those who are not terminally ill can die. She could have been murdered. She could have died as a result of what someone else unintentionally did or failed to do—accident or negligence. She could have been among the nearly 100,000 annual victims of medical mistakes (Wachter & Shojania, 2004).

Ida could have died as the result of euthanasia, another's action or omission undertaken with the intention of relieving her suffering and hastening a "good death." Active euthanasia would have involved someone taking active steps toward this end. Passive euthanasia would have involved their refraining from using life-prolonging procedures. Either could have been voluntary, carried out with Ida's consent. She could have given consent directly while conscious and capable of rational consent or indirectly through an advance directive, such as a written living will or through assigning power of attorney to someone to speak for her if she were to become unable to speak for herself. Active or passive euthanasia could also have been nonvoluntary, carried out without Ida's consent.

THE ETHICS OF SUICIDE SET ASIDE

Some who learn about Ida's story immediately want to say that what she did was morally wrong. They urge that, despite her suffering, intentional self-killing is always wrong, that suicide is self-murder. Others urge that what Ida did was morally justifiable. They admire her courage in making a difficult decision and respect her right to make it. Still others suspect that Ida must have been tragically irrational in ways not clear from the story. They contend that she was not morally responsible for what she did: Her suicide was neither wrong nor morally justifiable.

It is tempting to build moral condemnation into the term and to understand "suicide," as morally wrong self-killing. But we should resist this temptation. We apply terms like "wrong" and "justifiable" only to actions for which persons are morally responsible, that is, when they are in full command of their faculties, able to understand the consequences of their actions, and free of external coercion. But some who work in suicide intervention insist that all suicides are irrational. And many whose loved ones have died by suicide insist on saying that they "completed," not "committed," suicide, because they were not responsible for the act. If these interventionists and survivors are right—and they usually are—then the term "suicide" understood as morally wrong would not apply to these self-killings. We would need another term. Since we have no such term, we speak of irrational self-killings as suicides and debate whether *any* suicides are rational and subject to moral evaluation.

I describe suicide as 'intentional self-killing' in order to define it in a morally neutral way. The term 'self-killing' is neutral in the same way as the term 'killing' is neutral. Most intentional killing of our fellow humans is morally wrong—for example, murder, genocide, killing in wars of aggression, and killing that results from culpable negligence. But when killing results from unforeseeable accidents or irrational actions, we do not hold the agents morally responsible. And some intentional killing is held by all but the most stringent pacifists (and not those supported by the traditions of pacifism in the world's great religions) to be morally justifiable, even righteous, however regrettable it may be. Think, for example, of killing in just wars or killing in self-defense. Some self-killings also could be construed as justifiable—as acts of self-defense against intolerable life circumstances or irremediable suffering.

I have said that it is appropriate to evaluate the morality of only *rational* suicides. There is considerable controversy about whether any suicides are rational. Different views are pivotal in evaluating alternative positions on the ethics of intervention and assistance.

To focus on the ethics of intervention or assistance in suicide among the terminally ill, we will leave open the question of the ethics of suicide itself. The finest entrance into reflection on the ethics of suicide I know is found in the writings of Margaret Pabst Battin (1995). Here it suffices to say that there is serious disagreement on the subject.

The Ethics of Suicide Intervention

Workers in suicide prevention centers or suicide hotlines, first responders, health care professionals, hospice volunteers, and even average citizens are apt to encounter would-be suicides, including the terminally ill, in circumstances where they know little about them or the processes that led them to choose death. Often they must act before they can learn enough to determine whether intervention is appropriate. Interventions range from talking things through with someone contemplating suicide, to physically intervening to prevent an attempt, to using sophisticated medical procedures to revive persons in mid-attempt. Presumptions in the area of suicide intervention spell out when any such interventions are appropriate. *Presumptions* are general principles to guide action in circumstances where (1) knowledge about particular cases is lacking, and (2) there is not enough time to learn about all things worth considering before acting.

Intervention, Presumption, and Respect for Persons

The contrast between the views of those who oppose suicide intervention and those who favor it in such circumstances is marked. Opponents of intervention argue that it is reasonable to presume that all suicidal persons have their reasons and that it is never appropriate to intervene. Defenders argue that it is extremely rare for their reasoning to be rational, and therefore it is always appropriate to intervene.

At the core of the view of intervention opponents is respect for personal autonomy. The Western tradition has long defended personal autonomy, or liberty, against paternalistic interference. In the tradition of John Stuart Mill, only decisions that will harm others may be legitimately overturned. Intervention would be appropriate if a suicide would clearly harm another—for example, by causing injury or death to, visiting hardship upon, or violating a commitment to another. Intervention in the name of "the person's own good" would not be legitimate. Critics of suicide intervention have argued that no decision is more fundamental than that of whether to continue living. It is profoundly disrespectful to intervene in this intensely personal decision . . . even when it may involve a mistaken judgment concerning the worth of the life remaining.

But Immanuel Kant and his followers have insisted that only rational decisions are the proper objects of respect, since only they reflect a person's true character. Decisions that are known to be irrational may be overridden. Still, the burden of proof falls upon those who claim that irrationality is present. Without such proof or clear indication that a suicide would harm another, intervention would fail to respect personal autonomy. And it is proper to presume that the decision is rational unless proven otherwise.

The core concern of those who defend suicide intervention is to respect personal potential for future meaningful living, the vision of which may be obscured by irrationality in times of crisis. Death through suicide is so often tragic precisely because it short-circuits the full realization of that potential. Intervention in suicide is based on concern for the suicidal person's own best interest. It presumes at least temporary irrationality on that person's part.

The tension between opponents and proponents of suicide intervention, then, fundamentally reflects a tension internal to the concept of respect for persons. Each side calls attention to an element of what respect is. Opponents correctly point out that respect requires taking autonomy very seriously. Proponents correctly point out that respect requires taking prospects for continued meaningful living very seriously. Each position is deficient to the extent that it downplays or ignores the strength of the other.

Appropriate Presumption in Suicide Intervention

How, then, are viable presumptions in suicide intervention to be formulated? The ultimate goal is to preserve respect for persons. The challenge is to define a presumption, or guiding principle for conditions of uncertainty, that minimizes the likelihood of either undervaluing human potential or riding roughshod over human autonomy.

We normally presume that intervention in the decisions of others is illegitimate unless a compelling reason has been provided to justify it. In the area of decisions for suicide, however, compelling considerations pull us in the opposite direction. Here it is much more reasonable to presume that intervention is appropriate, for two reasons: (1) weighty empirical evidence indicates that it is highly likely that elements of irrationality are present in most decisions for suicide, and (2) decisions to intervene can be reversed, but decisions not to intervene seldom can. Where suicidal persons and their processes of choosing death are not well known, it is best to err on the side of respect for their potential for meaningful living at the risk of temporarily failing to respect their autonomy. Presuming, when little is known about them, that the suicidal terminally ill are irrational is respectful and appropriate. Had Ida Rollin been found still breathing after she took the pills, it would have been appropriate for her visiting nurse or emergency medical personnel to attempt to revive her.

When Presumption Is Inappropriate:
When to Intervene and When Not to

What is an appropriate response to would-be suicides (including the terminally ill) when much is known about their life circumstances, their characters, and their deliberations about killing themselves? Presumption, by definition, would be inappropriate. But it is still important to respect and weigh considerations of personal autonomy and potential for future meaningful living.

We can know a great deal about those contemplating suicide. We can know the challenges they face, the extent of their suffering, means of addressing it, whether they are in a temporary crisis, and whether their suffering is likely to persist or worsen. We can know their prospects of continuing to live meaningfully on their own terms. Temporary crises may arise in the lives of the terminally ill—for example, readily treatable painful injuries, recurrences of distressing symptoms, or setbacks in relationships with others. If they have found life with illness otherwise meaningful yet express a desire to die because of a temporary crisis, it is appropriate to override the desire.

But terminal illness itself is no temporary crisis. The suffering that it entails, or particularly devastating permanent reversals that can come as it unfolds, can cast a shadow over any prospects of the dying ever living in ways that they would consider meaningful. Intervention then finds no footing in respect for potential for meaningful living.

Palliative and hospice care can often relieve symptoms and provide comfort for, stabilize, and even improve the quality of life for the terminally ill. And intervention to the extent of insisting on discussion with them to clarify the quality of life that such services can provide is, of course, appropriate. Many who might otherwise be tempted to kill themselves find that such care enables them to live meaningfully until they die. They choose to take advantage of such services and die of natural causes.

However, high-quality palliative and hospice care is not always available. In the 1990s in the United States, a high percentage of those who died still did so with too little symptom control and inadequate support for their psychological, social, and spiritual needs (Institute of Medicine, 1997). When support does not reach particular individuals, it is not irrational for them to kill themselves just because it is generally available.

Even the best palliative and hospice care may fail to return the dying to a meaningful quality of life. They may conclude that life is no longer worth living. The right to refuse treatment includes the right to refuse palliative and hospice care. It is not irrational to exercise that right, either by declining to enter a program to begin with or by declining to continue with services once a program has been initiated. The estimation of the prospects for meaningful living must not be grounded in a search for a prospect that an interventionist caregiver might find meaningful. Rather, the point is whether the *would-be suicide* might find such a prospect meaningful. If, after careful consideration, he or she finds no acceptable prospect, it would be disrespectful to insist that since the *caregiver* could, *he or she* must. Respect for autonomy, then, would support non-intervention in such cases.

We can know a great deal about the personal history and character of those contemplating suicide. We can know their long-term convictions about what they wish to do given events affecting matters of vital importance to them. When such events come to pass—for example, they lose dignity or physical or mental well-being or become terminally ill—a decision for suicide is not necessarily the product of crisis-induced irrationality. The decision can be an expression of the suicidal person's character, an expression of long-held preferences, interests, values, purposes, meanings, or rationally developed convictions.

We can also know much about the process of deliberation that leads to decisions for suicide. The terminally ill may contemplate or undertake suicidal actions that run counter to their own best interests as they themselves would see them. Some, for example, may suffer so greatly from the side effects of chemotherapy or other intensive therapies that they are unable to envision a time when they could live meaningfully. Some may be unable to imagine how palliative care or other measures could alleviate their suffering and afford them a quality of life they would embrace. Some are compromised by various forms of dementia and unable to make major decisions for themselves. Some are gripped by irrational fears of life prospects that are not at all likely, such as fear of physical suffering from an illness that rarely entails such suffering, or fear of suffering that can be easily managed. Some are ambivalent, wanting very much to live if their suffering can be alleviated, but wanting to die in the mistaken belief that it cannot. Some are misinformed about their prognosis, unaware of the

possibilities of remission. Some misread the extent to which their continued illness burdens others. And some are tragically manipulated or coerced
into killing themselves by persons who stand to benefit from their death.

But sometimes, we may know the terminally ill well enough to know
that the marks of irrationality are absent. The presumption for suicide
intervention would not apply. When the terminally ill are known to be in
command of their faculties, deciding and acting in ways that express their
true selves, and not being coerced, respect for their autonomy requires
others to refrain from intervening in their decisions for death.

Betty Rollin's account left little doubt that Ida Rollin truly wanted to
die. No one pressed her to act against her will. Ida explicitly considered the
possibility of underestimating the potential meaningfulness of the time left
to her and dismissed it. She was quite happy about the 76 years she had
lived up until she decided to end her life. She perceived her illness as
making it impossible for her to remain the self she had always been and
wanted to continue to be. Her physician confirmed her judgments about
the futility of future treatment and her future life prospects. She saw suicide
as a final way of being true to herself, not as a way of betraying or harming
herself. She explicitly said that she could see no way that her action would
harm her or anyone else. As she looked ahead, she saw nothing but
worsening suffering, devoid of the cherished activities and interactions
with loved ones that she called "life."

Through many conversations with Ida, Betty and Ed concluded that
she was in full command of her faculties: She was not in a temporary crisis
frame of mind, not ambivalent, not depressed or overwhelmed by some
other emotion. She was well informed about her prognosis and the future
quality of life. Her decision reflected her true character and long-standing
convictions. They understood how she could conclude that her potential
for meaningful living on her own terms was limited, and they respected her
autonomy. They carefully observed their own behaviors to ensure that they
in no way encouraged Ida to do something she did not really want to do,
even to the point of adopting a rule that only Ida could bring up the
subject. Ida repeatedly initiated conversations on the subject and reiterated
her desire.

THE ETHICS OF ASSISTED SUICIDE

The ethics of suicide intervention has to do with principles about when it is or is not appropriate to take measures intended to keep another from carrying out a decision for suicide. The ethics of assisted suicide has to do with principles about when it is or is not appropriate to support others as they prepare to carry out such decisions.

Ida Rollin could not have killed herself without the help of Betty and Betty's husband Ed. From the time when it became clear that chemo-therapy would be futile and she was still in the hospital, Ida began to voice her desire to kill herself in conversation with Betty.

"Why can't they give me a pill that would end it?"

"They can't do that," I said, looking at the bed covers.

"Why can't they?"

"It's against the law."

"It shouldn't be. If a person wants to go, they should help."
Her lips were tight. She held the edges of the sheets in her fists
as if they were reins. "What's the point of trapping you in life if
you don't want it?" she said, trying to find my eyes which were
still pinned on the bed. "It's cruel. They don't care. They don't
care what a person really wants. They care about their profession,
not the people they practice it on" (Rollin, 1985, p. 139).

Some time later, after Ida was at home, bedridden, and cared for with the help of visiting nurses, she spoke with Betty of feeling trapped.

"It's the only relief I have now—sleep." Gently she took her
hand out of mine and looked at me, her eyes wide and hard.
"How am I going to get out of this?" she said. "Where's the
door?" (Rollin, 1985, p. 149).

Betty began trying to gather information about how her mother could kill herself. Doctors seemed an unlikely source of advice, given legal prohibitions against assisting suicide. So she turned to a book that contained stories about how people had killed themselves.

As she was reading, her husband Ed came home, and they began to talk about Betty's conversation with Ida. She told Ed, "My mother wants to kill herself, and I'm trying to find out how she can do it." Though Ida had spoken of doing so several times before, Betty had never paid much attention. "But she brought it up tonight in a way that made me think she means it." She explained,

> "She just sounded . . . serious. She didn't really ask me to help.
> I don't think she wanted to ask, but she did . . . . It's hard to
> imagine that she'd ever actually do such a thing. Besides, I
> don't see how she could do it. This book tells about all the
> different kinds of pills you can take, but she'd never be able to
> keep pills down . . . . She's very frightened . . . . She feels trapped
> in life, and I think she just wants to know there's a way out. She
> wants to know where the emergency door is; in fact, that's the
> expression she used. 'Where's the door?' she said. Even if she
> doesn't use it, I think she'd feel better knowing where it is . . . .
> Do you blame her? If you were in her shoes, wouldn't you want
> to know? I would. I do. I want to know in case it happens to me.
> I want to know for all of us" (Rollin, 1985, pp. 153–154).

Ed responded,

> "I agree with you . . . . I don't think she'd do anything either, but
> she'd certainly get some comfort knowing there was something
> she could do. So we should find out. We should find out as soon
> as we can" (Rollin, 1985, p. 155).

Assisting suicide does not involve killing others or taking steps that cause or hasten their deaths. Suicides kill themselves. Assistance involves such things as giving would-be suicides information about how to kill themselves, enabling them to secure the means of doing so, giving them realistic options, interacting with them as they choose among their options, assuring them that their choice will be respected, supporting them emotionally once they have decided, and protecting them from unwanted intervention. The would-be suicides themselves are entirely responsible for exercising the option and completing the act of killing themselves. So assisted suicide cannot be wrong because the assisting is wrongful killing.

Betty and Ed called every doctor they could think of. Ida was hospitalized temporarily, dehydrated after persistent vomiting. Pills seemed a bad idea since Ida could not possibly keep them down. They explored guns, poison, carbon monoxide, and other violent means. All were either logistically not feasible or something that Ida would never do. The issue was choice, and they agreed that she should have it. Betty asked Ed why he thought she might really commit suicide. Ed responded, "Because it makes sense, and your mother's sensible." Together they remembered Ed's mother's long, excruciating death. Ed recalled how in her last days, sitting by her bedside, he had thought of putting a pillow over her face. When Betty asked why he didn't, he replied, "You don't kill your mother." Betty asked,

> "What's the difference between that and what we're doing?
> I know, but I want you to tell me."

> He looked at me again. "There's every difference. We're not
> talking about killing your mother. We're talking about her
> killing herself. The other difference is that your mother wants
> to kill herself. My mother wanted God to do it . . . . She couldn't
> imagine that God would let her down" (Rollin, 1985, pp. 164–165).

Assisted suicide is not euthanasia. Those who assist suicide neither administer fatal doses nor withdraw life support. Rather, they put would-be suicides in a position to choose to use the means they select or not. And they do so with the full consent, indeed most often at the explicit request, of those they assist. The decisive moves are taken by the suicides themselves. So assisted suicide cannot be wrong as an instance of wrongful nonvoluntary euthanasia.

On October 6, Ida was able to eat. She told Betty, "If I can eat food, I can eat pills." Further conversation made it clear that Ida was still intent on killing herself and relieved to know that taking pills could work.

Because Ida's ability to eat might last only a few days, she wanted Betty and Ed to learn what they could quickly about how to use pills. They eventually connected with an American physician who had retired to Amsterdam. He was friendly, gentle, and very cautious. He wanted to know a great deal about Ida—her character, her illness, how lucid she was, her mental state, whether she was depressed, how persistent she was in her wish to die. He asked many medical, psychological, and practical questions. In a second call, he offered instructions about the drugs Ida would need, effective doses, and timing in taking them. Ida already had one of the sedatives and the anti-nausea medication, and he explained how she could ask her doctor for the other without raising suspicions.

In the next days the medications were secured. Betty and Ed won the dispute about being there when Ida took the pills. Ida got some of her things and affairs in order. They consulted further with the doctor in Amsterdam. Ida reiterated her desire to die. In fact, she was quite happy at the prospect, though she was concerned about her children being implicated in her death. They agreed that they had to be careful.

A few days passed, and they wondered if that was a sign that Ida did not really want to end her life. But when Ida insisted that Ed go to the bank and transfer assets to her children's accounts so that they would not be frozen after she killed herself, they had no more doubt. Ida rehearsed the Amsterdam physician's plan with them again and again, to make sure that she understood every detail and that it would be effective. Betty and Ed wanted to be in the apartment with Ida when she took her pills and long enough to ensure that nothing went wrong. The doctor assured them that if anything did go wrong, it would be within an hour or two. The doorman would be sure to see them leaving. They arranged for a willing friend to stay with Ida until she died, likely four to five hours after taking the pills.

The day before Ida killed herself, she, Betty, and Ed were working out such last details, and Betty was looking sad after her mother had given her the wedding ring she had not taken off for 52 years. Ida said to her,

> "Sweetheart, don't look sad. Your mother is doing exactly what she wants to do. Do you know how grateful I am to be getting out of this? Do you think I want to wait until somebody has to pull a plug? Believe me, I'm the happiest woman in the world that I can do this. But to do it alone—I admit it—that would have been much harder. This way, with my children near me . . . but what mother has such children? . . . What do people do when they don't have children? What if you want to get out and you have no one to help you?" (Rollin, 1985, p. 215).

On the day of her suicide, Ida spoke of being a burden to Betty and Ed, and Betty asked if she felt somehow obliged to kill herself because of them. Ida responded, "Obliged? Obliged to whom? I can't wait. I had such pain last night . . . . I thank God that I can swallow right now so that I can get out" (Rollin, 1985, p. 221).

In the hour before the time Ida had chosen to begin taking the pills, she invited Betty and Ed into her bedroom. Betty brought out a family photo album, and together they reminisced about years gone by. Ida interrupted, inquiring whether it was time for her to begin. And so it was.

As she prepared to take the pills, Ida struggled to open a bottle of water, and Ed offered to help. Ida insisted on doing it herself, not wanting there to be any evidence of his having aided her. She took all the pills as recommended. At first she did not feel sleepy, but when she did, in her last words she told Betty and Ed, "Remember, I am the most happy woman. And this is my wish. I want you to remember . . . . " And Betty told her, "I love you, Mother," fell on her neck crying, then sat sobbing in a chair, but not for long, because, in her words, "When I look up and see how still she is, I know that she has found the door she was looking for and that it has closed, gently, behind her" (Rollin, 1985, p. 236).

Ida Rollin's clear and persistent wish was to die rather than continue living within the limits her illness imposed upon her. Her story is especially poignant in that she asks her children to assist her. It puts the debate about assisted suicide and the terminally ill in a concrete and realistic context. The debate is not about abstractions; it is about flesh-and-blood persons living in desperate circumstances. I have always found it essential to insist that those who reflect on the ethics of assisting suicide ask how they would respond if someone near and dear to them were to ask for help.

WHEN ASSISTING SUICIDE MIGHT BE WRONG

Clearly, it is wrong to assist irrational suicides, actions that are inimical to the best interests of the suicides themselves. It is wrong to assist suicides that will clearly harm others, physically in the acts themselves or by visiting serious hardship upon dependents. And it is wrong to "assist" suicides in ways that are manipulative or coercive. But it is difficult to understand what moral objection there could be to assisting a suicide such as Ida's.

Some hold that suicide is inherently wrong. If this were clearly and universally agreed, then assisting suicide would be wrong because it supports action that is wrong. But we have argued above that self-killing is not wrong by definition any more than killing is wrong by definition. Just as some acts of killing are widely recognized as justifiable, so some acts of self-killing might be. Of course, not everyone sees it that way. Those who believe suicide is always wrong because life is sacred are free to refrain from killing themselves or assisting others. But respect for personal autonomy requires that even they refrain from intervening in others' rational suicides. And that same respect for personal autonomy allows those who have no moral objection to assist others as Ida was assisted.

THE LEGALITY OF ASSISTED SUICIDE

The ethics of assisting suicide is quite different from its legality. Currently, the majority of states prohibits assisting in suicide. Betty, Ed, and the local physicians with whom they consulted were rightly concerned that assisted suicide is a crime, and they risked prosecution in New York. Betty and Ed took several precautions to avoid arousing the suspicions of authorities. Remarkably, Betty published her book only two years after Ida killed herself, seemingly laying herself open to a prosecution that never materialized.

Paradoxically, while assisted suicide is widely banned, suicide itself is not illegal, though statutes against it were once quite common. It is difficult to think of any other type of behavior that is itself perfectly legal but illegal to assist another in carrying out. The statutory basis for prohibiting assisting in suicide is not grounded in concern about the immorality of suicide itself. Some statutes are designed to protect citizens from the manipulative and coercive actions. Clearly, protection against such pressures is entirely warranted. But such "assistance" is readily distinguishable from true assistance offered to those who ask for and wholeheartedly want it. Some statutes delimit the authority and responsibilities of physicians and other health care providers. In part, they protect citizens from inappropriate encouragement of suicide by such professionals (again, not truly "assistance"). And in part, they protect health care providers from pressures for true assistance that they do not want to be obligated to offer. It seems clear that no professionals should be required to perform services about which they have personal, moral reservations.

Some might argue that assisted suicide is morally wrong because it violates the law. But of course, this provides no argument that it is wrong where no statutes prohibit it. We are inclined to think that moral principles apply universally, but this view would suggest that assisting suicide is morally wrong in some jurisdictions but not in others. Here we set aside treatment of the ethics of obedience to the law and, in particular, whether it is ever morally justifiable to break a law that is perceived to be unjust. We merely note that Betty's story of assisting Ida is not the only story of surreptitious assistance in suicide. We leave it to the reader to determine whether it was morally wrong because it was illegal in New York at the time.

Because of laws that prohibit assisted suicide, some who are rational in their desire to end their lives are not assisted. They then suffer in ways they would not have suffered in the absence of the statutes. Some linger in intolerable circumstances because of a lack of information, lack of access to effective, acceptable means, or fear of failing in attempts and making things worse for themselves. Some persistently ask for assistance, are judged irrational, and are subjected to inappropriate interventions, including forced medications, confinement, and restraint. Some are shamed merely because they ask. Some fail in attempts to kill themselves and compound their suffering. Some are assisted, but inadequately, because their helpers are forced to avoid the eyes of authorities or are denied good information by health care professionals. Some family members or friends are prosecuted for doing what they were asked to do.

PHYSICIAN-ASSISTED SUICIDE: SPECIAL CONSIDERATIONS

Special ethical objections to physician-assisted suicide arise when many point to the Hippocratic or other oaths that doctors take. The oaths commonly require doctors to do all they can to preserve life and prohibit them from taking any deliberate steps to end it. But, as discussed above, assisting suicide does not involve anyone other than would-be suicides taking steps to hasten death. Doctors might provide information about means or the means themselves, but the would-be suicide, and not the doctor, chooses whether to use those means. If doctors took steps known to shorten their patients' lives, that would be active euthanasia, not assisted suicide.

The typical oath also requires that doctors take all measures necessary to relieve suffering. Clearly, in some instances the obligation to preserve life and the obligation to relieve suffering come into conflict. Sometimes suffering can be relieved only by taking measures to hasten death. There is no clear guidance in the oaths about what to do in such cases. Patient suicide is one alternative. And, although the ethics of euthanasia is not the subject of this chapter, it is well known that hastening death is practiced and approved in many ways in contemporary terminal care when suffering is extreme and irremediable—for example, by terminal sedation, by delivering pain relief sufficient to cause death by incidentally suppressing breathing, or by withdrawing nutrition and hydration. Given the obligation to relieve suffering, such practices are not incompatible with the physicians' oaths.

Still, physicians and other health care professionals may have personal, moral reservations about suicide and want no part of offering the kinds of true assistance discussed above. It would be inappropriate to force them to offer such assistance. It would, however, be appropriate to require them to inform the terminally ill about the availability of assistance from others and to refer a dying patient who is asking for assistance.

Because physician-assisted suicide is illegal in most jurisdictions, doctors who would otherwise be willing to assist dying patients may refuse to do so. And some patients, like Ida, feel abandoned by such refusals. If doctors choose to assist, they risk losing their licenses or facing criminal prosecution. And they are forced to avoid detection by legal authorities, even when it is ethically justifiable to offer assistance, because authorities want to protect the dying from themselves and from those who might coerce or manipulate them. The effect is an injustice, as some are helped surreptitiously by doctors willing to take the risk and others are not helped.

Timothy Quill, a professor of medicine and psychiatry, chief of medicine at a public hospital, a primary care general internist, and prominent author, urges that

Partnership and nonabandonment are the core obligations of humane medical care for the dying. Debate in the United States about the role health care providers should play in their patients' deaths too often has been superficial and polarized. It is a debate between those who feel that patients have a "right to die" (as if dying were an option to be chosen) and those who believe that "easing death is too dangerous to vulnerable populations" (as if keeping suffering persons alive against their will protected them from abuse). One side does not hear the true anguish experienced by some dying patients, and the other side minimizes the real potential for life-ending clinical decisions to be adversely influenced by social factors (Quill, 1996, p. 202).

He goes on to offer a set of guidelines for physician interactions with the terminally ill. They are compatible with both the ethics of suicide intervention and the ethics of assistance in suicide discussed above. And they are entirely respectful of the potential of palliative and hospice care to provide relief to many who might otherwise kill themselves. Here are Dr. Quill's guidelines in summary form (with my brief clarifications in parentheses):

1) Physicians, nurses, and other health care providers who care for severely ill patients must become experts in comfort-oriented care. (Lest patients fear abandonment if they ask that life-prolonging measures be stopped.)

2) We must learn how to talk openly with those who wish for death. (The meaning of such wishes can only be discovered, or irrationality detected, that way.)

3) Patients need an open-ended commitment from their physicians to help them find acceptable solutions to the vexing problems of dying. (Knowing there is a means to escape can be very important. Knowing doctors will respond to extreme suffering is reassuring.)

4) Dying patients should be given as much choice and control as possible according to the limitations of their disease. (With rare exception, effective palliative and hospice care suffices. But sometimes choices for death can be rational. Unfortunately, they can now be enacted only in secret.)

5) Physicians must be fully educated about currently accepted options for easing death. (Including a right to refuse treatment, use of pain relief that indirectly contributes to wished-for death, use of terminal sedation, and refusal to eat or drink.)

6) We must be sure that the current ethical distinctions between "active" and "passive" assisted dying and between physician-assisted suicide and euthanasia are clinically meaningful and morally worth preserving. (Medical procedures that hasten death should be used only as a last resort. Methods matter less than the process of caring and joint decision making.)

7) Safeguards must be defined and implemented for any and all treatments that result in a patient's death. (Patient decisions must be fully informed, patients must be rational and certified by a psychiatrist to be free of depression or mental disorder, suffering must be unbearable, palliative measures must be at least considered and preferably tried, the patient must have a terminal disease, and an independent second opinion must be obtained from someone who knows palliative care to verify that these criteria are met.)

8) The main public policy question is whether patients would be better served by safeguards controlling a more explicit, open process than they are by the current unstated policy requiring secrecy and ambiguity whenever death is eased. (The current requirement that easing death always be unintentional, indirect, or covert is dangerous for patients and erodes the integrity of medicine and law. Currently, the safest approach for doctors is to walk away from the most difficult end-of-life problems, leaving patients and families to act on their own.)

9) Managed care has the potential to disrupt the long-term patient-doctor relationship so central to end-of-life decision making. (If society sacrifices in-depth patient-doctor interactions to save money, we will lose something precious at the heart of medicine.)

10) A bad death should be considered a medical emergency. (When a patient's personhood and integrity are at stake in extreme suffering at the end of life, we must use all personal and medical resources to find a solution that is acceptable to the patient, just as we do in intensive care units when lives are at stake.)

11) Nonabandonment is fundamental to the long-term doctor-patient partnership. (Facing an uncertain future alone is far different from having a caring partner who will remain present no matter what happens.) (Quill, 1996, pp. 203–221.)

THE OREGON DEATH WITH DIGNITY ACT

Only one state, Oregon, has adopted a statute that endorses assisted suicide and establishes procedural guidelines designed to protect citizens from both their own irrationality and the abuses of others (Reagan, 2000). Oregon voters approved the Act in 1994 in a ballot measure that asked, "Shall law allow terminally ill adult Oregon patients voluntary informed choice to obtain physician's prescription for drugs to end life?" A legal injunction blocked implementation of the Act until late 1997.

The principal provisions of the Act are outlined here. They conform to most of the ethical guidelines governing practices of assisted suicide outlined above. And they address most of Quill's concerns. The Act requires that the dying who want assistance must officially request it, orally or in writing, from their physician 15 days before they obtain the drugs. They must reaffirm their requests in writing after that waiting period. The written requests must be witnessed by at least two individuals, at least one of whom is not a relative, entitled to any portion of the dying person's estate, or affiliated with the health care facility where the dying person is receiving care. The doctors must be well acquainted with the patients and their life circumstances, corroborate that they are terminally ill and have less than 6 months to live, find that they are competent and not clinically depressed or driven by outside influences that would create duress, and check that their decisions are fully informed before they can prescribe the drugs. They must also inform their patients of alternatives to physician-assisted suicide, including comfort, hospice, and palliative care.

A second physician must be consulted to confirm the primary physician's diagnosis and that the dying person is competent and rational, not depressed or suffering from a diagnosable mental disorder. Physicians must dispense the medications themselves if they are licensed to do so or submit a letter along with a prescription to the pharmacist explaining the purpose of the prescription. No health care provider has any duty to comply with a request for a lethal prescription. Written records of all of these matters must be submitted to state authorities. Family members are allowed to be present and assist the dying in preparing to take and taking the drugs, but not to administer them directly.

The requirements and provisions of the Act support respect for individual autonomy and informed consent, reinforce patients' right to refuse treatment, provide safeguards for individuals against irrationality and coercion, protect both physicians who are willing and those who are unwilling to assist, protect health care facilities that support or prohibit assistance, and insist on and protect the openness of the process of assisting suicidal persons. These provisions can all be construed as improvements over practices of assisting suicide in secret, away from public scrutiny. The Act also supports informing patients about good-quality end-of-life care. In so doing, it promotes respect for the potential of the dying to find meaning (on their own terms) in their last days that good-quality end-of-life care so often supports. The Act and guidelines for its implementation (Reagan, 2002) together conform strikingly to Quill's recommendations. ■

Thomas Attig, PhD, is the author of The Heart of Grief: Death and the Search for Lasting Love *and* How We Grieve: Relearning the World. *He has written numerous articles and reviews on grief and loss, care of the dying, suicide intervention, death education, expert witnessing in wrongful death cases, the ethics of interactions with the dying, and the nature of applied philosophy.*

Dr. Attig received his MA (1969) and PhD (1973) in philosophy from Washington University in St. Louis. He taught philosophy at Bowling Green State University for nearly 25 years, serving as the Department Chair for 11 years and leading efforts to establish the first PhD in Applied Philosophy in the world in 1987. Dr. Attig served as president of the Association for Death Education and Counseling and as vice-chair of the Board of Directors of the International Work Group on Death, Dying, and Bereavement. He invites you to visit his website at www.griefsheart.com

REFERENCES

Battin, M. (1995). *Ethical Issues in Suicide.* Englewood Cliffs, NJ: Prentice-Hall.

Institute of Medicine. (1997). *Approaching death: Improving care at the end of life* (M. J. Field & C. K. Cassel, Eds.). Washington, DC: National Academy Press.

Quill, T. (1996). *A midwife through the dying process: Stories of healing and hard choices at the end of life.* Baltimore: Johns Hopkins University Press.

Reagan, B. (2000). *The Oregon Death with Dignity Act: A guidebook for health care providers.* Portland: Center for Ethics in Health Care, Task Force to Improve the Care of Terminally-Ill Oregonians, Oregon Health and Science University.

Rollin, B. (1985). *Last wish.* New York: Warner Books.

Wachter, R. M., & Shojania, K. (2004). *Internal bleeding: The truth behind America's terrifying epidemic of medical mistakes.* New York: Rugged Land, LLC.

Privileged Information or Confused Communication?

Hospice and Palliative Care Associates
of Central New York, Liverpool, New York

Hospice personnel, like anyone in a specialty, are often perceived to be a "community resource" for free and thoughtful conversation on a whole range of end-of-life issues. Many of us serve on various community boards, participate in forums, are active in congregations, and have widespread professional contacts. Besides the psychospiritual issues that are more in my purview and the medical issues about which I can easily plead noncompetency, I am asked for advice on ethical issues.

A year ago, a therapist who is both an old friend and colleague ("Gwen") informally consulted with me about a patient of hers ("Evelyn") who was suffering from a chronic illness and who was contemplating suicide and had the means to do so with "little fuss"—with the tacit approval of her physician, but without his participation or assistance. Gwen asked me what I thought about this situation, how she should respond, and what was my own experience. She was struggling with Evelyn's possible decision, but ultimately believed in the patient's autonomy and capability to decide for herself, provided the therapist could be reasonably assured that she was not acting in either an impulsive moment or a chronic depressed state. We talked about Gwen's own philosophical and religious perspectives about suicide and how comfortable she was exploring those of her patient. We spoke about the legal and professional issues involved and whether she should talk further with the physician about this matter. I asked her to think about the patient's children's knowledge and reactions and how they would impact her as a professional. Also, I asked about her thinking about how an incomplete attempt might look or play out, with the many tragic possible consequences. She was grateful for this conversation and told me that she was going to think and talk further with her patient. She asked if she could call me for future discussion, to which I easily replied, "Certainly."

Six months later, Gwen called to say that Evelyn was being referred to hospice and had her permission to tell me—and me alone—so that I might visit with her. Evelyn knew that I had been apprised of the issue that we discussed and was still holding suicide as personal option. I had not thought about that possibility in our prior conversation and now was faced with knowing much more than would be revealed to the team at the time of admission or possibly even in subsequent visits. I told Gwen that I didn't know how to use this information with the team, since it would be relevant to our plan of care, and that it would not be professional, fair to the team or the patient, or perhaps even legal for me to have such knowledge and not share it in appropriate ways. Gwen understood the dilemma in which she had inadvertently placed me. She was very apologetic and offered to meet with Evelyn and me before Evelyn was admitted to hospice. I told her that I wasn't certain that I should even be a party to that conversation, but that I would talk with a supervisor about the question.

Gwen called me within a half-hour and said that Evelyn was adamantly opposed to my sharing this knowledge with anyone else and that she didn't want to meet with me at all if I was going to question her further about it. She said that if I in any way attempted to block her acceptance to hospice by sharing this information, she would somehow take revenge on both Gwen and me. Since the admission was scheduled for just two days hence, I told Gwen that I would not say anything at this point that would inhibit that interview or admission, but that this question would still have to be addressed.

DISCUSSION

The questions about confidentiality, roles, and boundaries are paramount in this scenario. There was surely confusion on all parts. Possible questions at this point in the process include the following.

- What is the responsibility of the chaplain to share this information with the rest of the team?

- Is there another type of communication involving the therapist or "backdoor" conversation that is professional, legal, and helpful?

- How does the chaplain balance the competing claims of confidentiality against the team responsibilities inherent to hospice, especially when the hospice chaplain may have information obtained confidentially as a chaplain in another role? ■

David E. Pasinski is Senior Chaplain at Hospice and Palliative Care Associates of Central New York. He holds Master's Degrees in Divinity, Theology, Marriage and Family Therapy, and Public Administration.

Ethics and
the Health System

Fife's chapter on ethical dilemmas in hospice care provides a transition from current ethical issues to their application in specific health care systems. Fife begins by delineating the common ethical decisions faced by hospice that actually apply concepts such as autonomy, futility, confidentiality, and assisted suicide. The issues involved with these decisions include withdrawing or withholding hydration and artificial nutrition, resuscitation of patients, palliation and the question of double effect, and protecting the rights of patients, families, and caregivers. Fife calls for a careful ethical process—clearly defining the ethical dilemmas, identifying the interests of varied stakeholders, and assessing the viability of all potential courses of action. He reaffirms that ethical decisions are a process rather than an event. Fife then roots such a process in hospice ethics committees. Not only is this good practice, it is inherent in the hospice philosophy of team-centered care.

These day-to-day dilemmas are illustrated in a case study from the Hospice of the Bluegrass. This case raises another ethical issue—whose agenda is it? Whether the issue is the need for aggressive treatment or staff desire that a person achieve certain psychological or relational goals prior to death, it is essential not only to critically examine the larger goals of treatment but also to question staff presumptions. What Fife would suggest is not so much a decision but a careful assessment of whether these issues were thoroughly vetted through an ethics committee.

This notion of process is critical because any book on ethics, even one specifically examining end-of-life ethics, is inherently selective. Other issues that can be addressed include the ethical issues inherent in terminal sedation, expanded discussion of the ethical debates and empirical evidence on double effects, and the myriad other issues that emerge in home care. Moreover, new technological advances will create new ethical issues even as this book (or any book on ethical issues) goes to press. The key lesson is not to attempt to resolve all these issues *a priori* but rather to create a process that allows for resolution of ethical dilemmas.

Klugman's chapter addresses another problem of the health system— the difficulties and ethical dilemmas inherent in pediatric care. The major issue is that children and adolescents are legally unable to offer consent— a right reserved to adults. Klugman introduces the useful concept of *informed assent*, which advocates that children, in ways appropriate to their developmental level, should be active participants in their own care, assenting or agreeing with decisions made in their name. The case presented by Huff, Milch, and Skretny roots this discussion in the reality of daily care. Just how determinative should this assent be for treatment decisions?

Johnson explores the other end of the life cycle—older persons, particularly those in long-term care facilities. Johnson begins with the premise that for many older persons, a long-term care facility *is* home. Older persons, then, she maintains, have the right to die in that home. She recognizes, however, the practical difficulties inherent in exercising that right. In recent years the culture of nursing homes and long-term care facilities has moved from custodial to rehabilitative. These institutions no longer view themselves as places where people come to die. For many homes, this view even translates to a discomfort with death. Johnson also notes that these institutions are highly regulated, complicating the provision of palliative care. For example, in the long-term care environment it may be difficult to withhold or withdraw nutrition or hydration. She also reminds readers that until some recent decisions on pain control, physicians who prescribed pain medication were more likely to face regulatory scrutiny than those who failed to prescribe. Although conscious of other dilemmas facing long-term care facilities, including questions of medical futility and the dilemmas of consent with patients with dementia, Johnson still affirms that persons should have the right to die in place—even if the place is a nursing facility.

Corr's chapter considers the ethical dilemmas posed by another technological advance—organ donation. Corr is sensitive to three different types of donations: organ donation after brain death, organ donation after cardiac death, and living donations. Corr not only addresses the ethical issues in each type of donation, he also makes the critical point that each type of donation creates distinct issues for grief. Implicit in this discussion is the ethical mandate for transplant organizations to acknowledge and provide appropriate support for individuals coping with grief.

Churchill's chapter concludes this section. Although it only tangentially deals with end-of-life ethics, the inclusion of Churchill's chapter follows the essential point of Jack Gordon, chair of the Hospice Foundation of America, that discussions of end-of-life ethics must be rooted in the larger ethical context of the American health care system—a system that Churchill describes as characterized by the paradoxical juxtaposition of excess and deprivation. Despite this larger emphasis, Churchill is sensitive to the point that poor policy creates issues that complicate the grief of survivors. These last two chapters provide a bridge to the next section, which examines how ethical decisions influence grief. ■

CHAPTER 11

Ethical Dilemmas in Hospice Care

Richard Fife

COMMON ETHICAL ISSUES FACED BY HOSPICE STAFF

Dying is no longer a matter simply between a patient and a physician. This is especially true in hospice, where there is a team effort among a patient, family, significant others, physicians, and providers. In addition, there are a multitude of questions about how a person may die and the variety of treatments and technologies that are available. There is a great deal of room for ethical dilemmas as the hospice staff member interacts with the community surrounding the patient and deals with the needs and desires of a particular patient. In addition to patient-related concerns, a staff member may face ethical questions involving work-related circumstances. In the author's two-year study of ethical dilemmas discussed in a formal setting in VITAS Healthcare Corporation, a hospice provider that has a dozen clinical ethics committees, the most common patient-related and work-related issues facing hospice staff members were the following, which are presented in the order of frequency:

- The question of suicide, assisted suicide, and euthanasia
- Working with patients who have been admitted without a do not resuscitate (DNR) order

- The question of whether or not to perform cardiopulmonary resuscitation (CPR) on a patient who does not have a signed DNR order or an advance directive stating that the patient does not want CPR

- Withdrawal or withholding of nutrition/hydration

- Family decisions to "prolong dying" versus an incompetent patient's previously expressed views

- Patient autonomy versus patient safety and physical needs

- The underdiagnosing of potentially treatable problems

- Confidentiality of AIDS patients versus safety of visitors and caregivers

- Treating a patient on a ventilator

- Removing a patient's life support system

- Conflicts with the patient's family or significant others

- Concern that the nursing home facility is not providing adequate care for the patient

- Ethics of being judgmental or accepting

- Religious objections regarding the treatment or lack of treatment given to a particular patient

- Conflict over whether to follow a patient's wish to be discharged from a hospice unit when the staff member feels that the primary caregiver is incompetent to take care of the patient

- Family needs and nursing home placement

- Pain medication—respiratory distress/consciousness— the question here being whether the pain is so great that it is necessary to adversely affect consciousness and cause some respiratory distress by the higher use of medications to suppress the pain. Is it better to control the pain or for the patient to be more alert?

- Dealing with the request of a white patient to have no black staff caring for the patient at home

- Deciding whether to honor a patient's request for total palliative sedation for "existential" reasons (i.e., psychological distress or suffering rather than uncontrollable physical pain)

- Suspecting that a patient or family caregiver is selling or sharing the medications provided by the hospice

- Having to go into a neighborhood recognized as dangerous in order to provide home care for a patient

- Being sexually harassed or sexually assaulted by a patient or family member

THE HOSPICE ETHICS COMMITTEE

Any of the issues above can become ethical dilemmas within the hospice program. Although the list is not exhaustive, it is fairly representative. The questions are what makes any of these issues an ethical dilemma and what is the most effective way of dealing with them. To take the second question first, there are several potential approaches. It is possible to ignore the conflict or dilemma, and this solution is one that is applied on a regular basis in all health care settings. It is also possible for the staff member to discuss the issue with the team physician or medical director, with colleagues at a team meeting, or with a designated ethicist or risk manager. Finally, the staff member may bring the issue to one of the gatekeepers in the hospice ethics committee. However, not all hospices have an ethics committee. In this case, the staff member may choose to use the ethics committee of a hospital or nursing home if the patient-related issue is involved with one of these.

Fortunately, more and more hospices are developing ethics committees, many of them along the lines recommended by the National Hospice and Palliative Care Organization. These guidelines include the development of a committee that draws members from the team, from the hospice management, and from the community at large. The committee members receive training in ethical theory and the principles of ethics. These committees meet regularly to provide education on ethical issues and concerns to their members, to the hospice staff, and to the community. They use case study methods and often seek a consensus by applying the major principles described below to the cases. By studying the principles and working together with cases, they can answer the question of what makes a particular issue an ethical dilemma. For example, take a look at the following case study.

THE ETHICAL PRINCIPLES

Ernest Young was 62 years old, a quiet, soft-spoken man, former salesman, father of three grown children, married to a woman named Inez for 34 years. Ernest was no longer working because recently he had been diagnosed as being in the end stages of lung cancer, and two weeks ago he was admitted to a hospice program. This particular hospice program had a great deal of experience with patients like Ernest, and staff prided themselves on their ability to manage the pain of such patients. Each week a team of professionals—nurses, home health aides, chaplains, physicians, social workers, volunteers—met and discussed the needs of the patients on their hospice team. They specifically discussed issues relating to pain management and emotional support.

It was only the second meeting in which the team discussed Ernest that Rosemary, his primary nurse, brought up the issue of pain control. "His pain is not under control," she said. When the team physician, who had not yet seen Ernest, inquired as to the reasons, Rosemary replied, "I don't think that he is taking his pain medications." Following a brief discussion and a request to send the social worker to Ernest's home, the team moved on to consider the next patient, as there were more than 50 patients and their families to discuss on this day.

Rosemary was a professional, an extremely sensitive and caring nurse who believed that she could relieve most of Ernest's pain if he would simply follow her instructions in relation to pain medications. Although Ernest was polite to Rosemary, he refused to discuss his choice either with her or with the social worker who came by the next day. Over lunch with a colleague, Rosemary expressed her frustration about Ernest, as well as her own need to make him comfortable. The colleague suggested that she take her concerns beyond the team to the program's clinical ethics committee. Rosemary decided to take this course of action, and she spoke with the chair of the committee, a chaplain. Before the ethics committee meeting, the chaplain visited Ernest at home and spoke with him at length. Gradually Ernest shared an interesting perspective on his own pain with the chaplain. He said that he had done many wicked things during his lifetime, and that now, as he approached life's end, he was in anguish about his mistakes. He described himself as a "lapsed Catholic" who believed that his faith required him to "make atonement for his sins." "I must suffer," he said, "or I shall never see paradise."

In a discussion of ethical dilemmas, it is necessary to determine exactly what an ethical dilemma may be. Most students of ethics recognize four established principles in the study of ethics: beneficence, nonmaleficence, autonomy, and justice. The briefest definition of these principles in relation to health care is to do what is best for the patient (beneficence), to do no harm (nonmaleficence), to respect the choice of the patient (autonomy), and to be fair and equal in treatment to all patients (justice). An additional principle used in health care is veracity or fidelity, which is essentially telling the truth to the patient. When two or more of these principles come into conflict, an ethical dilemma is created. These principles have enduring values, and an ethical conflict occurs when there is a conflict of values and no clear indication of right or wrong.

In the case study above, Rosemary is the person experiencing the ethical dilemma. Two of the values that she holds dear are autonomy and beneficence. She believes that a properly informed patient has the right to make a choice, even if she considers it to be a bad choice. Her professional training also tells her that she can provide the care that will benefit the patient, and that, in this case, taking the pain medications would be most beneficial to the patient. She comes before the ethics committee with these two values in conflict. Furthermore, although most Catholics would probably say that Ernest's view is incorrect—that suffering in and of itself has no value—it is still the belief that Ernest holds.

THE PRINCIPLE OF AUTONOMY

In end-of-life care many ethical dilemmas are created as the result of a patient or a family member (speaking for the patient) exerting autonomy in the face of treatment options. Take the case of Robert Bailey, who is suffering multiple complications and disability, principally from advanced diabetes and renal failure. He has both legs amputated above the knee and is functionally blind. He is not considered a candidate for a kidney transplant and faces dialysis treatment for the rest of his life. He is mentally alert, and his medical situation was fully explained to him by his attending physician. Robert seems to understand his condition very well. Two weeks ago he decided that he wanted no more painful dialysis treatments, knowing that this decision would most likely result in his untimely death within a few short weeks. He remained steadfast in his decision, but his physician refuses to stop the dialysis treatment, believing that it would be tantamount to killing the patient. It is at this point that many ethicists talk about the difference between "killing and letting die." But the real question is whether Robert actually has a choice. It is a question that hospice providers encounter frequently. The nursing home, the assisted living facility, or someone else insists that the patient continue to be kept on a ventilator or a feeding tube or receive dialysis. Many point out that there is no ethical difference between starting a procedure and stopping a procedure.

The more difficult question about withholding or withdrawing comes when the patient is no longer alert or oriented and the family caregiver requests that life-sustaining treatment be discontinued. If there is no advance directive, or if the directive is ambiguous, how does one know that the family caregiver is expressing the wishes of the patient? Take the case of Bertha Allen. She is 88 years old and a resident in a nursing home. For several years she has been in a persistent vegetative state (PVS). In PVS all upper brain function is lost, which means that a person is no longer able to control conscious actions such as speaking, thinking, and eating. The person is permanently unconscious, although not in a coma. In Bertha's case, PVS was due to numerous strokes over the years. She was unable to talk or recognize family. She lay curled up in bed, fed through a tube inserted into her stomach. The hospice staff gave her very good care, as did the nursing home staff, and she seemed comfortable.

Alice, Bertha's daughter, visited frequently and also gave her mother excellent care. Alice was a devout Catholic who had talked with her priest many times about her mother's condition. Gradually, Alice came to the conclusion that what was being done for her mother was not right, and that this woman was no longer the vibrant, active, beautiful person that she knew as her mother. She also did not believe that her mother would want to exist in this condition. Her mother was deeply religious and had told her many times that she would not want to linger needlessly in this life when there was a better life to come. So, Alice spoke with her physician and asked that the tube feeding be removed so that her mother could die in peace. The physician replied that he could not do that, because "it would be immoral and illegal. What you are asking me to do is wrong." This made Alice feel very guilty, especially since one of her own daughters had said essentially the same thing. However, although this daughter lived in the same city as her mother, she very rarely visited her grandmother. Alice tried to talk about withholding the tube feeding with the administrator of the nursing home, but she was told that only a doctor could make that decision.

Alice was feeling very confused and somewhat overwhelmed when she ran into the hospice chaplain during one of his visits to her mother. Alice discussed her concerns with the chaplain, who suggested that she take the matter before the ethics committee for further discussion and consideration. The ethics committee pointed out to Alice that in the state where she was living there was no law against withdrawing the feeding tube. Essentially, the physician was mistaken. With regard to the statement that the request was immoral, the committee pointed out that the physician was expressing his own opinion. Furthermore, even if there was no advance directive, Bertha had communicated her wishes to her daughter earlier. In this state, that type of statement was as valid as a living will. If the physician was not comfortable with this course of action, the committee pointed out that he could withdraw from the case.

THE PRINCIPLES OF BENEFICENCE AND NONMALEFICENCE

It is generally agreed that the principle of autonomy became the most vital of the ethical principles because of an event that happened in New Jersey in 1975. It was in April of that year that a young woman named Karen Ann Quinlan was rushed to a hospital. At the time of her admission she was already in a persistent vegetative state. Although the exact cause of her condition was never determined, she had ceased breathing for a long time, and there was apparent brain damage. In spite of that, there was obvious brain activity, and she was quickly placed on a ventilator to provide breathing and later on a feeding tube to provide sustenance. As her condition on the ventilator began to weigh on Joseph Quinlan, her father, her family made a decision that Karen would not want to be dependent on a machine for her breathing. The removal of the ventilator, especially in the face of brain activity, was contrary to what the medical establishment in the community considered to be acceptable care. Long fights in the courts began. The case became well known throughout the United States, and indeed the world, and for the first time there were many public discussions about living wills, DNR orders, and the right to die. When the Quinlans won thanks to the decision of an appeals court and a newly formed clinical ethics committee, the result came to be seen as a great statement about the principle of autonomy—the right to choose (even if the patient herself is not able to make the choice). Autonomy was underlined because Karen's parents were speaking for her in their belief that they were making her own wishes known. That it was not a right-to-die case became apparent because even after the Quinlans won the right to have the ventilator removed, and even after this was done, Karen did not die as expected. Her family never requested that the feeding tube be removed. Indeed, Karen continued to live for more than a decade.

The question for the Quinlans involved not only autonomy but beneficence and nonmaleficence. Although these two principles are not the same, they do share much common ground. The Quinlans believed that the ventilator was intrusive and harmful to Karen ("do no harm"). Likewise, they believed that the thing most beneficial for Karen was not her death but removal of the ventilator. If death were to come because of that action (which is commonly known as "double effect"), then the Quinlans had reconciled themselves to it.

The same question of beneficence and who decides what is most beneficial for the patient may still bring the same type of conflict almost 30 years after the Quinlan case. This is apparent in the story of Terri Schiavo in Florida. In 1990, Terri Schiavo, a 26-year-old, previously healthy woman, suffered a cardiac arrhythmia resulting in cardiac arrest. In 2003, she was 39 years old, had been on a hospice program for three years, and had remained for 13 years in a persistent vegetative state. Neurologists have certified that she is indeed in a PVS and unlikely to recover. Terri's husband claims that before the cardiac arrest, she had made statements consistent with a desire not to be kept alive in a PVS. Her husband, as the legal health care surrogate, decided to have her feedings discontinued.

Terri's parents claim that she never made such statements. They also claim that she has shown some evidence of cognition and they disagree with the diagnosis of PVS. Therefore, acting on the principles of beneficence and nonmaleficence, they oppose the removal of the feeding tube. Any ethics committee discussing this case would be faced with further complications, such as the following: The parents have been showing a videotape claiming that Terri is able to follow movement in a conscious way with her eyes, indicating cognition. However, there are also claims that this tape was made several years ago over a long period of time and spliced together. In addition, there are claims that Terri's husband has ulterior motives because of the presence of a girlfriend with his child and significant amounts of money won in a malpractice suit. There are also considerations relating to the faith body of the persons involved, which, in this case, is Catholic. The greatest complication, though, is that the governor of Florida joined the fight on the side of the parents in the case, and the legislative body wrote a law ("Terri's Law") that keeps the feeding tube in place. The legislators intended to write a very narrow law pertaining only to the Schiavo case but found this impossible to do. In effect, unless this law is ruled unconstitutional, all terminally ill persons in Florida will be affected if they are in dementia and have no living will. One court has already ruled the law unconstitutional, but an appeal in July 2004 has kept the feeding tube in place and the situation uncertain.

Aside from the actions of the legislative body, there are a number of ethical dilemmas in this volatile case. How do we deal with a person in a vegetative state in the absence of a living will? How is the right of self-determination decided? Who decides whether the situation is futile or not? In terms of beneficence, who gets to decide what is most beneficial for Terri? In terms of nonmaleficence, does the removal of a feeding tube "do harm"? It is interesting that in spite of all these questions and the ethical dilemmas involved, the case of Terri Schiavo was never taken before the hospice ethics committee or any other clinical ethics committee that might have had legitimate involvement in the case.

THE PRINCIPLE OF JUSTICE

The principle of justice is a little more nebulous than the other principles, but it generally involves fairness. Are like cases being treated the same? Are there circumstances that make a particular situation unfair? Take the case of an elderly white man who was being discharged from a hospital to home care in a hospice. Upon discharge from the hospice he told the hospice admissions nurse that he did not want black people to care for him in his home. Aside from the question of prejudice, one might consider whether a person has the right to decide who does and does not come into his own home. One way of dealing with this situation could be for the admissions nurse to tell the team manager to assign only white staff members to care for this patient. However, such an action immediately involves the principle of justice. Is it fair to the black staff members?

This brings up a larger question in relation to African Americans and hospice. The ethical question is related to fair access. African Americans make up only about 8% of the total hospice patient population, but make up about 13% of the total population, according to the U.S. Census Bureau. Part of the problem is related to the prejudice shown to African Americans and Hispanics in American health care. Whether it is because of a long tradition dating back to slavery and proceeding through a period of experiments in Tuskegee, as well as neglect, there are ample reasons for minorities to distrust health care in general. In a sense of justice, have hospices, which have been traditionally oriented to middle-class whites, done enough to remove the barriers to access to hospice care for minorities?

There is another side to fairness, which relates to an allocation of resources. Take the case of Diana Taylor, a 95-year-old patient at a nursing home facility. She has been a hospice patient for 18 months. She has two durable powers of attorney, which share responsibility for decision making. Her terminal diagnosis is myelodysplasia, and she has a history of cardiac and vascular problems. Diana has been bed bound with an extremely low level of consciousness for several months. She has decubitus ulcers, one of which is believed to be gangrenous. She has been receiving blood transfusions on a regular basis, along with frequent blood tests. The blood transfusions were to decrease with hospice, and the routine blood tests were supposedly discontinued. In early April a complete blood count was drawn, and Diana was found to be anemic. Her family asked the facility to have her transported for a blood transfusion. This request was approved, and she was to be transferred to the hospice inpatient unit for the transfusion and immediately returned to the facility and physician. She received four units of packed red blood cells. The hospice staff voiced some concerns. The team at the inpatient unit felt that they should be allowed to observe the patient post-transfusion as she was at risk for cardiac failure, and they had concerns about why such a patient would be transfused in the first place. This same situation recurred two months later, and Diana was again transfused. At this time, upon ordering the blood, the hospice received a call from the blood bank questioning why the hospice was using the last units of O positive blood available in the area. The hospice was trying to honor the requests of the patient's family, but was it just to give blood transfusions to a dying patient when so many in the larger community were in need? The question of allocation of resources is a particular ethical question for those dealing with dying patients.

THE PRINCIPLE OF FIDELITY

In health care, there is a principle related specifically to truth-telling. One is not supposed to knowingly lie to a patient. Furthermore, to give consent, the patient must be informed of diagnosis, prognosis, alternatives, and possible consequences. Fidelity takes on added meaning and additional ethical challenges in the hospice experience. There are questions up front about hospice eligibility. If a person can only be admitted to hospice during the final six months of life, how does one determine when admission should occur? What are the criteria? What about cultural or religious influences? For example, in certain cultures (specifically Hispanic and African American), one is not encouraged to speak directly with the patient about death and dying. If one speaks openly and truthfully about death and dying to persons within certain Asian cultures, especially many in Korea, China, Japan, and India, there is a belief that one is actually bringing about the patient's death. Furthermore, many of these traditional beliefs continue to be held by Asian Americans. In a recent presentation that concentrated on Chinese and Japanese grief processes, Stella Kwong-Wirth, Director of the

Asian Home Care Program of the National Association of Social Workers in New York, made the following statements: "In the Asian family, death is not discussed. It is a common superstition that talking about death may lead to it. Illness may be seen as evil and suffering as unavoidable" ("The End of Life: Coping with Death and Dying in the Asian Family", May 12, 1999 Roundtable Minutes posted by CAF on July 7, 1999). This author has heard the same pronouncements made by Asian social workers at the hospice meetings of the National Hospice and Palliative Care Organization in 2002 and 2003. If it is true that this superstition is part of the culture of a group such as first generation Asian Americans, then what is the ethical thing to do in such a situation?

Take the case of Maria Ramirez, an 84-year-old hospice patient. She speaks no English, but she is bathed and cared for most days by Rita, a home health aide who speaks fluent Spanish. Maria has pancreatic cancer, but she tells Rita that according to her family, she only has an ulcer and the care that she is receiving from the hospice is making her well. Rita believes that Maria is entitled to know her true condition. She tells the family that it is not right to lie about Maria's condition to her, but they tell her that it is done all the time in Colombia. Perhaps there are no real negative consequences in a case like this, as Maria probably knows that she is terminally ill anyway; or perhaps withholding the full truth in such a case is the kinder thing to do.

However, take the case of Ronnie Banks. When he was admitted to the hospice program, he was hospitalized in severe distress, neither alert nor oriented. He was diagnosed as HIV-positive and actively dying. When he was discharged to his parents' home, his condition was stabilized and he was once again oriented. His parents said that Ronnie was not aware of his true condition, that he thought he was being cared for by a home health team. Furthermore, his parents insisted that no one on the hospice team tell Ronnie that he was terminally ill. The social worker believed that since Ronnie was now alert and oriented, he should be making his own decisions about his health care.

CONCLUSION

In hospice care, staff members are constantly faced with the possibilities and realities of ethical dilemmas. How much do you tell the patient being admitted to a hospice program? If the patient elects to have a feeding tube or a ventilator removed and the facility refuses to allow it to be done on site, how much autonomy does the patient actually have? If the patient asks you to help assist with his or her dying, what are the limits to autonomy? If you know that morphine will quell the patient's pain but may suppress breathing, what is the beneficial thing to do? If the patient prefers full consciousness over medication, and the pain is great, what does this say about beneficence and nonmaleficence? If you sense that the situation of treatment is unfair for some, do you invoke the principle of justice?

Whatever the question or ethical dilemma may be, since caring for the terminally ill involves matters of ultimate concern, no one should struggle alone with these questions. Generally speaking, the ethics committee is a good place to take ethical dilemmas in hospice care. It is there that a wide variety of persons have become a moral community by working together on issues of mutual concern for patients, families, providers, and others. These persons are not ethicists, but they have been trained in the areas of ethical theory and practice, and bioethical principles. Unlike a hospice team that has only a limited amount of time to discuss a patient and his or her needs, the committee can focus on specific concerns for hours or even days if needed. It can bring together all the players in a particular situation. One of the greatest strengths of the committee is in the options that it discusses at the end of a case consultation. Often, one person looking at a conflict can see only one or two options. In the group setting, especially with persons who have dealt with many clinical cases, there can be a rich sharing and the possibility of multiple options. In the hospice, when the ethics committee works as it should, there is a rich opportunity to deal positively with the ethical dilemmas of hospice care.

Note: With the exceptions of Karen Ann Quinlan and Terri Schiavo, all of the cases discussed in this chapter are actual case studies from VITAS Healthcare Corporation, the largest provider of hospice care in the United States. The names of actual persons have been changed in all VITAS cases. ■

Richard B. Fife, PhD, is a United Methodist minister and Vice-President of Bioethics and Pastoral Care for VITAS Healthcare Corporation in Miami. An activist minister, he has written about his encounters with racism during the civil rights movement and was involved in the peace movement during the 1970's and 1980's. Most recently he has written on ethics, contributing chapters to Ethics in Hospice Care and 20 Common Problems: End of Life Care. *His newest book is* The Effect of Death and Loss on Health *(University of North Carolina Press, in press). He has also written on the other areas of his work—chaplaincy, pastoral care, and bereavement. Dr. Fife has trained ethics committees for the past 12 years and serves as an ethicist for 30 hospices.*

Suggested Reading

Beauchamp, T. L., & Childress, J. F. (2001). *The Principles of Biomedical Ethics* (5th ed.). Oxford, UK: Oxford University Press.

Colby, William H. (2002). *Long Goodbye: The Deaths of Nancy Cruzan.* Carlsbad, CA: Hay House, Inc.

Irish, Donald P., Lundquist, Kathleen F., & Nelsen, V. J. *Ethnic Variations in Dying, Death, and Grief: Diversity in Universality.* Philadelphia: Taylor & Francis, 1993.

Jennings, B. (1997). *Ethics in hospice care: Challenges to hospice values in a changing health care environment.* Binghamton, NY: Haworth Press.

Kinzbrunner, B., Weinreb, N., & Policzer, J. (2001). *20 common problems: End of life care.* New York: McGraw-Hill.

National Hospice and Palliative Care Organization. (1998). *Developing a hospice ethics committee.* Washington, DC: Author.

Urofsky, M. L. (1993). *Letting go: Death, dying, and the law.* New York: Charles Scribners' Sons.

Sarah: Autonomy and Medical Paternalism

Hospice of the Bluegrass, Lexington, Kentucky

"Sarah" was a 36-year-old woman, married with five young children, when she was admitted to hospice with late stage metastatic breast cancer. Friends had contacted a philanthropic organization and had arranged for Sarah and her family to receive an all-expense-paid holiday before Sarah's death. Sarah and her family were elated and talked about the trip and when they could go.

The oncologist, however, was opposed to the idea of a family trip. He continued to insist on aggressive chemotherapy treatments for Sarah, and the trip would interrupt her therapy. The oncologist was adamant that without these treatments, Sarah would have "no chance" and her disease would produce unbearable symptoms. He did not offer the option of discontinuing chemotherapy and providing palliative care. The treatments left her too weak and sick to travel. Sarah had great admiration for her oncologist and trusted him. He had treated her mom when she was dying of breast cancer, and Sarah felt a debt of gratitude for the care he had provided. When the hospice team asked Sarah what she wanted to do, she would look at her husband and say she had to keep trying for him and the children. She would repeat the doctor's statement that the chemotherapy was the only thing keeping her alive. Sarah insisted that the oncologist had her best interests at heart, but she really wished she could take the trip with her family.

As the disease progressed, the hospice staff struggled with what they were observing. Sarah's condition continued to worsen, and her chemotherapy treatments created intolerable side effects. Sarah spent much of her last few months going back to the hospital. She and her family were conflicted over the seeming lack of choice and their inability to leave town for a final trip. The staff wanted to support Sarah in her decision, but they were unsure if they would undermine her relationship with the oncologist. The oncologist insisted that the family would have time for the trip after the chemotherapy. The staff wanted to encourage the family to question the usefulness of the chemotherapy treatment. Sarah continued with the treatments until she died. The trip never happened.

DISCUSSION

- How much responsibility should staff assume when advocating for patients?

- Is the view of the staff any less paternalistic than the physician's?

- How do you promote autonomy when the care decisions are so complex?

- How do patients exercise autonomy when they are dependant on the physician for care options?

- Does the hospice team have the ability or responsibility to determine if the oncologist is truthful? ▪

Janet Snapp, MSN, OCN, CHPN, Vice President Clinical Services, and Bonnie Meyer, MDiv., Doctoral Candidate, Chaplain, of Hospice of the Bluegrass, submitted this case study on behalf of the Hospice of the Bluegrass Ethics Committee.

CHAPTER 12

A Life Cut Short:
When Children Die

Craig M. Klugman

The Centers for Disease Control and Prevention estimate that 40,008 children under the age of 15 died in the United States in 2002 (Kochanek & Smith, 2004). Most of them died from accidents, but many died from malignant neoplasms or congenital/chromosomal abnormalities (Kochanek & Smith, 2004). The death of a child seems to hit people harder than the death of an elderly person. Perhaps people see a child's death as the loss of potential—to love, to learn, to create, to succeed. Or loss of a child might indicate a loss of innocence or the loss of parents' sense of immortality—that their genes, values, and memory will live on into future generations. Or the loss of a child may bother people because it feels like an inversion of nature. In the United States, people believe that children should outlive their parents. According to the anthropologist Gaylene Becker (1994), Americans see any disruption in what they view as the normal life course as tragic and unnatural. For many reasons, the death of a child is particularly difficult to accept.

In addition to the psychological issues of dealing with a dying child, several ethical issues are unique to this situation. First, parents and other medical providers may be particularly reluctant to disclose a fatal diagnosis treatment options or to mention hospice to a child. Second, in the case of the pediatric patient, informed consent becomes a particularly sticky issue since the patient, as a minor, is incapable of giving consent to treatment or requesting that treatment be stopped. And third, as a result of this incapacity, advance directives (ADs) and do not resuscitate (DNR) orders are often overlooked or ignored. This chapter will examine these issues through the case of a 12-year-old hospice patient.

DISCLOSURE

Andrew Chang was a 12-year-old whose family had immigrated to Florida from China.[1] He suffered from an astrocytoma that had not responded to aggressive surgery, radiation, or chemotherapy. Because of China's one-child policy, Andrew was an only child, and his parents were now incapable of having another. Mr. Chang was an engineer and Mrs. Chang was an accountant. Although the Changs originally did not want Andrew to know he was dying, Andrew was aware of his condition. Andrew's hospice nurse, Denise, described him as a very bright child who feared that his parents would divorce after he died. Denise helped him to create a farewell video-tape for his parents. Andrew told her that his two regrets about dying were that he would never drive a car and that he would never have sex. Denise let him drive her car in the parking lot. She did not address his second wish, but did spend hours watching baseball with him. He died quietly in his sleep while his parents took a break from their bedside vigil.

The Changs, following the customs of their homeland, at first did not want Andrew to know he was dying. However, in the United States, a different ethos prevails: Health care providers have a moral duty to inform adult patients so that they can make decisions regarding treatment options (Jonsen, Siegler, & Winslade, 2002). The notion of autonomy, or self-governance as discussed by Immanuel Kant (1995) and later refined by Beauchamp and Childress (2001), says that a person has the right to make a well-reasoned choice. However, moral deliberation requires that a person have the requisite information, such as a terminal prognosis. U.S. court cases have ruled that physicians have a duty of reasonable disclosure to a patient who must have adequate information in order to make a well-informed choice (*Cobbs v. Grant*, 1972). In addition, honest disclosure is seen as a necessary component of maintaining trust in the physician-patient relationship (Jonsen, Siegler, & Winslade, 2002).

---

[1] Thanks to the Florida hospice nurse who relayed the details of this real case. Names have been changed to protect patient confidentiality.

Adults have things they need to do before they die. They must draw up wills, put their personal affairs in order, and often negotiate for the care of children. However, the case of a child is seen as different. Children do not usually have financial or legal matters to settle. Nor are they seen as having a large number of personal issues that need closure. In addition, they cannot legally make their own health care decisions. Parents and providers may argue that a child knowing of his or her imminent death loses all sense of hope of recovering and growing up. They believe that children will be fearful if they know that death is near. Most parents have a strong desire to keep their children safe from harm and thus see protecting the child from this knowledge of death as imperative. However, hiding such knowledge may also cause its own kind of harms.

The American Medical Association code of ethics states, "A physician shall . . . be honest in all professional interactions" (American Medical Association, 2001). Therefore, physicians have legal and ethical obligations to be truthful. The philosopher Sissela Bok (1989) suggests that most of the time truth is necessary for the functioning of a society. Bok says that without truth, there can be no trust, and without trust, the very foundations of a society crumble. Thus, according to Bok and many other theorists, truth-telling is a moral duty. To keep knowledge of his or her impending death from a child would require a complicity in lying from all members of the health care team, visitors, and family members. Neither Kant nor Bok would find moral justification for creating a situation that forced others to participate in a lie.

Such a belief in truth-telling to the dying is, however, thoroughly culture-bound. In many other countries, such as Italy, a dying adult is never told the truth. Instead, the family is given the information and then asked to make treatment decisions. The loss of hope that disclosure entails is considered barbaric (Surbone, 1992). Respecting a patient's culture is essential to a trusting and effective patient-provider relationship. A physician who disrespects a patient's culture and beliefs is unlikely to earn the trust of that patient and denies the patient the right to exercise autonomy. Therefore, whenever possible, cultural beliefs should be considered in health care decision making. Conflicts are inevitable when a culturally based request contradicts hospital policy, law, or standards of practice. In such situations, negotiations among patients, families, and care providers are important in resolving the conflict. For example, if Andrew's family had made a request for nondisclosure and Andrew had agreed that he didn't want to know his condition, then nondisclosure would be acceptable, since it resulted from Andrew exercising his autonomy. But in this case, Andrew did want to know, and his parents eventually agreed with his wishes.

Bok (1989) does suggest that there are some situations in which telling *a little white lie* might be acceptable. For example, if a woman asks her boyfriend if she looks fat in a particular outfit, he should probably be complimentary rather than truthful. Such small lies have less potential for harm than does the truth. The question, then, is whether informing a child that he or she is dying represents a greater harm to the child than not disclosing the truth. The justifications for not telling a child—loss of hope, fear, and the fact that the child is not the decision maker—remove any sense of control or autonomy from the child. The reality, at least according to Andrew's hospice nurse, Denise, is that, "They [children] are very intuitive, much more than adults. They know when they've had enough, when their body can't take anymore. They worry about their parents more than themselves. They do not get depressed like adults."

Not informing someone that he or she is dying is more than a little white lie. Indeed, it prevents a person from coming to terms with his or her mortality and bringing closure to his or her life. If Andrew had not known he was dying, he would not have had the opportunity to live his dream of driving a car. The age and comprehension level of the child will have an effect on whether and how he or she is told. A 4-year-old has a different ability to understand and reason than a 12-year-old. The assumption, however, should be in favor of telling a child who seems interested and developmentally capable of understanding. The child should be told in an age-appropriate manner, to offer him or her the same opportunities for closure and resolution that this society offers to adults.

CONSENT/ASSENT

Even though Andrew knew that he was dying and could come to terms with it and fulfill some of his lifelong desires, he still lacked the right to make his own health care choices. Informed consent means that a rational person, given sufficient information on risks and benefits, has the right to make a well-reasoned choice regarding his or her care. This notion derives in part from the Nuremburg Code, which states, "The voluntary consent of the human subject is absolutely necessary"(Nuremberg Military Tribunal, n.d.). Although the Nuremburg Code was intended for human research experimentation, many of its tenets have found its way into therapeutic practice. Other sources include a landmark 1891 U.S. Supreme Court case, where Justice Horace Gray wrote, "No right is held more sacred, or is more carefully guarded, by the common law, than the right of every individual to the possession and control of his own person, free from restraint or interference of others" (*Union Pacific Railroad Co. v. Botsford*, 1891). Justice Benjamin Cardozo wrote in his famous 1914 New York State Supreme Court opinion, "Every human being of adult years and sound mind has a right to determine what shall be done with his own body" (*Schloendorff v. Society of New York Hospital*, 1914).

In medical ethics, informed consent also derives directly from the idea of autonomy, that is, that the patient can self-govern. Autonomy allows a patient to express preferences and make choices regarding care. In order to achieve informed consent, several conditions must be met: (1) The patient must be legally competent to make his or her own decisions; (2) the patient must be medically capable of making his or her own decisions; (3) the patient must be informed of the treatment risks and benefits as well as alternative treatments available; (4) the patient must understand the information and make a well-reasoned choice; and (5) the patient must express a treatment preference and explain his or her reasons for that choice.

Competence and incompetence are legal determinations that designate whether someone has the legal authority to make his or her own decisions in finances, health care, business, and legal matters. In general, a person is considered competent unless he or she is declared incompetent by a judge. As a categorical group, in the United States, a person who is under the age of majority—16 to 18, depending on the state (Grisso & Applebaum, 1998)—is considered incompetent to make health care choices. Thus, by definition, children are unable to give informed consent since they almost always fail the age requirement. There are several exceptions to this rule, such as the minor who gives birth to a child or the minor who has been emancipated by a court. U.S. law holds that a child lacks the cognitive abilities and capacity to make the necessary judgments (Grisso & Applebaum, 1998). The legal decision-maker for a child is a surrogate acting *in loco parentis*, that is, as a parent, usually the child's parent or guardian (Grisso & Applebaum, 1998). At 12 years of age, Andrew is clearly a minor, no matter how bright and intellectually sophisticated he may be.

Technically, then, children could be subjected to endless bouts of treatments as long as their parents consented. But few people would feel comfortable with the image of physicians strapping down a squirming child, stabbing him with needles, pushing tubes down his throat, and forcing surgery on him. Such action toward an adult would be battery in most jurisdictions and toward a child would be child abuse.

This ethical discomfort is significant, and assistance may be found in the second requirement, decisional capacity. This concept is a determinant made by a physician or other health care provider that the patient can understand medical information, acknowledges the situation, and can communicate a well-reasoned decision regarding treatment at this particular time (Jonsen, Siegler, & Winslade, 2002). A physician could determine that a patient, even though legally competent, is not capable of making health care choices at a given time, such as a patient who is extremely agitated or in shock. However, when conditions change, capacity may return. Even patients with dementia have periods of lucidity when they can rationally talk and express preferences. During such episodes they have capacity.

Since capacity is determined by health care providers, it allows much greater flexibility. A 17-year-old who is in college may lack the legal ability to consent to medical treatment, but may have thought about and have much to say concerning his or her condition. A 2-year-old probably lacks the ability to understand and to reason about a medical condition. Twelve-year-old Andrew's health care providers decided that he had capacity and that therefore he should be involved in his medical decision making. A similar situation can be found in the area of research, where discussions over pediatric subjects have occurred for some time. As a research subject, a child is unable to give informed consent. Although only a parent or guardian can give this consent, the child's agreement and cooperation are considered important. Instead of legal *consent*, the notion of *assent* has been developed. Assent is "a child's affirmative agreement to participate in research. Mere failure to object should not, absent affirmative agreement, be construed as assent" (Department of Health and Human Services, 1991). Assent, then, is the child's permission. Although the child's assent carries no legal weight, it does carry considerable moral weight. After all, decisions affect the child's body and life. The federal regulation also says that absence of a child's objection to experiment does not indicate assent. Similarly, in a pediatric end-of-life situation, the child's assent should be sought for treatment, withdrawal, or withholding of treatment. Careful patience is necessary to get a response from the child; lack of an answer is not assent.

On a case-by-case basis, health care providers can decide how much weight the child's assent or lack of assent should carry in the final choice. An older child's preferences often merit more consideration than a younger child's. The decision of a pediatric patient who can offer a well-reasoned choice, and explanation for that choice, should carry more weight than that of one who cannot. Thus, the physician's and family's evaluation of the child's capacity for decision making determines the amount of consideration to be given to the child's assent. Andrew's intelligence, acumen, and strong communication abilities led his care providers to decide he had capacity, and thus his assent was seriously considered.

While assent is morally valuable, legally it carries little weight. Though parents, guardians, and providers still have the final say in treatment, the provider should make sure that choices are in the patient's, and not the surrogates', best interest. A provider who believes that a surrogate decision maker is not acting in the patient's best interest may have an obligation to pursue legal channels to have an appropriate guardian appointed. In cases where parental actions or decisions may be viewed as abusive, the provider has an obligation to contact child protective services to make sure that the best interests of the child are being upheld. For example, the greedy and disinterested guardian of a child who stands to lose control of a large trust fund if the child dies may not have the patient's best interests at heart. The provider would then be obliged to report such behavior and urge that a new guardian be appointed.

ADVANCE DIRECTIVES AND DNRS

Although informed consent is taken as the gold standard, when a patient is unable to express his or her choices, an advance directive (AD)—composed of a living will and medical power of attorney—can serve as a proxy voice. The AD has become a centerpiece in the patient rights movement. By preparing a legal document that states a patient's wishes and designates a surrogate decision-maker, the patient can exercise autonomy even when he or she cannot communicate. These documents were established in several court rulings such as Cruzan (*Cruzan v. Director, Missouri Department of Health*, 1990) and were codified in the 1991 Patient Self-Determination Act. In order to complete an AD, a patient must be legally competent. Therefore, by definition, a child cannot create an AD. However, parents and guardians along with health care providers can create an AD for a child. The AD is an expression of a patient's wishes, but only a physician's orders can direct treatment in a medical facility. Thus, a child with a life-shortening condition may also want to have a physician-written DNR order. This treatment order establishes that in the event of cardiac failure, neither cardiopulmonary resuscitation, electroshock, nor related drugs will be administered to the patient.

Many people are reluctant to write a document that suggests withholding or withdrawing life-sustaining treatment from a child. In a series of focus groups with clergy facilitated by this author, participants said that parents of a dying child have a deep sense of guilt and they wonder why God would allow this to happen to their child. These clergy also said that parents often feel responsible for their child's illness and have difficulty dealing with their emotions. Such turmoil does not create an environment for well-informed, well-reasoned decision making. Parents already feel guilty over their child's illness; they do not want the added burden of feeling that they ordered their child killed or allowed their child to die.

Even though ADs were created to protect and preserve patients' autonomy and desires, their use in the pediatric setting has been limited. In some suggested models, such as FOOTPRINTSSM, a conversation regarding end-of-life goals, patient and family wishes, social and religious needs, withdrawing life support, and setting limits to active care occurs early in the dying process. The results of this conversation are placed in a "written discharge order sheet," which is then widely distributed within the relevant communities, including emergency medical services, police, and funeral directors (Toce & Collins, 2003). Thus, even when formal ADs are not completed, some creative thinking can produce an equally effective and valuable document.

Other studies show that even when pediatric ADs and DNR orders are written, hospital personnel may be reluctant to carry out the orders if a parent or designated decision maker is not present (Walsh-Kelly et al., 1999). Another issue for providers exists if the child is very young, such as a newborn. Some health care providers may fear that failure to resuscitate would be considered problematic under the "Baby Doe Rules." These rules are part of the 1985 federal Child Abuse Prevention and Treatment and Adoption Reform Act, which dictates that handicapped newborns (in the case of the original Baby Doe, anencephaly) must be treated. However, Jonsen, Siegler, and Winslade (2002) note that these rules do not apply when further treatment would "merely prolong dying" or would be "futile in terms of survival of the infant." In addition, these rules apply to newborns, not to older children.

Reluctance to prepare advance care planning documents is also reflected in how late in the dying process children are referred to hospice. Studies show that only between 1% and 10% of all dying children receive hospice care (Morgan & Murphy, 2000). In a study of a pediatric intensive care unit, DNR orders were written an average of 6.9 days after the child was on the unit, and death usually followed DNR writing within a mean of 39 hours (Garros, Rosychuk, & Cox, 2003). The same study also found that life-sustaining treatment was removed only when death was imminent (within an average of 3 hours).

THE FUTURE

Andrew's family and caregivers felt that he died a good death. His care providers and family told him of his diagnosis and prognosis. As a result, he was able to fulfill one of his life dreams and to leave a lasting message to his family through a videotape. Because of his keen intellect and his age, he was able to take part in discussions about his treatment and limits to medical intervention. Although he did not have a formal advance directive, the results of the conversations regarding his future were noted in his chart and known by all who cared for him. Andrew had a good death because of foresight, planning, and his inclusion in the discussions.

Both the American Academy of Pediatrics (2000) and the Institute of Medicine (Field & Berhman, 2003) have produced reports calling for improved end-of-life care for children. Both reports suggest providing training for pediatricians and pediatric residents as well as improved counseling for families and patients. Both organizations are drawing attention to this often-neglected aspect of the end-of-life movement: the care of the pediatric patient. From an ethical perspective, justice dictates a sharing of the benefits and burdens across a population. Therefore, children should be able to benefit as much as adults from increased attention to palliative and hospice care to reduce the burdens of dying, including pain management, decision making, advance care planning, and truth-telling. Only by recognizing the unique ethical and medical situation of the most vulnerable of all patients can true comfort and care be said to be provided for those who are dying. ■

Craig M. Klugman is assistant professor of bioethics in the School of Public Health at the University of Nevada, Reno; chair of the Program in Health Care Ethics at the Nevada Center for Ethics and Health Policy; and clinical faculty in the Division of Interdisciplinary Medical Education at the University of Nevada School of Medicine. He holds degrees in the medical humanities from the University of Texas Medical Branch; bioethics and medical anthropology from Case Western Reserve University; and human biology from Stanford University. Dr. Klugman conducts research in end-of life-issues, public health ethics, literature and medicine, bioterrorism, and rural ethics.

REFERENCES

American Academy of Pediatrics, Committee on Bioethics and Committee on Hospital Care. (2000). Palliative care for children. *Pediatrics, 106*(2) Pt 1, 351–357.

American Medical Association. (2001). *Principles of medical ethics.* Retrieved August 30, 2004, from http://www.ama-assn.org/ama/pub/category/2512.html

Beauchamp, T. L., & Childress, J. F. (2001). *Principles of biomedical ethics.* New York: Oxford University Press.

Becker, G. (1994). Metaphors in disrupted lives: Infertility and cultural constructions of continuity. *Medical Anthropology Quarterly, 8*(4), 383–410.

Bok, S. (1989). *Lying: Moral choice in public and private life.* New York: Vintage Books.

Cobbs v. Grant. 1972.8 Cal. 3d 229; 502 P.2d 1; 104 Cal. Rptr. 505; 1972 Cal. LEXIS 278: California Supreme Court.

Code of Federal Regulations. 1985. U.S. Code 45 (1340). as quoted in Jonsen, A. R., Siegler, M., & Winslade, W. J. (2002). *Clinical ethics* (5th ed.). New York: McGraw Hill, 42.

Cruzan v. Director, Missouri Department of Health. 1990.497 U.S. 261; 110 S. Ct. 2841; 111 L. Ed. 2d 224; 1990 U.S. LEXIS 3301; 58 U.S.L.W. 4916: U. S. Supreme Court.

Department of Health and Human Services, National Institutes of Health, Office for Protection from Research Risks. (1991). Code of Federal Regulations Title 45, Public Welfare, Part 46, Protection of Human Subjects. In H. Y. Vanderpool (Ed.), *The ethics of research involving human subjects: Facing the 21st century* (pp. 449–500). Frederick, MD: University Publishing Group.

Field, M. J., & Berhman, R. E. (Eds.) (2003). *When children die: Improving palliative and end-of-life care for children and their families.* Washington, DC: National Academy Press.

Garros, D., Rosychuk, R. J., & Cox, P. N. (2003). Circumstances surrounding end of life in a pediatric intensive care unit. *Pediatrics, 112*(5), e371.

Grisso, T., & Applebaum, P. S. (1998). *Assessing competence to consent to treatment.* New York: Oxford University Press.

Jonsen, A. R., Siegler, M., & Winslade, W. J. (2002). *Clinical ethics* (5th ed.). New York: McGraw Hill.

Kant, I. (1995). *Foundation of metaphysics of morals* (L. W. Beck, Trans.). Library of Liberal Arts. Upper Saddle River, NJ: Prentice Hall, 1785.

Kochanek, K. D., & Smith, B. L. (2004). Deaths: Preliminary data for 2002. *National Vital Statistics Reports, 52*(13).

Morgan, R., & Murphy, S. B. (2000). Care of children who are dying of cancer. *New England Journal of Medicine, 342*, 347–348.

Nuremberg Military Tribunal. n.d. Permissible Medical Experiments. *Trials of war criminals before the Nuremberg Military Tribunals under control council law no. 10*: Nuremberg October 1946-April 1949. Washington: U.S. Government Printing Office, vol. 2, 181-182. In H. Y. Vanderpool (Ed.), *The ethics of research involving human subjects: Facing the 21st century* (pp. 431–532). Frederick, MD: University Publishing Group.

Schloendorff v. Society of New York Hospital. 1914. 211 N.Y. 125, 129-130, 105 N.E. 92, 93: N.Y. Supreme Court.

Surbone, A. (1992). Truth telling to the patient. *JAMA, 268*, 1661–1662.

Toce, S., & Collins, M. A. (2003). The FOOTPRINTS model of pediatric palliative care. *Journal of Palliative Medicine, 6*, 989-1000.

Union Pacific Railroad Co. v. Botsford. 1891. 141 U.S. 250, 251, 11 S.Ct. 1000, 1001, 35 L. Ed. 734: U.S. Supreme Court.

Walsh-Kelly, C. M., Lang, K. R., Chevako, J., Blank, E. L., Korom, N., Kirk, K., & Gray, A. (1999). Advance directives in a pediatric emergency department. *Pediatrics, 103*(4) Pt 1, 829–830.

Brian: Autonomy and Self-Determination of a Minor

The Center for Hospice & Palliative Care, Cheektowaga, New York

At the age of 15, Brian, a previously healthy and active high school sophomore, was diagnosed with a high-grade malignancy. Surgical removal of the tumor was followed by aggressive chemotherapy. Four months after surgery, a CT scan showed metastases to his lungs and liver. For the next three months, Brian received further chemotherapy, which failed to halt his disease. After much discussion among Brian, his physician, and his parents, a decision was made to discontinue chemotherapy. DNR orders were initiated and Brian was admitted into our hospice program.

Throughout the course of his illness, Brian, the youngest of three boys, insisted on being involved in decisions regarding his care. His parents struggled to balance the need to support their son's autonomy and right to self-determination with their own wish to keep him alive at all costs. A point of crisis in their relationship arose when Brian decided he wanted to stop all aggressive treatment, even though some "salvage" protocols had been identified that could be tried. Multiple case and family conferences were held with all the stakeholders around a number of issues.

DISCUSSION

- What standards should be used in making decisions for children? What circumstances modify considerations of the best interests or preferences of the child versus the interests of the family?

- What are the limitations or exceptions, if any, on the presumption of primacy of parental decision making? While not an emancipated minor, would Brian not be considered a "mature minor," and if so, how should his capacity be assessed?

- Would Brian's refusal of therapy be considered differently were the proposed therapies more effective or less burdensome, with fewer side effects? What would be the team's course of action under those circumstances?

- Could Brian stay in the hospice program if he elected such treatment and, if not, would this fact be considered coercive in the decision-making process? ■

Robert A. Milch, MD, FACS, is Medical Director for The Center for Hospice & Palliative Care.

Judith A. Skretny, MA, is Vice President for The Center for Excellence in End-of-Life Education, Research & Practice at The Center for Hospice & Palliative Care.

Susan M. Huff, MSN, is Director of Essential Care, for The Center for Hospice & Palliative Care.

CHAPTER 13

Living and Dying in Nursing Homes

Sandra Johnson

Most people, including health care professionals, experience discomfort when they talk about dying. Most people are also uncomfortable talking about nursing homes generally and especially about even the speculative prospect of nursing home admission for themselves or a family member. When "dying" and "nursing home" come together, double discomfort occurs and denial is often the default coping mechanism. In light of this embedded avoidance, any consideration of ethical issues in the care of the dying in nursing homes must begin by stating emphatically: *people die in nursing homes.*

More than 20% of all deaths of older Americans occur in long-term care facilities. More telling, perhaps, is that 30% of all persons who die in hospitals have been transferred there from nursing homes and die within three days of that transfer (Sloane, Zimmerman, Hanson, Mitchell, Riedel-Leo, & Custis-Buie, 2003). Of those whose primary residence is a nursing home, two-thirds will reside there until their deaths (Zerzan, Stearns, & Hanson, 2000).

In fact, people *should* be able to die in nursing homes, just as they should be able to die in their own homes. The call of the hospice movement—to see dying as a part of life rather something segregated and isolated—is as true for nursing home residents as it is for anyone else.

The assertion that death is a part of life in nursing homes, however, runs counter to hard-won ideals and standards of contemporary nursing home care. The unequivocal repudiation of the notions that physical and mental decline are unavoidable for nursing home residents and that nursing homes are way stations where people wait to die forms the basis of the framework for improving the quality of care and the quality of life for nursing home residents in the United States. Instead of being resigned to residents' inevitable decline, nursing home professionals and regulators are committed to the expectation that residents can maintain or improve their levels of social, psychological, and physical functioning. If this expectation has influenced the culture of nursing homes toward a more engaged and less pessimistic care model, it should be viewed as enriching the quality of life for nursing home residents.

This rehabilitative, health-promoting mission, however, may have unintentionally produced a death-denying culture. Regulations impose standards that assume that physical, mental, and emotional decline may indicate deficiencies in care of residents. The regulations implement those standards through a number of processes, including the federally mandated Resident Assessment Instrument, that identify evidence of decline as a flag for further investigation to ensure that the resident's deterioration is not due to inadequate care. The physical changes often associated with the dying process, such as weight loss, can become signs of failure rather than expected and normal occurrences in the dying process (Zerzan et al, 2000). Because nursing home administrators and caregivers are highly sensitive to both the risk of litigation and the risk of scrutiny by state and federal regulators, they will tend to avoid situations that may trigger inquiry or investigation (Kapp, 2003). The emphasis on positive indicators of improvement or maintenance of health status thus becomes an incentive for avoidance of situations that are likely to attract attention, including avoidance of assisting patients in the dying process.

This death-denying culture, whether resulting from the focus on health promotion or fear of legal risk, is evident in the numbers of nursing home residents who are transferred to hospital emergency departments when death is imminent. While transfer to a hospital may open the door for hospice services (although typically for only a short time before death), transfer to hospital may be a manifestation of avoidance and abandonment. Marshall Kapp describes a "popular motto" in the nursing home world: "When in doubt, ship them out. Make the patient the other guy's worry" (Kapp, 2003, p. 119). Denying death a place in the nursing home also explains in part why advance planning for the dying process is lacking even though the age and physical condition of most residents produces a death rate averaging about 25% of the bed count of a typical facility each year (Travis, Bernard, Dixon, McAuley, Loving, & McClanahan, 2002). The lack of advance planning results in decisions made under the stress of urgency, communication difficulties with families and among staff, and inappropriately intensive care or hospitalization (Mitchell, Kiely, & Hamel, 2004). Perhaps because care for the dying is in apparent conflict with the core mission of nursing homes, the quality of end-of-life care is often unsatisfactory (Cassel & Field, 1997).

THE NEED FOR A CULTURAL SHIFT

The importance of recognizing the cultural construct that limits good care for the dying in nursing homes operates on several fronts. For example, Rosalie Kane has focused a good deal of her prodigious efforts on behalf of nursing home residents on making sure that "everyday ethics" is recognized as central to ethical issues in nursing home life, as it is the "indignities and losses of ordinary life" that determine the quality of living, and dying, for nursing home residents (Kane & Caplan, 1990, p. 5). The ethical challenges for end-of-life care reside not only in the paradigmatic decisions regarding particular interventions such as resuscitation and medically provided nutrition, but extend as well to everyday matters. If a modification or expansion of culture and ideal is seen as a foundation for improving the care of the dying in nursing homes, the small, incremental things that form a culture will be valued. This approach would recognize the significance of expressions of sympathy both to family and to other residents, public marking of the death in the facility by more than redistribution of clothing, and attendance at funerals, for example.

Beginning with culture also shifts the focus from the physician-patient dyad, which in any case does not fit nursing home care as much as it does hospitalization, to the community of caregivers, family, and all of the home's residents (Travis et al., 2002). Most care for nursing home residents is provided not by physicians or even professional nurses, but rather by paraprofessional or nonprofessional caregivers. Often, the direct caregivers as a group differ from the residents in terms of race and ethnicity, socioeconomic class, and culture. If a death-denying culture is identified as an issue and enrichment of that culture as a goal, the clashes in behavior and expectation between residents and caregivers may be more broadly addressed and contextualized as a community issue rather than as individual and perhaps aberrant episodes. Conflicts in treatment goals between the paraprofessional and nonprofessional direct caregivers and medical professionals also negatively affect the quality of end-of-life care (Kapp, 2003); and they, too, can be addressed as larger questions rather than individual conflicts between staff and physicians.

Understanding that the culture of nursing homes is defined by regulatory standards also allows attention to be paid to public policy. Because regulation drives so much of the character of nursing homes, it is important to identify where the regulatory standards and practices may be impeding development of a richer environment of support for the dying resident and the surviving community. For example, many have proposed revising the mandatory Resident Assessment Index to better accommodate palliative care (Kapp, 2003; Zerzan et al., 2000), as well as financing initiatives that support end-of-life care in nursing homes (Casarett, Hirschman, & Henry, 2001). To date, public policy has not been supportive of the relationship between hospice and nursing home care, even treating it as an occasion of fraud at some points (Kapp, 2003; Zerzan et al., 2000).

No one would contend that the rehabilitative and health-promoting mission and regulatory standards for nursing homes should be abandoned or diminished. They are too important to the quality of life of most residents. Advocates for nursing home residents and nursing homes that are in the leadership of best practices have worked hard to transform the American nursing home from the stereotypical warehouse for those who are declining into death into a place of engagement and hope. Although the ideal may depart from the reality and from what is actually within reach in many circumstances, it is an ideal that should not be, and need not be, compromised.

Once dying is accepted as a natural part of living in a nursing home, it is clear that the nursing home should embrace the full course of life, including dying. The challenge is to encourage the system to accept death, and the physical and mental deterioration that accompanies the process, as well as the abandonment of interventions that would otherwise be fundamental, without creating a shield for neglect.

Although hospice and nursing home care generally have not had the most harmonious or synergistic relationship overall (Casarett et al., 2001; Zerzan et al., 2000), communication between the two modes of care may help to marry the health-promoting mission of nursing homes to the reverence for the dying process that characterizes hospice. For example, the recognition within hospice that the dying process can be a time of growth can provide a base for integrating care for the dying resident into the contemporary emphasis on active social, emotional, and medical care and can offset feelings of failure and inadequacy as a resident dies. Further, nursing home care is always intimate care, as is hospice care for the dying. That mutual experience of intimacy can be another channel for communication between the two approaches to care.

Nursing homes do indeed confront some of the same issues in caring for dying residents as do other health care providers. These issues include, for example, decisions concerning the provision of nutrition and hydration and pain and symptom management. In some ways, the fact that the dying patient is receiving care in a nursing home does not alter the essential principles at issue; however, the context of care often complicates the application of those principles.

For example, in discussions of end-of-life care, there is often an unspoken assumption that the patient can be identified as having entered the dying process. In caring for nursing home residents, however, the process often is so subtle, so incremental, that it is hard to conclude with any certainty that a patient is dying (Travis et al., 2002). Is this pneumonia or this infection the one that signals imminent dying? Or is it treatable and will the patient return to her previous health status? Is the mental disorientation or psychosis seen in a particular patient upon admission to the hospital a permanent change, or will he recover when brought home?

CARING FOR RESIDENTS WITH DEMENTIA

The ambiguity of the prognosis for patients who do not have inoperable or chemotherapy-resistant cancer or a similar condition has been a familiar challenge for hospice. This ambiguity is endemic with nursing home residents. When has the dying begun? This may be an even more serious problem among patients with dementia, as one study documented that only 1.1% of residents with advanced dementia were assessed as having a life expectancy of less than 6 months, whereas 71% of those patients went on to die within that timeframe (Mitchell, Kiely, & Hamel, 2004). Of course, it might be easier, and at least partially true, to say that all nursing home residents are dying, but that broad definition is hardly useful so long as whether the patient is "dying" is viewed as a critical element for making treatment decisions. The vestiges of the requirement that death be imminent or that the patient fall securely within the category of "dying" before withdrawal of life-sustaining treatment need to be reexamined in the context of patients suffering certain types of conditions, such as advanced dementia, whether in a nursing home, hospital, or at home (Travis, Loving, McClanahan, & Bernard, 2001). This is especially true when the categories are used as gateways to care that is consciously end-of-life care.

Nursing home residents also experience a significant incidence of dementia or other mental disorders that may compromise their decision-making capacity. In fact, 55.6% of the nursing home residents in one study were unable to speak or write in the last month of life, limiting the scope of end-of-life support that could be of benefit (Sloane et al., 2003).

Dementia presents a number of challenges to end-of-life care. First, a diagnosis of dementia does not necessarily mean that the resident has lost all decision-making capacity; special efforts may be needed to enable such residents to direct their own care. Second, dementia complicates treatment at all times, including at the time of dying. Patients with advanced dementia may be physically combative, which can be misinterpreted as voluntary rejection of treatment. Seriously impaired patients may not be able to communicate discomfort and pain. Finally, caregivers tend to distance themselves from patients with dementia, as they do from dying patients and patients in pain, and this distancing impedes care.

Recommendations for appropriate decision making in the context of life-sustaining treatment at the end of life often rely on surrogate decision makers, especially family members. Patients with no family or patients with a family in sharp conflict are customarily viewed as difficult cases because of the absence of reliable, or even simply cooperative, surrogate decision makers. This scenario is quite common in nursing homes. In addition, caregivers in nursing homes often refer to their own paradigm of the distant family member who shows up only sporadically and disruptively or the family member who does not seem to have the resident's best interests at heart.

Nor do advance directives ordinarily provide much guidance in directing the care of nursing home residents. The large majority of nursing home residents do not have a living will. Most studies report that Do Not Resuscitate orders exist for approximately half of nursing home residents (Mitchell et al., 2004; Sloane et al., 2003; Travis et al., 2002), but that as few as 20% of residents have living wills (Sloane et al., 2003). Even when the resident has a living will, the document is not likely to be responsive to the range of treatment issues that will arise (Francis, 2001; Johnson, 1987). Living wills tend to be focused on particular episodes of life-sustaining treatment that fit the scenarios that have characterized high-profile disputes, such as resuscitation, ventilator support, and medically provided nutrition and hydration for the anticipated circumstances of dying or permanent unconsciousness. Living wills are not very likely to be directive, although they may be suggestive, regarding such questions as whether a urinary tract infection or pneumonia should be treated with antibiotics.

PAIN MANAGEMENT

Pain and symptom management are the foundation of good end-of-life care, as unrelenting pain and related symptoms can interfere so completely with rational thought, emotional engagement, and social relationships as to rob the individual of the experience of being human. Treatment of pain remains a challenge in palliative care generally, even after serious efforts have been made to improve the situation. Even more so, pain is undertreated in nursing homes, with studies reporting that 30% to 80% of residents receive inadequate pain management (Sloane et al., 2003).

Certainly, aggressive treatment for pain, especially for the terminally ill patient, is totally consistent with the focus on rehabilitation and health promotion. Pain management in nursing homes, however, is challenged by the tendency on the part of both health care providers and family members to underestimate pain in the elderly (Matulonis, 2004) or to view pain as an unavoidable consequence of aging (Sheehan & Schirm, 2003). In addition, older adults generally may underreport pain for fear of being a burden (Sheehan & Schirm, 2003), and assessing pain in individuals with cognitive impairment requires more intensive efforts (Matulonis, 2004; Sheehan & Schirm, 2003).

The ethical duty to relieve pain is widely recognized and well established. Until recently, however, health care providers who neglected their patients in pain faced no substantial legal risk, while those who treated patients in pain with controlled substances feared legal sanctions (Johnson, 1996; Rich, 2000). Nursing home providers also report that fear of legal risk negatively impacts the treatment of pain in residents (Kapp, 2003). Health care professionals can no longer neglect active treatment for pain without fear of legal consequences. Two lawsuits filed in California resulted in substantial payments to surviving family members where the only injury complained of was the suffering experienced as a result of seriously deficient pain management (Fishman, 2004). In one of these cases, the patient, Mr. Tomlinson, had been discharged from a hospital to a nursing home for care in the final stages of terminal lung cancer (Tucker, 2004). He suffered excruciating pain from the cancer and received clearly inadequate treatment for pain. The discharge orders for Mr. Tomlinson's transfer from the hospital to the nursing home did not include appropriate pain medication even though severe pain had been documented during the hospital stay. Once at the nursing home, even though Mr. Tomlinson reported pain at the level of 10 on a 10-point scale, Demoral was the strongest pain medication provided to him. The family's lawyers sued the hospital, the hospital physician, the nursing home, and the nursing home physician using California's elder abuse statute, which provided for attorney's fees and punitive damages. Some of the defendants agreed to pay damages to the family before trial. The case against the remaining defendants was brought to a jury, and the jury awarded the family $1.5 million. The trial judge subsequently reduced the verdict to $250,000 but awarded attorney's fees of approximately $500,000.

NUTRITION AND HYDRATION

Many of the challenges of competent and effective pain management in nursing homes are experienced in other settings as well, including hospice. So too are issues relating to the medical provision of nutrition and hydration, but in nursing homes the context for these decisions is different.

Medically provided nutrition and hydration for patients who are in a persistent vegetative state (PVS) has been the paradigm case for end-of-life care and has been the legal test case for nearly 30 years, from Karen Ann Quinlan through Nancy Cruzan, and including Helen Wanglie. Of course, this "classic" case occurs in long-term care settings, perhaps more frequently than elsewhere. This scenario is used for teaching and for testing the law because it places competing ethical positions in stark contrast and illustrates essential conflicts. PVS, although relatively rare compared with the many other more complicated ways of dying, is a *relatively* "clean" medical condition presenting little uncertainty and little change over time. The apparent or total absence of consciousness puts the spotlight on what it means to be human and where human dignity lies. Medical provision of nutrition and hydration, because of its deep association with nurture and human relationships, triggers responses concerning what it means to care.

Concerns relating to nutrition and hydration—food and water— are heightened in nursing homes compared with other health care settings, including hospitals, home care, and hospice. Food and water are a core symbol of the ethic of care in nursing homes. Poor food service and inattention to encouraging fluid intake are key indicators of poor nursing home care. The better nursing homes understand the social and emotional power of eating, and nursing homes are exhorted to encourage residents to eat and drink well. Food and water—even medically provided nutrition and hydration—always bear emotional and symbolic content, but even more so in the nursing home setting, where they are enmeshed with the basic obligations of the facility.

Deficiencies in diet and hydration are commonly viewed as the root cause of substantial physical and mental impairments and of injuries ranging from bedsores to pneumonia. This widely accepted view is not entirely accurate. Increasingly, evidence indicates that a common intervention for tube feeding—percutaneous endoscopic gastrostomy (PEG)—does not reduce the risk of pneumonia or infection and may not reduce the risk of bedsores (Finucane, Christmas, & Travis, 1999). This new knowledge presents a challenge analogous to the earlier work on the use of physical restraints in nursing homes (Braun & Capezuti, 2000). The two developments are similar in that the common practice (of restraints and PEGs) has been supported by a "common knowledge" (that restraints keep residents safe and PEGs keep them healthy) that has proved to be largely mistaken and concomitantly by the ethical duty of beneficence toward the patient (Johnson, 1990). Just as with restraints, new knowledge about medically provided nutrition and hydration should modify practice while maintaining the values underlying the current practice.

Although the scenario of the patient in a PVS occurs in nursing homes, the much more common scenario involves a resident who is seriously cognitively impaired with some minimal level of consciousness. Even more than PVS, this scenario raises serious issues of appropriate treatment. In fact, one of the more influential court cases involving life-sustaining treatment is the case of Claire Conroy, a nursing home resident in exactly that position (*In re Conroy* 1985). During the course of litigation, advocacy groups for nursing home residents argued that the court should not allow the withdrawal of nutrition and hydration because of the vulnerability of nursing home residents. In response, the court mandated a government surveillance system to ensure that persons in Conroy's position would not be neglected while allowing for individual choice in the matter.

We assume that individuals can have different views on providing nutrition and hydration through surgical or other medical intervention when the individual has lost the ability to swallow and is either irreversibly comatose, dying, or in a merely minimal level of consciousness. With respect for pluralism and freedom, we have a legal framework that largely relies on individuals to express, before incapacity, their own views of what should be done or on the court to decide in each individual case what this particular patient's wishes would be or what is in this particular patient's best interests. Our laws do not hold that tube feeding persons in a persistent vegetative state or with advanced dementia violates the goals of medicine or virtue and that, therefore, it shall not be done. Nor have we even adopted the position that surgical interventions to maintain tube feeding should not be done unless there is evidence that this patient would have chosen this course of treatment. Such a position may be more ethically sound and better represent majority views, but it is not the one we have chosen. The reliance on individual choice for opting out is particularly problematic in the nursing home context, and, of course, an opt-in default would face the same issues (Finucane, 2001).

HOSPITAL TRANSFER

If nursing homes have a distinctive paradigmatic case that expresses key ethical issues, however, it is the decision whether to transfer the dying resident to a hospital. The decision to transfer may be motivated by an assessment or intuition that the resident requires hospitalization for adequate care; however, nursing home residents hospitalized when death is imminent do not necessarily receive better care than they would in their own nursing home (Bottrell, O'Sullivan, Robbins, Mitty, & Mezey, 2001). Care may be more acute than is desirable because of a lack of familiarity with the patient's medical condition or desires (Jacobs, Bonuck, Burton, & Mulvihill, 2002). Transfer also presents risks of discontinuity of care, as in the Tomlinson case, that could result in absent or unclear transfer orders for pain and symptom management or orders that are delayed in the handoff between physicians at the two facilities. Nursing home-to-hospital transfers may also be motivated primarily by legal concerns, adequately perceived or not (Kapp, 2003). Finally, the structure of treatment decision making and communication in the nursing home is also implicated in the rate of transfers of dying residents, as the order to transfer is likely to be secured through a telephone conversation with the physician (Bottrell et al., 2001).

CONCLUSION

Efforts to improve care for the dying must extend to the nursing home setting, where a large number of elderly persons experience the dying process. If we can move beyond the recognition that people *will* die in nursing homes toward an understanding that people *should* die in nursing homes, just as they die in their own homes; if we can view the ideal of caring for the dying as quite compatible with caring for elderly nursing home residents, perhaps we can move care for dying residents to parity with health-promoting care. ■

Sandra H. Johnson holds the Tenet Endowed Chair in Health Care Law and Ethics at the School of Law and the Center for Health Care Ethics at Saint Louis University. Professor Johnson also holds faculty appointments as professor of law in internal medicine at the University's School of Medicine and professor of health care administration at the School of Public Health. Professor Johnson is a co-author of Health Law—Cases, Materials and Problems *(5th ed. Thomson West),* Bioethics and Law *(5th ed. Thomson West) and the treatise* Health Law *(2d ed. Thomson West), which has been cited several times by the United States Supreme Court. She is the Director of the Mayday Project on Legal and Regulatory Issues in Pain Relief at the American Society of Law, Medicine & Ethics. She is a Fellow of the Hastings Center and a Fellow of the American Bar Association and has received numerous awards in recognition of her work in health law and ethics, including the Distinguished Health Law Teacher Award from the American Society of Law, Medicine & Ethics. Professor Johnson received a BA from Saint Louis University, a JD from New York University, and an LLM from Yale University.*

REFERENCES

Bottrell, M. M., O'Sullivan, J. E., Robbins, M. A., Mitty, E. L., & Mezey, M. D. (2001). Transferring dying nursing home residents to the hospital: DON perspectives on the nurse's role in transfer decisions. *Geriatric Nursing, 22*(6), 313–317.

Braun, J. A., & Capezuti, E. A. (2000). Legal and medical restraints and bed siderails and their relationship to falls and fall-related injuries in nursing homes. *DePaul Journal of Health Care Law, 4,* 1–72.

Casarett, D. J., Hirschman, K. B., & Henry, M. R. (2001). Does hospice have a role in nursing home care at the end of life? *Journal of the American Geriatrics Society, 49,* 1493–1498.

Cassel, C., & Field, M. J. (Eds.). (1997). *Approaching death: Improving care at the end of life.* Washington, DC: National Academy Press.

In re Conroy, 486 A.2d 1209 (N.J. 1985).

Finucane, T. (2001). Thinking about life-sustaining treatment late in the life of a demented person. *Georgia Law Review, 35,* 691–705.

Finucane, T. E., Christmas, C., & Travis, K. (1999). Tube feeding in patients with advanced dementia: A review of the evidence. *JAMA, 282,* 1365–1370.

Fishman, S. (2004). The debate on elder abuse for undertreated pain. *Pain Medicine, 5*(2), 212–213.

Francis, L. P. (2001). Decisionmaking at the end of life: Patients with Alzheimer's or other dementias. *Georgia Law Review, 35,* 539–592.

Jacobs, L. G., Bonuck, K., Burton, W., & Mulvihill, M. (2002). Hospital care at the end of life: An institutional assessment. *Journal of Pain and Symptom Management, 24*(3), 291–298.

Johnson, S. H. (1987). Sequential domination, autonomy and living wills. *Western New England Law Review, (9),* 113–137.

Johnson, S. H. (1990). The fear of liability and the use of restraints in nursing homes. *Journal of Law, Medicine & Health Care, 18,* 263–280.

Johnson, S. H. (1996). Disciplinary actions and pain relief. *Journal of Law, Medicine & Ethics, 24,* 319–327.

Kane, R. A. & Caplan, A. L. (Eds.). (1990). *Everyday ethics: Resolving dilemmas in nursing home life.* New York: Springer Publishing Company.

Kapp, M. B. (2003). Legal anxieties and end-of-life care in nursing homes. *Issues in Law and Medicine, 19,* 111, 1–23.

Matulonis, U. A. (2004). End of life issues in older patients. *Seminars in Oncology, 31,* (2), 274–281.

Mitchell, S. L., Kiely, D. K., & Hamel, M. B. (2004). Dying with advanced dementia in the nursing home. *Archives of Internal Medicine, 164*(3), 321–326.

Rich, B. A. (2000). A prescription for the pain: The emerging standard of care for pain management. *Wm. Mitchell Law Review, (26),* 1–90.

Sheehan, D. K., & Schirm, V. (2003). End-of-life care of older adults. *American Journal of Nursing, 103*(11), 48–58.

Sloane, P. D., Zimmerman, S., Hanson, L., Mitchell, C. M., Riedel-Leo, C., & Custis-Buie, V. (2003). End-of-life care in assisted living and related residential care settings: Comparison with nursing homes. *Journal of the American Geriatrics Society. 51,* 1587–1594.

Travis, S. S., Bernard, M., Dixon, S., McAuley, W. J., Loving, G., & McClanahan, L. (2002). Obstacles to palliation and end-of-life care in a long-term care facility. *The Gerontologist, 32*(3), 342–349.

Travis, S. S., Loving, G., McClanahan, L., & Bernard, M. (2001). Hospitalization patterns and palliation in the last year of life among residents in long-term care. *The Gerontologist, 41*(2), 153–160.

Tucker, K. L. (2004). Medico-Legal case report and commentary: inadequate pain management in the context of terminal cancer. The case of Lester Tomlinson. *Pain Medicine, 5*(2), 214–228.

Zerzan, J., Stearns, S., & Hanson, L. (2000). Access to palliative care and hospice in nursing homes. *JAMA, 284*(19), 2489–2494.

CHAPTER 14

Organ Donation: Ethical Issues and Issues of Loss and Grief

Charles A. Corr

The donation and transplantation of human organs and tissues is a complex subject. It touches in the most intimate ways the lives of donors, donor family members, transplant candidates, transplant recipients, and family members of both transplant candidates and recipients, as well as the professionals who work with any or all of these individuals. Because issues related to the transplant side of this field, as well as those associated with tissue donation, are complex and distinctive in nature, it may help to note from the outset that this chapter will be confined to a discussion of issues related to organ donation. Further, its special concern will be to explore ethical issues in human organ donation and those related to loss and grief.

This chapter begins by describing three basic types of organ donors. Thereafter, it will explore various ethical issues, along with issues related to loss and grief, as they apply to each of these types of organ donors.

ORGAN DONORS

There are essentially two broad categories of human organ donors: living donors and nonliving or deceased donors. The latter may be further divided into individuals who become donors after brain death and those who become donors after cardiac death. Each of these three types of donor will be considered in turn.

Living Donors

Living donors are individuals who choose to donate one of their twinned organs (e.g., a kidney) or part of one of their organs (e.g., a liver or lung) for the purposes of transplantation. They may be "directed donors" whose donation is made to help a specific transplant candidate or "nondirected donors" who donate for the benefit of any transplant candidate who might need their gift.

From 1988 through 2003, there were a total of 63,651 living donors in the United States (all data in this chapter come from the United Network for Organ Sharing [UNOS], 2004; www.unos.org). In 2003 (the most recent full year for which data are available as this is written), there were 6,815 living donors. The increasing number of individuals who are willing to offer themselves as living donors is strikingly indicated by the fact that in 2001, for the first time, there were more living than nonliving organ donors in our country (6,570 living donors versus 6,080 nonliving donors).

When human organ transplantation was first attempted in the 1950s, techniques for matching donors to recipients were limited and there were no modern immunosuppressive medications to fight rejection on the part of recipients (Dowie, 1988; Fox & Swazey, 1974, 1992). As a result, it has rightly been said that pioneering efforts in human organ transplantation involved "the courage to fail." At that time, the donation of human organs for transplantation was feasible only between close living relatives such as twins or other siblings. As time has gone by, increasingly sophisticated scientific and clinical interventions (e.g., immunosuppressive pharmaceuticals) have enabled transplants to be successful in many instances between complete strangers.

Further, additional strategies have been developed to facilitate organ donation and transplantation. For instance, it is now possible for a potential living donor who might desire to donate to a particular individual (transplant candidate A), but who is not biologically compatible with transplant candidate A, to arrange to donate to a second individual (transplant candidate B) with whom he or she is biologically compatible, in return for which a potential living donor who is incompatible with transplant candidate B will donate to transplant candidate A (with whom he or she is biologically compatible). So-called "swapping" donations like this, and even more complex stratagems, indicate one aspect of the flexibility made possible by living organ donors.

As a general rule, living donors are restricted to donating an organ or part of an organ that is not uniquely vital to the donor's health. Recovering an organ or a portion of an organ from a living donor has several advantages. For example, the donor's medical history will be known and can be investigated in advance of donation, an extensive evaluation of the donor and the organ in question can be conducted before donation, consent to donate can be obtained directly from the potential donor rather than from some substitute decision maker, the organ will be removed under elective circumstances, and the donated organ will be out of the body for a very short time, which is preferable because shorter time outside the body (ischemic time) maximizes the efficacy of the organ. In the case of a directed donation, the donor can find satisfaction in knowing that his or her donation will go to a specific recipient that he or she has chosen to help (e.g., Hamilton & Brown, 2002). In the case of a nondirected donation, satisfaction rests upon the donor's sense of having done a good deed to help an unknown human being in need.

Nonliving Donors: Organ Donation after Brain Death

The largest number of nonliving donors (sometimes called "deceased donors") consists of individuals who have died and whose bodily functions are being maintained by external support. In most instances, these nonliving donors will have died of a cerebrovascular incident (for example, as a result of a cerebral hemorrhage or stroke) or of external trauma to the head (for example, as a result of an accident, homicide, or suicide). Typically, such potential donors will be presented in an emergency room or other critical care situation. At that point, external support will be initiated to stabilize their bodily functions and to allow time for medical investigation and diagnosis. At some later time, these individuals will have been pronounced "brain dead" or dead by a neurological event, most often on the basis of clinical examinations including tests involving arterial blood flow.

At that point, external support will be continued. It is important to be clear that such support is not intended to keep the dead individual "alive." That would be impossible and a contradiction in terms. Rather, the purpose of renewing external support is to sustain bodily functions for a limited period in order to preserve the quality of the organs that might eventually be transplanted. During this limited period, an approach will be made to family members to offer the opportunity of donation, and next-of-kin will be permitted to consider decisions about donation (Albert, 1994). If the donation decision is favorable, external support will be continued while a search for appropriate recipients is undertaken, arrangements are made for organ recovery and transportation, and a potential recipient is prepared to receive a transplant. After appropriate organs (and tissues) are recovered or if next-of-kin decide against donation, external support will be removed and procedures for handling any dead body will apply.

In the United States from 1988 through 2003, there were a total of 84,187 nonliving donors. In 2003 itself, there were 6,455 nonliving donors.

Because nonliving donors no longer need their bodily organs or tissues, they can donate multiple transplantable organs and tissues. Among organs, these might include as many as two kidneys, two lungs, a liver, a pancreas, a heart, portions of an intestine, and in some cases combinations of a kidney-pancreas or heart-lung. This is why it is often said that nonliving donors can help save the lives of as many as six to eight other persons.

All of this depends upon several important variables, such as agreement by next-of-kin to permit recovery of multiple organs (in some instances, as explained later, as a result of a legal document of intent such as a signed donor card on the back of a donor's driver's license); the fact that conditions preceding, at the time of, and immediately following the death did not damage the organs in question or render them unsuitable for transplantation; and the suitability of those organs for transplantation within stipulated time frames.

In 1988, a government regulation called the Medicare and Medicaid "Conditions of Participation for Organ, Tissue, and Eye Donation" became effective that requires hospitals to (1) have a memorandum of agreement with their local or regional organ, tissue, and eye banks concerning organ donation; (2) report to their local or regional organ procurement organization (OPO) all patients whose deaths are imminent or who have died in the hospital; (3) permit the OPO to determine the suitability or eligibility of such patients for donation; and (4) arrange for trained personnel (such as members of the OPO's staff or hospital personnel who have been trained by the OPO for this purpose) to offer the opportunity to donate (U.S. Department of Health and Human Services, 1998, 2000). The goal of this "Conditions of Participation" regulation is to increase the number of donated organs while also ensuring that family members are given an appropriate opportunity to know about and carefully consider donation.

Nonliving Donors: Organ Donation after Cardiac Death

Individuals in persistent vegetative states and others who are not expected to progress to brain death may become candidates for organ donation after cardiac death. By definition, such individuals are not yet dead. That is, tests have not shown them to be brain dead. They do display ventilatory and circulatory functioning, but the question is whether such functioning is an artifact of the external support they are receiving (e.g., via respirators) or an ability they retain in their own right. In order to test which alternative applies in any given case, one would have to remove the external support to find out if the individual can continue functioning unsupported.

For many individuals in our society who are in persistent vegetative states—quite apart from any issues of potential organ donation— competent decision makers (such as next-of-kin or individuals who are authorized by such documents as durable powers of attorney in health care matters to act as substitute decision makers) may decide that no useful purpose is served by continuing external support. With the permission of a competent decision maker in these circumstances, medical personnel would withdraw external support and things would be allowed, as is said, "to take their natural course." That is, the individual in question would either continue life-sustaining functioning on his or her own or would be allowed to die.

For such individuals to become organ donors, a competent decision maker would need to grant permission for recovery of one or more organs after cardiac death. In these circumstances, an attending physician (who is not part of a transplant team) would withdraw external support and determine that the individual had died. Subsequently, after a relatively short time (during which family members are often allowed to be present), that individual would be pronounced dead by the attending physician and external support would be removed. After those events, members of an independent organ recovery team would become involved to recover stipulated organs (usually kidneys and liver).

It is useful to note that a procedure much like this would have been the familiar route to organ donation for nonliving donors before the passage of brain death legislation. Since that time, this procedure was continued in some (not all) areas of the United States, but it has received renewed emphasis in recent years.

From 1993 (when UNOS began collecting data on these donors) through 2003 in the United States, organs were recovered from a total of 1,229 individuals following cardiac death (sometimes called "non-heart-beating donors"). Such individuals represented less than 2% of all nonliving donors from whom organs were recovered during this period. The fact that efforts are made to seek out this small number of nonliving donors is testimony to the need to increase the pool of available organs for transplantation to the ever-increasing number of transplant candidates on the national waiting list. At the end of April 2004, there were 84,641 transplant candidates on that waiting list. More than 16 of those candidates die each day while waiting for a transplant.

ETHICAL, LOSS, AND GRIEF ISSUES IN ORGAN DONATION

Ethical, loss, and grief issues in organ donation take many forms. This section examines some of the most prominent of these issues in relation to the three types of organ donors.

Living Donors

The principal ethical issue that arises in relation to living donors is whether it is acceptable to approve a surgical intervention into the body of an otherwise healthy individual in order to remove an organ or a part of an organ for no direct benefit to that individual and in a way that will leave the donor permanently impaired. On its face, that practice would seem to violate the familiar medical injunction to "Do no harm." That issue is ordinarily resolved in two ways: first, in terms of the potential life-saving benefit that recovery of the organ can have for a transplant recipient; and second, in terms of an informed decision on the part of the living donor to permit the intervention.

In our system, the first of these considerations is never permitted to override the second. In other words, informed consent on the part of the potential donor is critical to all forms of living donation. To that end, medical professionals seek to establish that the potential donor is given all the information necessary to understand clearly the current situation, the risks that may be involved in the proposed surgery, and its likely outcomes—for both donor and recipient. The screening and evaluation process for living donors also seeks to determine that their blood and sensitivity to antibodies or rudimentary antigens is a good match to the potential recipient, that they are likely to be able to withstand the surgical donation process, and that they can be expected to cope effectively with the aftermath of the experience, however it may work out (The Authors for the Live Organ Donor Consensus Group, 2000).

In addition, it is particularly important to ensure that the potential living donor gives consent to donate freely and not as a result of any inappropriate motivation or pressure. For example, one might want to exclude from donation directed donors who are being improperly coerced by their family members to donate to a sibling when they really do not want to do so. Similarly, one might want to exclude nondirected donors who are covertly seeking to harm or mutilate themselves. Finally, while living donors are permitted to direct their donation to particular individuals, it is not acceptable in our system for such donors to impose ethnic, religious, or other conditions upon their donation by directing that the donation not be given to certain individuals or members of specific groups.

In addition, a promise is typically made to potential donors that, if at any time in the future their decision to donate might compromise their health status—for example, if they donated one kidney and later discovered that their other kidney was failing—they would be put at the head of the list for an appropriate organ transplant.

Loss and grief issues related to living donation concern both the donor and the recipient. For donors, however pleased they might be with their decision to donate and with the good outcomes to which it might lead, there still may be some sense of loss and grief at the removal of a healthy organ and what that will mean for their future. In addition, a living donor may feel a sense of loss, grief, and guilt if the donated organ should be rejected by the recipient's body ("Wasn't my kidney good enough for him?") or if the recipient should die following transplantation. All these issues need to be anticipated and addressed in advance of donation.

Nonliving Donors: Donation after Brain Death

The first ethical issue related to nonliving donors concerns determination of death. That determination must be carried out properly and in accord with commonly accepted medical standards. In our system, the implications of determination of death are addressed by "decoupling" them from issues associated with organ donation. Thus, health care professionals who are not part of the transplant team and who are not involved in caring for potential transplant recipients will care for the individual who is presented to them. In accordance with accepted medical standards, they will make every effort to save the life of that individual. It will be the additional responsibility of that team to determine whether or not (and when) that individual is dead. Normally, they will also be the ones who communicate that determination to the individual's next-of-kin. Meticulous attention to caring for and determining the death of every individual in these circumstances responds to the legitimate responsibilities of the care team, as well as to the medical, ethical, legal, and human interests of such individuals and their family members.

Second, the American death system does not recognize a generally accepted policy of "presumed consent" for donation of major organs, such as is found in some other countries. Presumed consent would mean that organs can be retrieved unless there is a written directive to the contrary from the decedent or next-of-kin. In contrast, our system requires explicit permission for organ donation. In accordance with the provisions of the Uniform Anatomical Gift Act (UAGA, 1968, with amendments in 1987; see Wendler & Dickert, 2001) and subsequent legislation in all the states and legal jurisdictions in this country, individuals may make their wishes about donation of organs known before they die. Under the provisions of the UAGA, an individual who is of sound mind and 18 years of age or older can donate all or any part of his or her body, the gift to take effect on his or her death and to be made for the purposes of health care education, research, therapy, or transplantation.

In recent years, extensive efforts have been made to

- Inform and educate the public about organ donation and transplantation (*"Don't take your organs to heaven . . . heaven knows we need them here."*)

- Promote discussion among family members about this subject (*"Share your life. Share your decision."*)

- Encourage potential donors to sign, date, and have witnessed an organ donor card (which is obtainable from the federal Division of Transplantation [tel. 888-90-SHARE; www.organdonor.gov], from local, regional, or national organizations, such as the Coalition on Donation [tel. 800-355-SHARE; www.shareyourlife.org], from UNOS [800-355-SHARE; www.unos.org], or from the National Kidney Foundation [800-622-9010; www.kidney.org], or which appears on the back of many state driver's licenses)

- Help individuals indicate willingness to donate by registering that fact when they obtain or renew a driver's license in many states that offer that option

When an individual has not formally declared his or her wishes regarding organ donation and in the absence of actual notice that a decedent did not wish to donate, donation decisions are most often made by next-of-kin or a health care surrogate. If so, it will be important to inform such decision makers of the death of the individual, to give them time and assistance to help them come to terms with that hard fact, to offer them the opportunity to donate, and to give them time and assistance in making that decision.

In most jurisdictions in the United States, even a formal declaration of a desire to donate made by an individual before death and communicated in one of the foregoing ways will not override a negative decision by next-of-kin or a surrogate decision maker. The basis for this appears to be the view that once a person has died, he or she no longer "owns" his or her body. In addition, the practical reality is that outsiders (such as organ procurement organizations and hospitals) would ordinarily be unwilling to enter into conflicts between family members on such a sensitive matter when there is usually only a relatively short time for its resolution. Nevertheless, some in the organ procurement community have advocated overturning this position so that a formal, signed declaration of intent to donate made by a competent individual should become legally definitive, sufficient in itself to authorize organ recovery, and not subject to being overruled by next-of-kin. That view has not yet become general policy in the United States, although it is practiced in Virginia and certain parts of Pennsylvania, and other areas of the country are considering adopting it.

The principal grief issues surrounding nonliving donors following a declaration of brain death involve family members. Issues related to organ donation frequently arise in the immediate aftermath of sudden and often traumatic deaths. For instance, not long after a college-age son rides off on his motorcycle to visit a friend or go to work, his parents may be informed of his death in a motor vehicle accident. How difficult must it be for them to absorb and cope with that fact? Understandably, they will need to have explained to them—often more than once—what has happened. That explanation must be done in a knowledgeable, authoritative, and caring way. Nothing can be done to alter the hard fact of the death.

However, something can be done to care for those who have encountered sudden bereavement. Skilled professionals can "offer the opportunity of donation." This is done, in the first place, as a gesture of caring for the bereaved persons. Members of the National Donor Family Council (NDFC) of the National Kidney Foundation (NKF) have encouraged procurement and critical care professionals not to speak of "requesting donation." Their view is that requesting something from family members in these circumstances means asking to take one more thing away from them and is implying that if family members were to deny such a request, the requester would have failed in his or her initiative. By contrast, it is thought that "offering the opportunity of donation" puts the family members back in control of at least one aspect of a situation in which they have little else to control. It enables them to determine that this may be an opportunity to do such things as

- Act in accordance with the previously expressed or perceived wishes and values of their loved one who has died
- Give some meaning to the death of their loved one

- Find some good or solace for themselves in a time of great difficulty

- Help others in need by offering something of benefit as a free gift of love

- Act upon their generally favorable attitudes toward donation

Offering an opportunity of this type should be consistent with a view that respects whatever decision the potential donor family makes. It recognizes that a decision not to donate does not take away from the care embodied in offering this opportunity. Indeed, the only failure in this regard would be not even to offer such an opportunity. Imagine the horror and sadness felt by family members who have reported that they had wanted to respect their loved one's wishes to donate but simply did not think of it in this time of great confusion, or who recognized too late that they would have wanted to make a decision to donate, but nobody mentioned it at the time!

One additional ethical and grief responsibility follows upon this discussion of donor family members. Since the early 1990s, the National Donor Family Council has advocated that donor family members should receive comprehensive follow-up bereavement services from the agencies that initiate discussions of organ donation with them. This is consistent with the view that "offering the opportunity of donation" is, in the first instance, one of the early interventions in a program of good bereavement care (Holtkamp, 2002; Maloney & Wolfelt, 2001). From the perspective of the NDFC, no such family members—whether or not they have chosen to donate—should be disregarded or left without support after their donation decision.

Among other things, the NDFC has initiated its own program of such care and advocacy. That program includes a quarterly newsletter (*For Those Who Give and Grieve*), a booklet with the same name (now in its third edition in English plus a Spanish edition), a "Bill of Rights for Donor Families" first published in 1994 (2nd ed., 2004), several short brochures on such subjects as brain death and various specific types of bereavement, a National Donor Family Memorial Quilt, educational and support meetings, and other activities. In cooperation with the federal Division of Transplantation, the NDFC and its parent organization, the National

Kidney Foundation, have helped to sponsor annual National Donor Recognition Ceremonies and the biennial Transplant Games. In addition, the NDFC and the NKF have been leaders in developing *National Communications Guidelines* concerning communications between donor families and transplant candidates/recipients and in guiding professionals in their roles in facilitating such communications (National Kidney Foundation, 1997, 2nd ed., 2004). The NDFC has also worked cooperatively with the Association of Organ Procurement Organizations to encourage similar activities at local levels. Clearly, things have changed greatly from a time not so long ago when shortly after donation, family members all too frequently became "disenfranchised grievers."

The NDFC has also encouraged professionals and all who become involved with organ donors of any type to be careful and considerate in how they speak about donation and nonliving donors. For example, the NDFC and many other organizations and individuals have advocated that talk about "harvesting" of organs is inappropriate and should be done away with. More recently, the NDFC has recommended that terms such as "cadaver donors" be replaced by phrases like "nonliving donors" or "deceased donors." However accurate the phrase "cadaver donors" may be from a technical point of view, it is offensive to family members who do not wish to hear their loved ones described in this way.

Nonliving Donors: Donation after Cardiac Death

Withdrawal of life-sustaining interventions from any individuals, even those in persistent vegetative states, is fraught with ethical issues. Opponents and proponents of such actions frequently express strong opinions, appealing to a variety of ethical, religious, or philosophical principles and values, along with personal feelings. This is so despite the fact that many mainline religious and philosophical positions do not object to withdrawal, or "forgoing" as some would prefer to say, of interventions that are no longer relevant to sustaining what some call "quality of life" and others refer to as "human life with its potential for meaningful relationships." In these circumstances, some argue that high-tech interventions are merely prolonging biological life, a form of life that would not in the past have been able to persist and that would not now be able to persist in the absence of such interventions.

However, these are broader issues than those that fall within our purview here. Questions related to possible organ donation are secondary in these circumstances to those related to the legitimacy of withdrawal of external support of life.

Once a decision has been made to withdraw external support, organ donation after cardiac death is possible only if determination of death can be made quickly (in a matter of minutes or less than an hour). If more time is taken, the organs that might be donated may begin to deteriorate and become unsuitable for transplantation. As a result, attending physicians are challenged to come to a clear and unambiguous determination of death before an organ recovery team attempts to recover transplantable organs. Specific details about how these processes do or should occur deserve careful attention on the part of all involved. Once they have been carried out, however, organ donation following cardiac death is no longer distinguishable from other forms of nonliving donation.

For those who acted as decision makers in relation to donation following cardiac death, however, there may be distinctive issues of loss, grief, and guilt. Unlike other donor family members, they will ordinarily have had more time to consider both withdrawing life-sustaining interventions and permitting organ donation. In addition, they may have had opportunities to discuss these matters in advance with the individual in question, especially if they had been appointed to act as that individual's health care surrogate.

Nevertheless, even when acting in accordance with the clear directions of a prior discussion or formal appointment as a health care surrogate, decision makers can still feel unsure that they have carried out the individual's wishes correctly, and they can still need reassurance that they have done the right thing. Making what they consider to be the proper decisions does not relieve them from a potential sense of loss or even of (possibly unjustified) guilt. In addition, even in these circumstances, most survivors face the implications of the death of someone they loved.

ALLOCATION OF DONATED ORGANS

Once organs have been donated and recovered, questions remain as to how they should be allocated. The overall framework for discussion of these questions is the National Organ Transplant Act (NOTA), passed by the United States Congress in 1984, which established the national Organ Procurement and Transplantation Network to facilitate the procurement and distribution of scarce organs in a fair and equitable way (Prottas, 1994). This network is currently administered by the United Network for Organ Sharing (UNOS) under contract to the Division of Transplantation in the Department of Health and Human Services.

Within this general framework, questions concerning the allocation of these scarce resources have intensified in recent years as the need for transplantable organs has increasingly exceeded their availability. For example, from 1988 through 2003, the number of patient registrations on the national transplant waiting list increased by well over 400%, while numbers of actual transplants increased only 100% and overall numbers of organ donors increased only about 125%. In other words, during this period the United States has witnessed something like a doubling of organs available for transplant, while there has been a quadrupling in the need for such organs. Consequently, *the single largest obstacle to organ transplantation today is the scarcity of transplantable organs.*

With respect to allocation of donated organs, as a general rule organs are allocated in terms of matching blood types, the size of the organ(s) needed, the time that an individual has spent waiting for a transplant, and the distance between the donor and a recipient. In the case of certain organs, allocation depends upon the medical urgency of the recipient, the degree of immune system match between the donor and a recipient, and whether the recipient is a child or an adult.

That said, in our system organs are usually made available to transplant centers and potential recipients first on a local or regional basis and only then on a national basis if no suitable match is found at the local or regional level. Recently, it has been argued that at least certain organs should be allocated first to those on the national waiting list who are in greatest need, regardless of geographical considerations. The argument for the traditional form of allocation is that consent to donate will more likely be obtained if the donor believes he or she is supporting members of a local or nearby community and that this form of allocation offers greater likelihood of long-term success in transplantation than the proposed alternative. The argument for dispensing with geographical considerations is that they may have the effect of disadvantaging the sickest transplant candidates and favoring candidates who are otherwise healthy enough to wait longer. Because of the typical pool of patients which each serves, it has also been suggested that the traditional allocation system tends to favor smaller, local transplant centers, while the proposed alternative tends to favor larger, regional or national transplant centers.

CONCLUSION

Ethical, loss, and grief issues related to organ donation are complex and many-sided. Because they differ for different types of donors, this chapter has described three principal types of donors. It has then identified and described ethical, loss, and grief issues in relationship to each type of donor.

Perhaps the most important thing to note about the ethical issues identified here is that they can all be managed with sufficient care and attention. Loss and grief issues can also be managed, both for living donors and for the family members of nonliving donors, if they are anticipated and proper support is provided to the individuals involved. In particular, for donor family members, the opportunity to donate must be presented as part of a comprehensive program of bereavement care. ■

Charles A. Corr, PhD, CT, is professor emeritus, Southern Illinois University Edwardsville, and a member of the following organizations: the Board of Directors of the Hospice Institute of the Florida Suncoast; the ChiPPS (Children's Project on Palliative/Hospice Services) Executive Committee of the National Hospice and Palliative Care Organization; the Executive Committee of the National Kidney Foundation's transAction Council; and the International Work Group on Death, Dying, and Bereavement (Chairperson, 1989-93). Dr. Corr's publications include 30 books and booklets, along with more than 80 articles and chapters, in the field of death, dying, and bereavement. His next book will be the fifth edition of Death and Dying, Life and Living, *co-authored with Clyde M. Nabe and Donna M. Corr, to be published in summer, 2005.*

REFERENCES

Albert, P. L. (1994). Overview of the organ donation process. *Critical Care Nursing Clinics of North America, 6,* 536–556

The Authors for the Live Organ Donor Consensus Group. (2000). Consensus statement on the live organ donor. *JAMA, 284,* 2919–2926.

Dowie, M. (1988). *"We have a donor": The bold new world of organ transplanting.* New York: St. Martin's Press.

Fox, R. C., & Swazey, J. P. (1974). *The courage to fail: A social view of organ transplants and dialysis.* Chicago: University of Chicago Press.

Fox, R. C., & Swazey, J. P. (1992). *Spare parts: Organ replacement in American society.* New York: Oxford University Press.

Hamilton, M. M., & Brown, W. (2002). *Black and white and red all over: The story of a friendship.* New York: Public Affairs.

Holtkamp, S. (2002). *Wrapped in mourning: The gift of life and organ donor family trauma.* New York: Taylor & Francis.

Maloney, R., & Wolfelt, A. D. (2001). *Caring for donor families before, during and after.* Fort Collins, CO: Compassion Press.

National Kidney Foundation. (1997; 2nd ed., 2004). *National communications guidelines regarding communication among donor families, transplant candidates/recipients, and health care professionals.* New York: Author.

Prottas, J. (1994). *The most useful gift: Altruism and the public policy of organ transplants.* San Francisco: Jossey-Bass.

U.S. Department of Health and Human Services, Health Care Financing Administration. (1998). Medicare and Medicaid programs; hospital conditions of participation; identification of potential organ, tissue, and eye donors and transplant hospitals' provision of transplant-related data. *Federal Register, 63,* 33856–33874.

U.S. Department of Health and Human Services, Health Resources and Services Administration and Health Care Financing Administration. (2000). *Roles and training in the donation process: A resource guide.* Rockville, MD: Author.

Wendler, D. & Dickert, N. (2001). The consent process for cadaveric organ procurement: How does it work? How can it be improved? *JAMA, 285,* 329–333.

CHAPTER 15

The Ethics of Excess and Deprivation: Implications for End-of-Life Care

Larry R. Churchill

TWO SCENARIOS

In April 2004, L. J., age 90, died at a nursing facility in Connecticut. During his early 80s he was admitted to the hospital several times, for a shoulder fracture following a fall, for pneumonia, and subsequent to a small stroke. A widower without family, L. J. lived alone and described his quality of life as "just tolerable." He indicated to physicians that he did not want to be "tied to machines," but he never signed a living will or other advance directive. A major stroke seven years ago had left him in a persistent vegetative state, and he remained in custodial care in the nursing facility with artificial feeding and skilled nursing care until his death. The total cost of his care over the last decade of his life exceeded $700,000.

In July 2003, U.S. postal workers in North Carolina found an envelope with the word "anthrax," addressed to the President. Authorities traced the envelope back to an unlikely terrorist—Rhonda Smith, an indigent woman who suffered from diabetes and lung disease. She was dependent on oxygen and a variety of prescription medications, and her medical bills left her little to live on. Smith told the Secret Service that she hoped to be caught and sent to jail because once incarcerated she would be provided with free health care (*Raleigh News and Observer*, Nov. 9, 2003).

A PARADOX OF EXCESS AND DEPRIVATION

The U.S. health care system has been described by two of its most prominent analysts as "a paradox of excess and deprivation" (Enthoven & Kronick, 1989). While few Americans would consider devising such an elaborate and dangerous scheme to get their health needs met, Rhonda Smith's problems are a typical story of deprivation. She is one of 44 million persons in the United States who have no health insurance. These uninsured Americans constitute a long-neglected medical underclass that Uwe Reinhardt (1997) has dubbed "health care beggars."

The general dimensions of the health care access problem are well known, but there are also hidden vulnerabilities. At any given point in time only about 84% of Americans have insurance for health services. In addition to the 44 million uninsured, as many as 85 million (38% of the non-elderly population) were without health insurance at some point during 1996–1999, and at least 30 million persons are *under*insured (Short, Graefe, & Schoen, 2003). The underinsured are those with sufficient gaps, exclusions, and limitations in their policies that a major illness would be financially ruinous. But even many of those with insurance, while avoiding bankruptcy, often struggle with costs and delay seeking care. A survey of patients at community health centers conducted by the nonprofit Access Project and Brandeis University found that 40% of all patients at these clinics had a medical debt and that 30% of those with a medical debt are insured (Lazar, 2004).

Eighty percent of the uninsured in the United States are workers, or live in families of workers (Institute of Medicine, 2001). In some cases employees simply cannot afford the coverage their employers offer (a quarter of the American workforce make less than $9 per hour), or their employer does not offer coverage. Most important, the uninsured are generally in poorer health than the insured and see doctors later in the course of an illness, when effective treatment is less likely. Not surprisingly, the uninsured receive about half as many health services as the insured, and they have shorter life expectancies. Recently the Institute of Medicine calculated that lack of insurance accounts for 18,000 premature deaths in the United States annually (Institute of Medicine, 2004). Children are among the most profoundly affected by lack of insurance. One survey indicated that uninsured children are more likely to receive no care at all for sore throat, tonsillitis, ear infection, and asthma (Newacheck, 2000). In sum, being without health insurance in America is hazardous to one's health, or more candidly, lack of insurance leads to poor quality of life, and the extended absence of coverage leads to preventable death. This is, intermittently, a source of national embarrassment, but to date not a sufficient source to mobilize for major changes.

In contrast to health care beggars like Rhonda Smith, insured Americans have access to an unprecedented array of medical technologies, such as magnetic resonance imaging, and superbly equipped intensive care units, operating theaters, and emergency rooms. Indeed, medical technology is so widely available, even in ambulatory clinics and long-term nursing facilities, that many observers worry that those with good insurance coverage receive too many services. Many would consider the last seven years of L. J.'s life just such a problem of "too much." The problem of excess, strikingly, can even be a hazard, since an estimated 44,000 to 98,000 deaths per year in the United States are attributable to medical mistakes (Institute of Medicine, 1999). This number exceeds the death rate from motor vehicle wrecks, breast cancer, and AIDS and costs billions of dollars each year. Most of these deaths occur in hospitals and are the result of mistakes in diagnosis or drug dosage, failure to monitor patients appropriately or to respond to monitoring, wrong-site surgery, and a host of other preventable errors. Still, the American assumption has steadfastly been that more medicine is almost always better medicine, promoting the development of a system in which health is equated with more sophisticated personal medical services. Accordingly, American society expends a greater percentage of its gross domestic product for health care than any other nation, and its physicians are substantially better paid than their European, Japanese, or Canadian counterparts.

Excess in capacity and services, of course, translates into excess costs. Cost escalation is such that in the 19-year period between 1980 and 1999 expenditures for health care quadrupled, from $1,000 per capita to more than $4,000 per capita and from 9% of the gross domestic product to more than 13% (Bodenheimer & Grumbach, 2002). While the rate of health care inflation did subside during the late 1990s owing to the economic boom and the short-term efficiencies of managed care, double-digit inflation for health expenditures had returned by 2000 and has remained constant (Iglehart, 2002). Americans spend roughly 15% of their national wealth on health care, and medical inflation continues to rise at more than double the rate of other goods and services.

A variety of factors contribute to the steep escalation in costs. Among the chief forces at work are financing patterns and cultural beliefs. Until roughly 20 years ago, medical services were almost always delivered by practitioners on a fee-for-service basis. Fees were paid mainly through employer-based policies or government programs, both of which functioned like traditional indemnity insurance. This practice of cost reimbursement rewarded physicians for doing more and bigger procedures, since each procedure could be billed for a separate fee. It also shielded patients from the true costs of care and discouraged questions about the value of services rendered, since third-party payers received the bill. Neither doctors nor patients had an incentive to think about costs.

In the wake of the failed federal reform proposals in 1994, the nation turned to commercial managed care to solve the cost problem. The change was swift and dramatic, so that by the late 1990s less than 20% of U.S. health care was fee-for-service (Freudenheim, 1998). The efficiencies of managed care slowed—and for a one-year period actually reversed— the cost escalation. However, the administrative and oversight changes of managed care were one-time remedies, and were so unpopular with both providers and consumers that some of the most effective cost-control aspects of managed care have been abandoned. Managed care was never a good fit with the traditional physician ethic that stressed care of individual patients, one at a time, rather than concern for fair and efficient allocation of limited services to enrolled members, which was the avowed aim of managed care. Nor were the utilization and cost-control strategies of managed care a good fit with most patients' cultural expectations that more care is usually better care, and that the application of scientific technology in medicine (rather than their own health behaviors) is the chief means for achieving better health. And even during its most successful period in the mid-1990s, managed care's stress on parsimony and cost-effective practices was no match for the continuing technological intensification of medical practice, a major driver of costs.

In the end, the effort to control costs through managed care was not just ineffective, it amplified the problems of access. Many of the cost reductions from managed care were the result of cost shifting, rather than true cost control (Fuchs, 2002). Health care insurers learned from the life and accident insurance business that the easiest way to control costs and increase profits is by careful selection of risks. Translated to the health care business, this means that those most likely to need health services (excluding Medicare patients) will be the least likely to be insured and the first to lose their insurance, and that they will also bear the greatest proportion of what costs are incurred. The "savings" from the efficiencies of managed care were largely the result of insuring healthy people, thereby providing fewer services, shifting the heavy utilizers to other providers; and also shifting more of the cost of services used to patients, in the form of increased deductibles, co-insurance, and more exclusions, and to physicians, in the form of lower reimbursements. In summary, the managed care revolution, while it did reduce costs for some managed care organizations and large employers, increased costs for providers and patients and—except for one brief period in the mid-1990s—did nothing to control the overall cost escalation. Insofar as it shifted costs to patients, it aggravated their lack of access, especially for lower- and middle-income families.

THE PARADOX RESOLVED:
PREDICTABLE EFFECTS OF AN AIMLESS SYSTEM

The pattern of "excess and deprivation" is conspicuous and troubling, but hardly paradoxical. Imagine a health care system conceived as a major engine of the economy, and therefore designed to protect health insurers from adverse risks and to expand the profitability of health-sector markets. Imagine, further, that this system seeks to infuse even the most marginal improvements in drugs and devices into routine medical practice and disseminates them as broadly as possible. Finally, imagine a system that values the income potential and practice options for providers above any rational assessment of how medical services are needed socially. A health care system ordered by such goals is not a speculation, but a reality. It is a fair description of the American system in the early 21st century. Excess and deprivation are the predictable results of such a system.

It is not, of course, the case that these goals and aims were debated and won the approval of the public or its elected representatives. Rather, these goals and aims can be discerned simply by asking who is best served by the current system. If one were to look at the present arrangements and ask, "What are these arrangements designed to achieve? What purposes do they serve?" no responses would fit better than those sketched above. Let me illustrate.

For more than 30 years, federal, state, and local governments have intervened in health care to insure persons whom private insurers did not want—the elderly, the poor, veterans, and more recently, persons whose diseases make them "bad risks," such as HIV, renal failure, and Hanson's disease. The protection of insurers from these liabilities, consistently undertaken for decades, is not just a by-product of our health care system, but one of its goals. The Bush administration's recent efforts to move a portion of Medicare to the private sector are more evidence for the durability of the conviction that private providers are inherently efficient and are an essential part of solving the cost overruns in health care. Yet there is no evidence to support this conviction, especially for Medicare, which returns 98 cents out of every dollar to patient care. Corporate health care programs, which must advertise and show a profit for shareholders, typically incur overhead costs between 10% and 25%. Commenting on the Bush administration's insistence on federal subsidies to entice corporate participation in the new Medicare program, Reinhardt (2003, p. 24) put it succinctly: "To an economist there is something both puzzling and troubling about the idea that a privatized Medicare will be 'viable' only if it is bolstered by a huge tax-financed subsidy for prescription drug coverage that would be largely denied elderly Americans who prefer to stay in the traditional Medicare program."

Also, there can be little doubt that one of the fundamental aims of the U.S. system is to translate pharmacological and technological innovations, even those promising the most marginal of improvements, into routine practice at a rapid rate. Americans are particularly enamored of technological innovations, and both physicians and patients routinely interpret a new therapeutic technique or drug as "better medicine." Hospitals often use their technological prowess to great advantage in marketing. The infusion of public funds into research through the National Institutes of Health, and the impressive spending of pharmaceutical firms for both developing and advertising their products, feeds the American appetite.

Physicians may question how much their professional autonomy has been valued or protected in light of the managerial curtailment of clinical judgment under managed care. Yet patient groups joined professionals in the backlash against managed care during the late 1990s, and one of their most insistent points was that if medical services are denied, the judgment must come from physicians and not from managers or bureaucrats. Also, for the past several decades public funds have paid for a large portion of the costs of medical education, including postgraduate training, and more than 40% of physician fees. Yet physicians remain largely free from public accountability for the uses of their time and talents. There are very few constraints on specialty choice and no restrictions on where a physician may choose to practice, despite the increasing maldistribution of physicians. Eli Ginsberg (1994) reports that in affluent metropolitan suburbs the physician-population ratio is 1 to 250, while in low-income urban areas it is 1 to 15,000. In most areas of the country, physicians practice without competitors in facilities designed for their convenience and often under their control or influence. Despite recent managerial inroads into physician autonomy, the current system clearly protects and greatly rewards physicians.

It is typically assumed that the chief goals of the American health care system are to treat illness, alleviate suffering, and generally improve the health of the population. Regrettably, there is little evidence for this. To be sure, illnesses are treated, suffering alleviated, and health improved, but I believe an impartial observer would conclude that these goals are secondary to the ones I have adumbrated above, which are the de facto purposes of our system. The lofty assumptive goals of better health for the population can be accepted as the real aims of the American system only so long as the uninsured are left out of the picture and costs are ignored.

The most that can be confidently asserted is that a primary purpose of the U.S. system is to meet the personal medical needs of *paying* patients. The uninsured receive fewer health services in both ambulatory and hospital settings, and as noted earlier, they have more morbidity and a shorter life span than their insured counterparts (Davis, 1991). Moreover, the health status of Americans does not compare favorably with that of citizens of other industrialized democracies when measured in terms of life expectancy, infant mortality, cancer and stroke rates, and a variety of other indices. In terms of overall health status, the United States has for some time ranked behind Canada, Japan, Scandinavia, and Western Europe. If meeting the health needs of the population is the chief goal, the U.S. system must be judged a failure.

It could be argued that Americans understand their system and have the one they want; and that when all the evidence is in, there will be no discord between American values and the current arrangements. It is more likely that Americans have not thought much, or at all, about explicitly defining a larger purpose against which the performance of the health system could be measured. Most of us worry about health care only in the short term—whether we and our families will have access to affordable services when we are sick. The issues we are concerned with are typical patient concerns—waiting times; respectful and attentive treatment; explanations of our problem we can understand; whether our illness is serious, and if serious, treatable; and the extent of insurance coverage. It may simply be that most of us will not ask critical questions about the system as long as our own personal health care is secure. If this is accurate, then understanding how far off course the current arrangements are will provide impetus for change. A sober look at the American system indicates the extent to which our access to health care depends on fortuitous events, such as not being born with handicaps or a chronic condition, and the continuation of fragile circumstances, such as our job stability and good health. Very few Americans can look at the current arrangements and believe that their own health care access, or that of their family, is secure. I have argued this point in detail elsewhere (Churchill, 1994).

In sum, excess and deprivation—far from being paradoxical—are predictable outcomes of a system with the de facto priorities enumerated above. The U.S. health care system lacks a guiding social purpose (Reinhardt, 1997). It is an "aimless system" in the sense that its primary mission is not the health of the citizenry. In the absence of this public and socially sanctioned aim, the most ambitious and powerful players—pharmaceutical firms, health care insurers, hospital corporations, and to a lesser degree, organized medicine—are allowed freedom to achieve their own private ends. The result is a great deal of needless suffering.

It is important here not to succumb to the rhetoric of villainy or glibly point to scapegoats for the problems we face. The premature deaths and suffering of those who get into the system too late, or not at all, are not problems created by commercial insurers, pharmaceutical firms, or physicians. Neither commercial insurance nor pharmaceutical and medical technology firms have ever had equity in allocation as their goals. Physician professional associations have only occasionally been advocates for the underserved. These actors are simply playing the roles permitted to them by the vacuum in political leadership regarding the social aims of health care. That America remains the single industrial democracy without a provision for ensuring all its citizens even a modicum of care is the responsibility of our government leaders. The persistence of our aimless system is finally a political and social issue, not a matter of financing or efficiency schemes, profit margins, or professional prerogatives.

BENCHMARKS FOR A BETTER SYSTEM

In January 2004, the Institute of Medicine (IOM) issued its fifth and final report on the uninsured in America. This series of reports, from IOM committees chaired by Mary Sue Coleman and Arthur L. Kellerman, is the most systematic and detailed examination yet available of the nature, scope, and consequences of lack of insurance for individuals, communities, institutions, and the nation as a whole. The fifth report, entitled *Insuring America's Health: Principles and Recommendations*, does not argue for specific changes to remedy the problem, but offers a set of five guiding principles for evaluating the various strategies that have been or will be proposed (Institute of Medicine, 2004). These five principles constitute the missing aims for American health care:

1) Health care coverage should be universal.

2) Health care coverage should be continuous.

3) Health care coverage should be affordable to individuals and families.

4) The health insurance strategy should be affordable and sustainable for society.

5) Health insurance should enhance health and well-being by promoting access to quality care that is effective, efficient, safe, timely, patient-centered, and equitable.

The current system meets none of these benchmarks, or at best meets some of them, some of the time, for the insured population. Currently we are 44 million people away from achieving universal coverage. The stability and continuity of services is thwarted by risk-rating health policies (Light, 1992), by "churning" (Short et al., 2003), by the patchwork of complex eligibility requirements from state and federal bureaucracies, by employers dropping insurance benefits, and by the changing demographics of work, income level, marital status, residence, health status, and other factors. As noted above, over a four-year period as many as 85 million people undergo change in one or more of these features of insurability that renders them at least temporarily uninsured. Affordability is, of course, one of the chief causes of lack of insurance. Moreover, as Daniel Callahan (1990) and others have forcefully argued, our current path in health policy is not sustainable, since constantly escalating costs threaten other realms of social needs and national priorities. Finally, effectiveness is threatened by pressure to market medical products with only marginal improvements; safety is a major concern given the 44,000 to 98,000 annual patient deaths from medical mistakes; and timeliness, being patient-centered, and equity are all contingent on a workable system of access. Universal coverage is the cardinal principle and the key to achieving each of the other four.

Of signal importance, the IOM report is very clear that incremental reforms of the past have failed and are very unlikely to be successful in the future. Take, for example, the State Children's Health Insurance Program (SCHIP). In the 12 states with the largest numbers of uninsured children, fewer children were covered under the combination of SCHIP and Medicaid in 1999 than were covered by Medicaid alone in 1996 (Families USA Foundation, 1999). Gains in SCHIP were offset by losses in Medicaid, to some extent by poor organization in the states, by misunderstanding of the complex requirements for implementation, and by changes in state eligibility rules. The confusion and ineffectiveness of piecemeal programs, usually designed for some especially deserving population—which often curtails use and sometimes stigmatizes those who eventually gain access—typically end in failure, or at best only modest success. The IOM report eschews targeting special groups and creating stopgap benefits at the margins; it calls for a basic rethinking of the system; and it calls for the federal government "to take action to achieve universal coverage and to establish an explicit schedule to reach this goal by 2010" (Institute of Medicine, 2004, p. 14).

IMPLICATIONS FOR END-OF-LIFE CARE

It is hardly surprising that many of the same difficulties that mark the health care system as a whole also impede care at the end of life. Roughly 2.5 million deaths occur in the United States every year, but hospice admissions account for only about 30% of those who die (Jennings, Rynes, D'Onofrio, & Baily, 2003). From one perspective this is a remarkable achievement, since the first U.S. hospice opened its doors only in 1974, and Medicare reimbursement dates only from the early 1980s. Yet given the growing need, 30% is far too low a number.

Cultural attitudes still bar the way to good care for many persons at the end of life. Both physicians and patients and their families often see a referral to hospice as "giving up" rather than providing the right care at the right time in life. For physicians in cancer research, hospice is a competitor; a candid conversation about the probabilities for recovery directly conflicts with the oncology researcher's need for participants in clinical trials (Miller, 2000). This conflict is exacerbated by the current tendency of both investigators and patient-subjects to see research—even early phase dose toxicity studies—as therapeutic (Churchill, Collins, King, Pemberton, & Wailloo, 1998; Daugherty et al., 1995; King et al., in press). Hospice is still not part of the medical mainstream, even for those health professionals without research careers and even sometimes for those within "palliative care" programs, which may or may not offer the full range of holistic social and spiritual supports characteristic of hospice. These cultural and professional factors, combined with the American penchant for optimism and death-denial, go a long way toward accounting for the fact that the average length of stay in hospice is short and has been declining steadily since the early 1990s (Jennings et al., 2003). This declining length of stay means more intensive professional services per day per patient—as patients and their families and other caregivers learn and gain confidence in this new form of care—and therefore higher costs per admission. Hence, a recent analysis of hospice costs nationwide indicated that they exceed revenues by 10% to 20% (National Hospice and Palliative Care Organization, 2001).

An equally important factor that inhibits end-of-life care, especially hospice, from being fully accessible, continuous, and effective is the philosophy under which services are offered and reimbursed. Eligibility for hospice is now based on a prognosis of 6 months or less. While eligibility for the Medicare Hospice Benefit can be recertified if people outlive their prognosis, this is not well understood, and in the past it was a contentious point with the Center for Medicare and Medicaid Services, which initially approached this question with worries about fraud and overuse, rather than an understanding of the uncertainties of prognosis and the need for a continuum of care. The fact that the original intent of hospice legislation was to provide for short-term care at the very end of life has curtailed opportunities for integrating hospice and palliative care into ongoing chronic illness care at all stages of life. Unless changes are made, this loss will be magnified many times over the next three decades as the boomer generation ages.

The report of the Hastings Center's Project on Increasing Access to Hospice Care points in the right direction. The report correctly observes that "hospice is now based on a medical prognosis of remaining length of life as a portal to an isolated package of services offered in essentially an all-or-nothing fashion. This approach must give way to a more flexible assessment of the patient and family's condition within a continuum of services coordinated to meet changing needs over time" (Jennings et al., 2003, p. S27). This will require not just rethinking eligibility, but rethinking the place of hospice and palliative care in the health care system as a whole and displacing the priority of prognosis in favor of a more patient-centered approach.

CONCLUSION: THE NEEDLESS GRIEF OF POOR POLICIES

Learning to live with loss and grief is an inevitable part of growing up, and we are not whole and mature persons until we have. Yet certain kinds of grief—grief resulting from losses incurred because of an inhumane system of health care—should provoke our indignation. They are not the subject of psychological and spiritual maturity but of basic human decency and justice in social policy.

Among the most egregious losses are the 18,000 annual premature deaths attributable to lack of health insurance. These are losses from deprivation. Next on this list are the staggering 44,000 to 98,000 annual deaths from medical mistakes. These are at least in part losses from excess. Beyond are the morbidities associated with the uninsured and the victims of error. There is no official record of these morbidities, but the pain and suffering, lost opportunities, diminished lives, and gnawing anxieties over lack of stable access to physicians and medications are substantial. As Michael Walzer (1983) has argued, lack of access to needed health services is not just dangerous; it is also degrading. Arguably the biggest ethical issue in health care is the absence of a system that puts the health needs of the population first, and the continuation of a system that is increasingly brutal and inequitable to those who help to pay for it.

The current policies play havoc with end-of-life care as well, creating ethical problems where they would not otherwise exist. Patterns of aggressive and technologically intensive care for those with poor prognoses and the consequent failure to refer to hospice or palliative care services are a source of needless grief for many. To be sure, not everyone would choose hospice, even if all barriers were eliminated. Yet given its manifest success, it is reasonable to assume that many with severe illnesses and limited prognoses would elect hospice if their physicians were more open to recommending these services and if families were more aware of what hospice can provide and more accepting of human finitude. Many of the vexing problems at the end of life with which caregivers and medical ethicists routinely struggle are products of too much intensive technology, arriving too late to be effective, accompanied by too much guilt in families and caregivers for an earlier pattern of deprivation. We cannot make up at the end for a lifetime of neglect. ■

Larry R. Churchill is Ann Geddes Stahlman Professor of Medical Ethics, Vanderbilt University. He has authored and edited several books on ethics, social justice, and U.S. health policy, including most recently Ethical Dimensions of Health Policy, *with Marion Danis and Carolyn Clancy (Oxford University Press, 2002). Dr. Churchill also helped to conceptualize and wrote the Introduction to* Parting: A Handbook for Spiritual Care at the End of Life *(University of North Carolina Press, 2004).*

REFERENCES

Bodenheimer, T., Grumbach, K. (2002). A primary care home for Americans. *JAMA, 288*, 889-893.

Callahan, D. (1990). *What kind of life: The limits of medical progress.* New York: Simon and Schuster.

Churchill, L. (1994). *Self-interest and universal health care: Why well-insured Americans should support coverage for everyone.* Cambridge, MA: Harvard University Press.

Churchill, L., Collins, M., King, N., Pemberton, S., & Wailoo, K. (1998). Genetic Research as therapy: Implications of "gene therapy" for informed consent. *Journal of Law, Medicine and Ethics, 26*, 38–47.

Daugherty, C., Ratain, J., Grochopwski, C., Stocking, C., Kodish, E., Mick, R., & Siegler, M. (1995). Perceptions of cancer patients and their physicians involved in phase 1 trials. *Journal of Clinical Oncology, 13*, 1062–1072.

Davis, K. (1991). Inequality and access to health care. *Milbank Quarterly, 69*, 253–274.

Enthoven, A., & Kronick, R. (1989). A consumer choice health plan for the 1990s. *New England Journal of Medicine, 320*, 29.

Families USA Foundation. (1999). America is taking one step forward and one step back in covering children's health. Retrieved October 20, 1999, from www.familiesusa.org

Freudenheim, M. (1998, September 29). (Loosely) managed care is in demand: Provider plans zooming over restricted HMOs. *New York Times*, p. C1.

Fuchs, V. (2002). What's ahead for health insurance in the United States? *New England Journal of Medicine, 346*,1822–1824.

Ginsberg, E. (1994). *Medical gridlock and health reform.* Boulder, CO: Westview Press, 69.

Iglehart, J. (2002). Changing health insurance trends. *New England Journal of Medicine, 347*, 956–962.

Institute of Medicine. (1999). *To err is human.* Washington, DC: National Academies Press.

Institute of Medicine. (2001). *Coverage matters.* Washington, DC: National Academics Press.

Institute of Medicine. (2004). *Insuring America's health.* Washington, DC: National Academies Press.

Jennings, B., Rynes, T., D'Onofrio, C., & Baily, M. (2003). Access to hospice care: Expanding boundaries, overcoming barriers, report of the National Hospice Workgroup. *Hastings Center Report* (Special Suppl.), S3–S59.

King, N., Henderson, G., Churchill, L., Davis, A., Hull, S., Nelson, D., et al. (in press). Consent forms and the therapeutic misconception. *IRB: Ethics and Human Research.*

Lazar, K. (2004, February 18). High costs cause some to forgo health care, survey finds. *Boston Herald*, p. 9.

Light, D. (1992). The practice and ethics of risk-rated health insurance. *JAMA, 267*, 2503–2508.

Miller, M. (2000). Phase 1 cancer trials: A collusion of misunderstanding. *Hastings Center Report, 30*, 34–42.

National Hospice and Palliative Care Organization. (2001). The costs of hospice care: An actuarial evaluation of the Medicare Hospital Benefit, report from Milliman, USA, Inc. Retrieved, April 20, 2004, from www.nhpco.org

Newacheck, P., Hughes, D., Hung Y., Wong, S., Stoddard, J. (2000) The unmet health needs of America's children. *Pediatrics, 105*, 989-997.

Reinhardt, U. (1997). Wanted: A clearly articulated social ethic for American health care. *JAMA, 278,* 1446–1467.

Reinhardt, U. (2003). *A primer for journalists on Medicare reform proposals.* Princeton, NJ: Woodrow Wilson School of Public and International Affairs.

Short, P., Graefe, D., & Schoen, C. (2003, November). Churn, churn, churn: How instability of health insurance shapes America's uninsurance problem. *Commonwealth Fund Issue Brief.*

Walzer, M. (1983). *Spheres of justice: A defense of pluralism and equality.* New York: Basic Books.

Conclusion

This final section, as with the other books in the Hospice Foundation of America's *Living with Grief*® series, ends with a list of resources. McGahey Veglahn does more than compile a list of associations and organizations that can offer assistance. She reminds readers that these decisions need not be made alone—suggesting that individuals consult their family, friends, and faith communities.

That comment echoes Doka's suggestions. Doka reaffirms that ethical decisions have consequences that may reach far beyond the end of a patient's life. These decisions may complicate or facilitate the grief of survivors. Doka suggests that a deliberative, consultative process may mitigate some of the deleterious effects of ethical decisions on the mourning process.

The case study submitted by Alive Hospice illustrates this. This case also explores the difficulties that technology presents to end of life care. Hospices often struggle with how to proceed with such care when external devices such as cardiac implants are involved. Beyond these questions, this case raises another issue. How will the possibly hastened death affect the grief of the surviving husband?

Kastenbaum's chapter considers future issues in end-of-life ethics. Like a Janus mask, he looks both backward and forward. Kastenbaum recounts how ethical debates moved from "Should the dying person be told?" to more complicated considerations of medical futility, autonomy, and consent. As he peers into the future, he sees two potential dilemmas. The first is a catastrophic plague that would put ethics to the test as health care providers struggle to maintain moral principles in the face of a calamitous epidemic. The second is already upon us—the challenge that the rising toll of Alzheimer's disease and other dementias will have on such ethical issues as autonomy and futility.

There may be one more future challenge. New reproductive technologies are already intersecting with end-of-life concerns. Can a family secure genetic material from an unconscious patient to maintain a biological line or legacy? Who determines the fate of a frozen embryo if the parents are no longer capable of making decisions? As the introduction to Section I noted, technological advances have eroded the historic consensus on when life begins and ends, creating a continuing context for ethical controversy and political debate. ■

CHAPTER 16

Ethics, End-of-Life Decisions, and Grief

Kenneth J. Doka

This chapter is based upon and draws from the author's paper "Ethics, End-of-Life Decisions and Grief," published in Mortality.

End-of-life decisions do more than prolong or terminate a life. These ethical decisions may haunt survivors long after the death occurs. They may complicate grief, creating family dissension, inhibiting support, and increasing ambivalence over the nature or circumstances of the death. Conversely, end-of-life decisions need not always be negative. In other circumstances, they may facilitate the grief process, allowing survivors a meaningful end to the story of a loved one, providing survivors a modicum of control that ends a person's pain, following the deceased's wishes, or simply seeming to survivors like the right thing to do.

A letter I received a number of years ago illustrates that point. The author of the letter, identified only as John, wrote that he had assisted in the death of his mother. She had been diagnosed with a virulent form of cancer. In great pain, she asked that her children aid her as she ended her life. John and his siblings agreed. What John did not realize was that the ethical dilemma would deeply influence his subsequent grief.

He wrote,

> The "normal grief" of losing a parent was further aggravated by a sense that there are some in society that would disapprove of her decision or feel it was improper or even criminal for us to assist. Some prosecutors might have a hard time overlooking it. In Minnesota it's a felony to assist in suicide, subject to 15 years in prison. I don't know that what we did fits a legal definition of "assist," but we supported her in the decision. It seems incongruous that we all might be part of a criminal conspiracy. Even though I don't think a jury would convict us, we don't want to have to defend ourselves in a court of law or even to the public.
>
> Perhaps someday, if Congress doesn't try to protect us from ourselves, we'll be able to talk about it publicly. My siblings and their spouses are all highly educated, mostly professional people, respected in our fields and not used to being muted by controversy. At this time we don't want to be poster children for assisted suicide. Unlike Kevorkicide (can I coin a term?), it was a very private, very personal act of love and compassion. And I have come to understand that the resulting grief is disenfranchised.

In this case, John faces an ethical dilemma. On the one hand, his mother is in pain and wishes to end her life. On the other hand, John realizes that assisting his mother places him in legal jeopardy. While he understands the act to be merciful and has the support of his siblings and extended family, his decision still generates ambivalence. He believes the action might arouse investigation and legal prosecution. The letter indicates a need to process his grief, and, in doing so, to explore his role in his mother's decision to terminate her life. Yet, well aware of the potential limits to confidentiality, he has to do it anonymously in a letter— unable to even seek a reply. Counseling seems precluded by the ambiguity of Minnesota's laws.

Positively or negatively, the end-of-life decisions that survivors make influence subsequent grief. This chapter explores that influence. It begins with three central assumptions.

The first is that the end-of-life decisions, like so many of the factors that affect grief responses, can be facilitating or complicating, perhaps even at the same time. The chapter explores both aspects of end-of-life decisions.

The second assumption is that professional caregivers—medical and nursing staff—as well as families have a stake in these ethical decisions. They may have opinions as to the best course of action. Staff, especially in long-term care institutions, may develop attachments to the patient. Hence, ethical decisions may influence the course of bereavement in both family and staff. In addition, each group may influence the other's decisions. For both family and staff, the aftermath of these actions or subsequent behaviors may generate doubt as to the wisdom of these decisions.

The third assumption is that these decisions cannot be understood apart from their context. Prolonged illnesses or sudden deaths in and of themselves each create complications to grief. Moreover, these contexts are not mutually exclusive. As Rando (1993) reminds us, persons even within the context of a lengthy illness can die "suddenly"—that is, at an unexpected time or in an unanticipated manner. The person slowly dying of cancer is not immune to a sudden deterioration or even a heart attack or stroke. In short, then, end-of-life decisions cannot be viewed apart from the context in which they occur. This context will eventually influence the experience of grief.

There is one additional assumption. There are strategies both during and after the decision making that can be helpful to families and staff. These strategies can enhance the possibility that this decision-making process can be facilitative of grief while mitigating complicating features. A final section of the chapter considers these strategies.

COMPLICATING FACTORS

As stated earlier, end-of-life decisions can both facilitate and complicate grief—sometimes simultaneously. In addition, end-of-life decisions cannot be separated from the context in which they occur. Research has indicated that sudden deaths as well as deaths that follow long-term illness each create their own complications (Rando, 1993).

Sudden deaths often occur from circumstances such as an accident, suicide, or homicide. While each circumstance creates unique issues for bereavement, all share complicating factors, such as a sense that the death was preventable and a lack of forewarning. These factors also can complicate reactions to a sudden death from natural causes such as a heart attack, aneurysm, or stroke. Here, too, there is preventability and lack of forewarning. In such circumstances, ethical decisions such as terminating treatment or stopping heroic measures are often undertaken in both shock and grief, with little forethought.

There are other factors when the illness is prolonged. Family caregivers may be highly stressed as they cope with the incessant physical, financial, social, and psychological demands of life-threatening illness. It may be difficult to witness the slow deterioration and pain of the dying patient. The illness may generate considerable ambivalence as family members simultaneously wish for death and an end of the person's and family's suffering and wish that the person would remain alive. There also may be ambivalence as the person's physical appearance deteriorates to such an extent that family members are repulsed even as they seek to care and to comfort. Ambivalence has long been identified as a factor that complicates grief (Rando, 1993; Worden, 2002).

End-of-life dilemmas themselves can reflect and even generate considerable ambivalence. The individual or family making the decision can be torn between a desire to end suffering and a continued quest to retain hope even in the face of impending death. Individuals or family members may experience conflict between following their own beliefs and choices and honoring the expressed wishes or beliefs of the deceased. The following case, drawn from clinical experience, illustrates this conflict:

> My husband had made it clear that he did not want continued treatment when we knew it to be futile. However, it was hard to accept that. I believed that when there is life, there is always hope. He would not want anything more. Yet, I felt I should continue. I followed his wishes and he died shortly afterward. I still wonder if I should have kept on going.

This passage suggests another potential factor in end-of-life decisions. Normally, one person within the family system may hold the health proxy. In the United States, such a proxy authorizes a given person to make medical decisions for an individual incapable (perhaps because of unconsciousness or diminished capacity) of making such decisions. Family members may differ in their abilities to communicate with one another and in their opinions about what should be done. Thus, end-of-life decisions can create or revive family conflicts. These conflicts in turn can render the process of decision making more complex. They may limit subsequent support while generating concurrent crises such as family fights that complicate the grief process. In some cases, family disagreements and subsequent legal actions can generate considerable publicity and debate can even polarize communities, further limiting support and generating increased ambivalence about the decision process. These factors, too, complicate grief (Rando, 1993; Worden, 2002).

> I held his [her father's] health proxy. My sister came in from California. She wanted [artificial] feeding to continue. I had kept it so she could be there when he died. Now I knew it was time to stop. She did not agree. I told her this was Dad's wish. She knew that but still could not let go. Finally after four days, I said "stop." Because there was family disagreement, the ethics committee became involved. Dad died a day later. I felt one more painful day. My sister felt she was right since he died naturally— whatever that means—the day before the committee would decide. She left right after the funeral. We have not spoken since the funeral.

Some of the decisions that may be made, such as assisting a suicide, can create additional issues for survivors. They may lead to legal investigations that add to the stress of the loss. The decision may isolate the proxy from other family members. It may, as the opening letter indicated, *disenfranchise grief.*

Disenfranchised grief refers to a loss that cannot be openly acknowledged, socially sanctioned, or publicly mourned (Doka, 2002). The individual experiences a loss but can neither share the full circumstances of the death nor receive subsequent support. Thus, the end-of-life decisions that individuals make may alienate others within the family system or even risk public censure—disenfranchising their grief.

The manner of death, too, may complicate subsequent grief. Even the decision to terminate life support may not ensure an easy death. Family members may interpret or misinterpret the final actions of the dying person as evidence of pain. Even when the death does not occur with signs of evident distress, families and especially decision makers may still worry about the way the person died. For example, it is generally believed by the medical community that neither artificial feeding nor hydration is always necessarily palliative. Yet, decision makers or other family members may still perceive the patient as suffering from thirst or starvation. These images can haunt subsequent bereavement.

Even decisions to continue treatment may generate issues. Families may feel, in retrospect, that they have let the person suffer needlessly. They may sense the active disapproval and even isolation of medical personnel. In other cases, the pain experienced by the dying individual may cause family decision makers to wish that they had taken a more proactive role to end the suffering. This may be one reason that Swarte, van der Lee, van der Born, van den Bout, and Heintz (2003) found that in the Netherlands, family and friends of individuals who died by euthanasia seem to have less intense grief manifestations than those of individuals who died by natural death from cancer.

FACILITATING FACTORS

End-of-life decisions may not always compound bereavement. In some cases, active decision making at the end of life can be a facilitating factor, easing the strains of grief. Parsons and Lidz (1967) have challenged the notion that contemporary Western societies deny death. Instead, the authors suggest that Western societies take an activist orientation toward death—accepting its inevitability but trying to control its timing and nature.

The hospice and palliative care movements, as well as the movement toward physician-assisted suicide, can be seen as extensions of this orientation. While these movements accept that death occurs, they attempt to assert some control over the way the person dies, trying to make that death less painful, and in physician-assisted suicide, timed to the patient's choice.

Individual end-of-life decisions also can provide that sense of control at an otherwise uncontrollable time. This notion of control may mitigate the sense of powerlessness that one often feels in the face of death.

Moreover, these decisions may be the end result of a process that in and of itself is therapeutic. The best end-of-life decisions are made in a reflective process wherein the individual consults with medical personnel as well as other family members. The process can do much to ease subsequent grief. It can allow consensus building that can generate support and ease isolation. It can offer increased information and discussion that acknowledges the inevitability of death and the futility of further medical interventions and so can assist survivors in accepting the reality of death. The decision-making process can provide an opportunity to confront painful emotions and finish unfinished business. In some cases, this process provokes strong spiritual reflection as one assesses not only how one's philosophy or theology addresses the ethical issues involved but also how one's spirituality more directly speaks to the very loss. All of these factors may ease the tasks that one struggles with in grief (Worden, 2002).

Product as well as process may have a role in facilitating grief. Neimeyer (2001) notes that the reconstruction of meaning is a major factor in coping with grief. An individual may define the decision-making process as enabling a loved one to die a good death, perhaps by easing pain or fulfilling that person's wishes and reaffirming the individual's own responsibility. These inferred meanings might offer subsequent comfort.

Even if one cannot find meanings in the nature of death, one might see decisions, for example, to allow an autopsy or donate tissue or organs, as conferring subsequent benefits, incidental to the death. A person may see that these decisions benefited others or allowed medical science to find or to confirm new information. Finding benefits also facilitates the grief process (Frantz, Farrell, & Trolley, 2001).

PROFESSIONAL CAREGIVERS: BEYOND ETHICAL ROUNDS

Family members are not the only ones with a stake in decision making. Professional caregivers also may be in deep distress over ethical decisions.

A number of years ago, there was a case in a local nursing home of a woman in the advanced stages of Alzheimer's disease who was dying of cancer. The woman thought everyone who worked around her was a son, daughter, or parent. She treated them as such. She endeared herself to the staff. Her husband, old and infirm himself, barely visited. There came a point when he asked that treatment cease. The staff felt considerable distress at her death. The ethics committee reviewed the decision, showing the woman's advanced directives and reminding staff that artificial feeding and hydration are not always palliative. At the conclusion of the discussion, one of nurses stood up and said, "If it is so damn ethical, why do I feel so bad?" (Doka, 1994).

Staff members had become deeply attached to the woman. They experienced grief at her death. The initial intervention simply served to explain the ethical process that led to a decision to terminate all treatment, including nutrition and hydration. The staff had not been consulted before the decision was made. A review of the decision and a reaffirmation that it had been carefully made in conjunction with an ethics committee did little to mitigate staff grief.

The point is that ethical decisions cannot be dealt with only at a cognitive level nor be seen as the responsibility only of families and ethics committees. Caregiver grief can often be disenfranchised (Doka, 2002). Caregivers can become highly attached to patients. In fact, Fulton (1987) applied the "Stockholm syndrome"—the long-accepted concept that captive can identify with captors—to the care of the dying. To Fulton, the essence of the Stockholm syndrome is that crisis situations intensify the process of bonding. When patients die, caregivers may experience profound grief. This grief may be exacerbated when caregivers feel power-less over the decisions that may govern a person's death. Both the lack of a formal role in this decision-making process and subsequent inattention to caregiver grief can complicate that bereavement, engendering distress and compassion fatigue (Doka, 1994; Puntillo et al., 2001).

IMPLICATIONS FOR PROFESSIONAL AND FAMILY CAREGIVERS

Though ethical decisions at the end of life can have significant effects on the grief reactions of both family members and professional caregivers (Richmond & Ross, 1994; Swarte & Heintz, 1999; Walwork & Ellison, 1985), there has not been much discussion of how the process by which end-of-life decisions are made and implemented can be made more therapeutic. A few points seem to be central.

The grief of family members is facilitated when they are encouraged to have a deliberative and inclusive process. Decisions to terminate treatment arouse strong feelings of ambivalence (Richmond & Ross, 1994; Walwork & Ellison, 1985). In addition, Foster and McLellan (2002) found that individuals report that they rely on family and friends to help make their end-of-life decisions. Such consulting is critical, as it develops a greater level of consensus and subsequent support. However, such a process does take time. This time allows the family an opportunity to weave their decisions into a consistent narrative of the patient's illness and death (Gilbert, 2002).

This process cannot be rushed. When families are engaged in the process, it is critical that physicians and others do not attempt to apply pressure to quicken that process. Two comments, drawn from clinical experience, illustrate the role of that deliberative process.

> His physician [i.e., the client's father's] kept pushing for us to make decisions to continue treatments long after it was necessary. We continued to ask, "How is this palliative?" He never could answer. Finally he simply said, "It's what I would do for my father." I said, "Fine, but you give us no compelling reason to do it to my Dad." Even now I am still troubled by his intrusion. My mother, though, was fearful—feeling we should listen to the doctor.

While in this case, the doctor's interference with the decision-making process created a note of distress, in the next case, the physician's respect for the family process was clearly appreciated.

The doctor was wonderful. She laid out the facts, all the options, patiently answered all our questions. It seemed clear that Mom would not emerge from her vegetative state. Yet, we still decided to wait a few days before disconnecting life support. We decided as a family that we would rather wonder if we waited too long rather than worry we terminated support quickly. This doctor understood. When Mom died, we were ready and at peace with our decision.

Moreover, the process may not end and with the patient's death. After the death, decision-makers may need to review the decisions that they made in the course of the illness. Physicians need to understand that this is a critical aspect of care and one that is both necessary and facilitative of the grief process.

This process, however, should not be restricted to family members; staff members, too, have a stake in ethical decisions. They, too, need to be debriefed when patients die, especially when that death follows end-of-life decisions that may be seen as either prolonging suffering or hastening death. These debriefings should not only concentrate on the ethics of the decision-making process but should acknowledge the ways that these decisions may influence caregiver grief (see Doka, 1994; Puntillo et al., 2001).

Ethical decisions never arise in a vacuum. Culture, technology, social and individual values, spiritual and religious traditions, and legal struggles are among the many factors that frame ethics. It is critical, then, to recognize the complement of that fact. Ethical decisions do not proceed in a vacuum either. Decisions that have been made may continue to be reconsidered and reviewed long after the choice and its consequences. ■

*Kenneth J. Doka is a Professor of Gerontology at the Graduate School
of The College of New Rochelle and Senior Consultant to the Hospice
Foundation of America. A prolific author, Dr. Doka has authored or edited
17 books including The Hospice Foundation of America's* Living with Grief®
*series. In addition to these books, he has published over 60 article and book
chapters. Dr. Doka is editor of both* Omega *and* Journeys: A Newsletter for
the Bereaved.

*Dr. Doka was elected President of the Association for Death Education
and Counseling in 1993. In 1995, he was elected to the Board of Directors
of the International Work Group on Dying, Death and Bereavement and
served as chair from 1997-1999. The Association for Death Education and
Counseling presented him with an Award for Outstanding Contributions in
the Field of Death Education in 1998.*

REFERENCES

Doka, K. J. (1994). Caregiver distress: If it is so ethical, why does it
feel so bad? *Critical Issues in Clinical Care Nursing, 5,* 346–347.

Doka, K. J. (Ed.). (2002). *Disenfranchised grief: New directions, challenges,
and strategies for practice.* Champaign, IL: Research Press.

Foster, L., & McLellan, L. (2002). Translating psychosocial insight into
ethical discussions supportive of families in end-of-life decision-making.
Social Work in Health Care, 35(3), 37–51.

Frantz, T., Farrell, M., & Trolley, B. (2001). Positive outcomes of losing
a loved one. In R. A. Neimeyer (Ed.), *Meaning reconstruction of the
experience of loss.* Washington, DC: American Psychological Association.

Fulton, R., (April, 1987) *Anticipatory Grief,* Presentation to Association
for Death Education and Counseling.

Gilbert, K. (2002). Taking a narrative approach to grief research:
Finding meaning in stories. *Death Studies, 26,* 223–239.

Neimeyer, R. A. (Ed.). (2001). *Meaning reconstruction of the experience
of loss.* Washington, DC: American Psychological Association.

Parsons, T., & Lidz, V. (1967). Death in American society.
In E. Shneidman (Ed.), *Essays in self-destruction.* New York: Aronsen.

Puntillo, K., Benner, P., Drought, T., Drew, B., Stotts, N., Stannard, D., et al. (2001). End-of-life issues in intensive care units: A national random survey of nurses' knowledge and beliefs. *American Journal of Clinical Care, 10,* 216–229.

Rando, T. A. (1993). *The treatment of complicated mourning.* Champaign, IL: Research Press.

Richmond, B., & Ross, M. (1994). Responses to AIDS-related bereavement. *Journal of Psychosocial Oncology, 12,* 143–163.

Swarte, N., & Heintz, A. (1999). Euthanasia and physician-assisted suicide. *Annals of Medicine, 31,* 364–371.

Swarte, N., van der Lee, M., van der Born, J., van den Bout, J., & Heintz, A. (2003). Effects of euthanasia on the bereaved family and friends: A cross sectional study. *British Medical Journal, 327,* 189–192.

Walwork, E., & Ellison, P. (1985). Follow-up of family of neonates in whom life support was withdrawn. *Clinical Pediatrics, 24*(1), 12–20.

Worden, W. (2002). *Grief counseling and grief therapy* (3rd ed.). New York: Springer.

Withdrawal of Implantable Cardiac Devices

Alive Hospice, Nashville, Tennessee

Marilyn is a 61-year old with a 7-year history of pacemaker implantation secondary to a fatal arrhythmia. Three years later she was diagnosed with amyotrophic lateral sclerosis (ALS). One year before hospice admission, upon the advent of a rapid decline in clinical status, she requested deactivation of her pacemaker, knowing that her death would be imminent. Her cardiologist refused. On admission to hospice, she again requested that her pacemaker be turned off. She was now completely paralyzed and totally dependent, nutrition was provided via a percutaneous endoscopic gastrotomy (PEG) tube, and bi-level positive airway pressure (Bi-PAP) was being used to supplement her impaired respiratory status. She experienced depression. Her husband, though saddened by the prospect of a hastened death, was amenable to her wishes. Communication was possible only via a communication board, but it was clear that Marilyn retained sharp intellect and appropriate decision-making capacity. It was her intent to hasten her death, relieving herself of further suffering from her ALS. She related that shortness of breath and fear of suffocation prompted her decision and request. The plea was posed directly to the team nurse, social worker, chaplain, and medical director on various visits. Appropriate psychospiritual, nursing, and medical interventions were instituted to address the depression, angst, and dyspnea.

A case conference was convened, followed by an ethics consultation, a full ethics committee discussion, and an agency grand rounds. At each level of this process, the patient's wishes and intent were identified, and the medical and psychospiritual ramifications were discussed. A number of issues and questions were raised.

Discussion

- Are there specific life-sustaining devices or procedures that could be considered for withdrawal, and others that cannot or should not be evaluated for this purpose? While ventilator withdrawal, refusal of chemotherapy, or discontinuation of dialysis in futile circumstances are generally accepted by the medical and lay communities, what about devices that carry a trivial symptom burden to the patient and have a clear opportunity to sustain life?

- What is the relevance of such devices or procedures to the primary hospice diagnosis? Is the relationship of the device to the hospice diagnosis of significance? Must the process of discontinuation or withdrawal be relevant to the terminal disease process for it to be considered? Does withdrawal of devices unrelated to the terminal diagnosis constitute the practice of assisted suicide or euthanasia?

- Is there a substantive difference between external devices or interventions versus those that are implanted and unseen?

- What would be the practical and psychological impact of withdrawal of nutrition or Bi-PAP as opposed to deactivation of her pacemaker, since withdrawal of those interventions would likewise hasten death? Is it appropriate to forward that recommendation to the patient in preference to pacemaker withdrawal?

Hospice traditionally operates under a rubric that focuses on quality of life and eschews a primary intention of either hastening death or artificially prolonging life. The decisions under consideration in this case require that the hospice team adjust to the potential that if the pacemaker is deactivated, the patient's life is shortened as a direct impact of that action—the ALS would have no opportunity to "run its natural course." Conversely, continuation of the pacemaker along with the tube feedings and Bi-PAP interventions would allow the patient's life to be extended beyond what the natural process would dictate.

Conventional hospice philosophy provides for "self-determined life closure," in which the patient is able to script an end-of-life scenario as much as the disease process and law might allow. That ethic comes into sharp focus in a case such as Marilyn's, in which hospice team members must negotiate their own personal reactions to the possibility of hastening death or prolonging life. ■

John Mulder, MD, is Medical Director for Alive Hospice, and is an assistant professor at Vanderbilt University School of Medicine. Dr. Mulder submitted this case study on behalf of the Alive Hospice Ethics Committee.

CHAPTER 17

Emerging Ethical Issues in the 21st Century

Robert Kastenbaum

The past is an uncertain but indispensable guide to the future. Its lessons must be interpreted by people who are caught up in the present. Society is often unprepared for catastrophic new (or renewed) threats to life and their accompanying challenges for care of the dying. It is reasonable, then, to learn from the past but to exercise caution with the inferences we draw. This chapter first reviews ethical issues that have arisen since the modern death awareness movement announced itself. Those ethical debates can help us develop perspective on current and possible future controversies. At least they will remind us that the issues of the moment are often superseded by other concerns. And perhaps we will be able to discern a historical pattern in these transitions. Those ethical debates arose within particular socio-medical contexts that we should recall.

We begin a visit to a past that many readers will recognize.

...AFTER A LONG ILLNESS

We are in the middle of the 20th century. Our local newspaper reports all known "passings." Every expired Somebody has a place within the alphabetical procession of death notices. Several notables (mostly men or the very, very old) receive obituaries (Moremen, 2003). The certified causes of death are seldom identified. Heart disease has recently become the leading cause of death in the United States, so it becomes the best-guess default. It is not the most disturbing cause, however.

There are two causes of death that we definitely don't want to encounter. Suicide is still widely regarded as shameful or sinful (Colt, 1991). Physicians, coroners, and editors try to shield us from such troubling reports with verbal sleight of hand.

Cancer is even more frightening. The second most common cause of death, cancer is free to stalk the imagination, neither restrained by fact nor comforted by sharing. *Somebody, therefore, passed away after a long illness* (don't ask what).

Biomedical ethics exists, but as a marginalized specialty. A few protothanatologists notice the disquieting quiet that surrounds dying, death, and grief. But they are pretty much ignored—so no harm done to prevailing attitudes and practices.

As we turn the corner into the 1960s, the concealing mist starts to dissolve. A movement of the wounded, the grieving, and the compassionate is arising from the embers of World War II. There has been too much loss to ignore. This grassroots movement is fueled by the resolve to take back our lives—and deaths—from a world that has become increasingly indifferent to human values (Kastenbaum, 1993). The international hospice movement, peer support groups, death education and counseling, and other manifestations of a maturing societal response to death will soon surface.

THE FIRST "SHOULD?"

What most commands our attention here is the articulation of a "should" followed by a question mark. This is dangerous syntax for the status quo. The first ethical question is *"Should the patient be told?"* More refined inquiries will follow, such as *"How much should the patient be told—and by whom?"* (Dodge, 1963). The ensuing discussions will contribute to a broader awareness of patient rights and physician responsibility; informed consent, for example, is just down the road. There is an immediate effect as well. Question will follow question, and answers will be subjected to intense cross-examination. Here, perhaps, is a working principle about ethical principles: *Questions beget more questions, and then practically everything can come into question.* Totalitarian leaders have long been aware of this principle.

Family members, physicians, and nurses had been persuading one another that they were doing the right thing in protecting dying people from knowledge of their condition. This had been an uncomfortable act for most. The prohibition engendered its own anxiety-provoking questions, for example, "What should I say when I'm not saying what I shouldn't say?" The resulting tension often led to physical and emotional distancing from terminally ill people. The prospect of now "having to be real" with a dying person could be terrifying for those who had been trying to avoid everything connected with death in their own lives. If telling—or simply acknowledging—the truth were to become the next "right thing," then many people would have to confront their own anxieties. Yet there was often a sense of relief in shedding the burden of pretense (Glaser & Strauss, 1966) and a sense of rightness in preserving the integrity of the relationship through honest communication.

THE 11TH COMMANDMENT

Mainline medical opinion insisted that telling the dying person the truth would destroy hope and precipitate a collapse into despair. Many nurses who were active at this time can recall scoldings about leaking the truth in an unguarded moment.

Seldom were specific ethical principles articulated or invoked. It just seemed obvious that we should keep hope alive—it would be cruel to do otherwise. This proposition was bolstered by the "11th commandment": "Thou shalt not get personally involved!" So ubiquitous was this teaching in schools of medicine and nursing and so stringently was it enforced by supervisory and peer pressure that most professional caregivers felt obliged to seal off their feelings of empathy, compassion, and personal distress in working with people whose lives they could not save.

The situation was complicated, though, by the fact that the physicians who enforced the prohibitory norm often supported the principles of honesty and admired a serene acceptance of mortality. Some physicians (e.g., Kasper, 1959) were starting to call attention to the misplaced application of "scientific objectivity" to the care of dying people. Physicians' personal values often were at war with unrealistic expectations to "cure death." Physicians increasingly recognized avoiding truth-telling and not "getting involved" as strategies for managing their own anxieties, which would be intensified if patients and their families fell apart. Unquestionably, physicians wanted to "do right" by their patients. One could wonder, however, whether their actions and attitudes were based on clearly articulated ethical principles or on the understandable desire to minimize their exposure to stressful interactions.

THE MODEL DEATH AND THE PRIMARY ETHICAL ISSUE

During this early phase of the death awareness movement, the model dying patient had "incurable" cancer and would suffer for an extended period until released by death: what Glaser & Strauss (1968) described as a "lingering trajectory." The ethical question centered on information control. In practice, this question was frequently reduced to the "tell/don't tell" issue, ignoring the many other facets of interpersonal communication.

Learned discussion of ethical principles would become more prominent in the years ahead. At this point, though, one had to cast about for a principle that might serve the purpose. There was an obvious candidate: the Hippocratic Oath demands that physicians do no harm to patients and limit professional involvement to matters of health. However, this ancient authority no longer wielded significant power in medical practice (Lamers, 2003). Furthermore, "do no harm" might be interpreted as "deceive not, so patients may contemplate their lives in possession of the truth."

Consider some of the psychological and sociocultural processes involved. Begin with two implicit propositions:

- Sick people need hope to recover or at least to hold on as long as possible.
- Telling the truth to an incurable patient has the force of a death sentence that will destroy hope and therefore worsen the already perilous condition.

Add a set of operational propositions:

- It is right to tell the truth. But it is "more right" for the physician to act in the patient's best interest.

- It is right for physicians to make the decision because they know what is best for patients. And the patient wants and trusts them to do so.

- Patients won't know they're dying if they aren't told.

- Getting involved personally is wrong because it can interfere with performance of physicians' professional duties and is not helpful to the patient.

Is there a problem here? How about the super-assumption that threads through all the propositions: *"We know."*

We know, for example, that the patient doesn't know. We also know that "hope" can mean only expectation of cure or remission, and that hope is easily crushed. Patients have no spiritual, personal, or interpersonal sources of value or support and no worldview that enables acceptance of death. We also know that the physician knows best and that the patient concurs with this belief, even if it includes misrepresentations and evasions. Furthermore, we know that dying patients are unable or unwilling to recognize their fate unless a physician or nurse lets slip the truth. We know that communication with a terminally ill person is most effective when physician speaks and patient listens. Finally, we know that health care personnel do more harm to themselves by "getting involved" than by keeping a cool professional distance. *All this we know because we know!* This knowledge certainty was not earned through open and intensive ethical dialogue or empirical research. That it might not be ethical to impose moral judgment on others without due process was itself not an ethical question—or so it seemed.

These propositions had no foundation in established fact. Professional journals and books were not bursting with studies that confirmed such assumptions. Lack of verified knowledge about the dying process and terminal care was still pervasive in the middle of the 20th century, so the dearth of supportive data was not surprising. The *attitude* toward verification was, however, a striking departure from the supposed commitment to scientifically based medical practice. The pioneering thanatologists were aware that there was very little to go on other than opinion and unsystematic observations. They set to work, realizing that there was almost everything to learn.

By contrast, the mainstream health system displayed little recognition either of the absence of a database or of an obligation to test its assumptions against reality. Physicians generally were devoted to their frequently updated databases in deciding on a course of treatment. Here was medical science in action! Yet the same physicians perpetuated sweeping generalizations that were raised to the level of moral imperatives without feeling the need for verification. Mainstream physicians were not concerned about the lack of empirical grounding for their strictures against becoming "involved" with terminally ill people. In most areas of practice, this seeming indifference to verification and discovery would have marked a physician as slothful and inept. But it was acceptable when dealing with end-of-life situations. Was there an ethical issue in the systematic neglect of the principles of testing assumptions and practices? I heard not a peep of "ethical discomfort" with the lack of verification for the approach prescribed for interactions with terminally ill patients and their families.

ANXIETY AS AN ETHICS INHIBITOR

Anxiety about facing mortality led to a tense constriction of communication. This was a self-perpetuating arrangement: not telling, not listening, and not getting involved was an effective dodge. Patients and family would have little opportunity to express doubts, fears, and unwelcome questions. Terminal patients therefore could be downsized as terminal patients— not as individuals with distinctive personalities, embedded in family and community. The essential link between the humanity of the physician and the patient could be obscured. In consequence, dying patients and their families, feeling stressed, uncertain, and abandoned, heightened physicians' own anxieties.

This attitude would become less prevalent as the grassroots death awareness movement and observations by early thanatologists started to take effect. It would be learned, for example, that many terminally ill people, including children, are aware of their situation (Bluebond-Langner, 1996). There would be increased recognition of the terminally ill person's total life situation, including the strengths and values that individuals and families could bring with them to the final phase of life; the need to affirm or repair significant interpersonal relationships; and the opportunity to participate in decision making regarding property distribution, funeral arrangements, and many other matters. "Management of the incurable patient" was starting to give way to comprehending "end-of-life" situations in all their complexity.

Gradually, it would also be realized (though still incompletely) that the circumstances of terminal cancer are not an adequate model for understanding the dying process in general. Other terminal pathways often have distinctive challenges that require close attention.

ETHICAL PRINCIPLES: WHAT WAKES THEM UP?

Ethical principles are not always on active duty. Some lie dormant for years. For example, truth-telling to a terminally ill patient was a non-issue for decades. Apparently a pattern of distress is not sufficient to activate the "ethical issue" reflex. It seems to take particular circumstances and mind-sets to arouse active ethical concern. Consider a familiar case history from this perspective.

The "tell/don't tell" controversy has been superseded by other life-and-death issues such as abortion, euthanasia, rational suicide, physician-assisted death, right to die, cryonic suspension, and certain aspects of organ harvesting and transplantation. With the ripening of these issues, ethical principles were called into service and also received more expert attention (e.g., Emanuel, 1998; Florencio & Keller, 1999; Keyes, (1995). For example, the "sacredness of life" position can be pitted against the utilitarian tradition with its communal emphasis, and both against the "liberty" or "autonomy right" that asserts the inherent rights of individuals. But the sharp edge of the issue became *Who should make the decision?* This question led to the implicit prior question *Who gets to decide about who decides?* The core ethical question remains *What is the right thing to do in a terminal care situation?* It would be naïve to assume that "the best principle will win." Vested interests have already lined up behind their preferred version of moral philosophy. For example, the U.S. Justice Department and the state of Florida have made repeated attacks on the individual autonomy right to discontinue medical treatment.

Major cultural institutions had largely neglected end-of-life concerns in the early days of the death awareness movement. It was soon realized, however, that significant economic and political stakes were on the table for vested interests that could claim moral leadership and thereby control legislative and regulative strongholds. Thus, economic, political, and religious interests brought their longstanding disputes into the realm of death and dying. It seems a mixed blessing for the dying person to be exposed to the heat of partisan causes.

"Conscience" often rests easy until tradition and routine are sufficiently disturbed. Rituals have governed the performance of both mundane and momentous activities through much of history (Grimes, 2000). The healing arts were very much in partnership with the reigning deities; medical rituals have evolved and endure to the present day, though with attenuated links to the sacred. The foundational beliefs and principles were affirmed every time a ritual was performed (Kastenbaum, 2004a).

History suggests that ethical principles become "hot" when a threat arises to the habitual way of doing things. For example, many societies have carried out normative practices as extreme as cannibalism, infanticide, mutilation, slavery, and torture. "This is what our people do. So—what's the problem?" The problem announces itself through confrontations from a variety of sources. In parts of the Americas, human sacrifice and canni-balism were strongly opposed by people arriving with a different religious and moral sensitivity, and also with more lethal weapons. The newcomers also had an ethical conflict of their own: Should the "natives" be treated with respect, or were they eligible for slaughter or enslavement?

In our day, biotechnology has generated a continuing series of options that have exposed underlying rifts within Euro-American culture. Demand for self-termination options increased exponentially when it became possible to keep people somewhere between life and death for an extended period. Can it be ethical both to keep people in persistent vegetative states and to legalize euthanasia or physician-assisted suicide? Why shouldn't people choose cryonic suspension over burial or cremation? What's really so wrong about purchasing body parts from third world donors, if the result is a financial boon for the donor and extended life for the recipient? Isn't this option in line with the tradition of providing superior health care to elite members of society?

Questions such as these call for clear and timely answers. Health care professionals and others on the front lines cannot be expected to sort out a shifting array of alternative ethical positions; they have critical decisions to make in the immediate situation. The pressure is on, then. Ethical positions make a difference—and the religious, political, and economical establishments they represent are being tested. Optimists believe that the high stakes will result in wise and humane ethical approaches. Pessimists believe that the realities of terminal illness and care will become secondary to the power struggle among ethical positions.

EMERGING DEATHS: WHAT RESPONSE?

Death on the Wing

Now let us consider some of the emerging modes or contexts of death that will further challenge our ability to judge and to do the right thing.

Public health experts have been warning us that worldwide pandemics are highly probable. The next pandemics could take many forms. The avian flu virus is one of the most likely pathogens, and it is taken here as an example of the looming challenges to terminal care. Recent "bird flu" (Influenza Type A, H5N1) outbreaks have been controlled thanks to public health response and a bit of luck. The outbreaks were alarming enough, though, to serve as reminders of the influenza pandemic of 1918 and to turn responsible people toward increasing prevention and management efforts.

Much can be learned from the devastation and panic brought on by the "Spanish flu" that caused 200,000 deaths in one month and nearly 700,000 altogether in the United States—and at least 40 million worldwide (Kolata, 1999). The hospice movement has improved care for many terminally ill patients and their families. But can the hospice system—or any other—cope with an epidemic that even approaches the 1918 pandemic in lethality and magnitude? The fact that we now have higher expectations for terminal care might even contribute to distress if our measures fall short.

How would we respond today if we confronted a pandemic on the scale of the 1918 flu? Consider characteristics such as these:

- Sudden onset, massive debility, and an agonizing death within days.

- Health care systems overwhelmed by the number and severity of those afflicted.

- No precise knowledge of cause; no effective medications or procedures.

- No clear idea how long this scourge will continue or what its final toll will be.

- General societal breakdown in the workplace, in transportation, and at home: public meetings suspended because of contagion fears—and health care personnel themselves among the most vulnerable.

- Expectations for both normal life and proper death shattered. Ordinary civility eroded by fear and grief; care of the dead collapses under the pressure—even a shortage of coffins, and a moratorium on memorial services.

Two ethical issues could become acute. *Should priority be given to never-say-die treatment or to comfort and support?* This familiar issue has continued to arise in considering the hospice option. Under catastrophe conditions, however, the decision-making process becomes confused and distorted. During the 1918 flu pandemic, it was exceedingly difficult to exercise case-by-case judgment in the absence of either effective treatment or a comfort care alternative. Perhaps a viable ethical principle is that ethical principles should not replace clinical judgment. Nevertheless, firm ethical guidance might prevent disintegration and despair on the part of health care professionals and other emergency responders.

Should priority be given to containing a pandemic or to affirming individual, interpersonal, and religious values? Here we draw on recent experiences. The 2004 outbreak of severe acute respiratory syndrome (SARS) in Hong Kong resulted in the hospitalization of people critically ill with the infection. Public health authorities were taxed to the utmost to limit spread of the contagion. At the same time, though, service providers came up against an urgent plea from family members: They had to be with their dying loved one. If not, it would be a dereliction of duty that would stain their own lives forever (Chan, 2004). How could the need to prevent further infections and deaths be balanced with respect for deep family and religious values?

There is no way to make this decision easy. Nevertheless, serious reflection and discussion of ethical principles and decision points before an emergency arises could provide a clearer guide and some relief from moral anguish. The isolating effects of a contagious, life-threatening condition have been experienced repeatedly throughout history, as in visitations of the bubonic plague and cholera and the long reign of tuberculosis as a leading cause of death.

Thanatologists have generally affirmed the value of close interpersonal support for terminally ill people. These interactions are recommended for several reasons: (1) comfort instead of social isolation for the dying person; (2) the opportunity to affirm relationships and perhaps resolve lingering grudges or misunderstandings; (3) in some cultures, contributing to the "safe conduct" of the dying person's soul to the next realm of existence; (4) a valuable early step toward grief recovery and "continuing bonds;" (5) the chance for the survivors to feel at peace, knowing they have met their obligations as family members or friends; and (6) in some cultures, the belief that the survivors' own fate at and after death will be more favorable if they have stayed with the dying person and done all that was possible. As Chan (2004) has observed, the bird flu outbreak in Hong Kong was especially stressful for family members of the victims because it included fear of after-death consequences for themselves if they were not at the bedside. Health care professionals had to make immediate and consequential decisions between two incompatible choices: respect cultural tradition and relieve anxiety and guilt on the part of relatives, or control a lethal contagion before it could turn into pandemic.

There a consensus among public health experts that situations of this kind are almost certain to recur. Is it possible to come up with credible ethical positions in advance of medical catastrophes that may exceed our experience? Are traditional ethical positions perhaps too distant from emerging realities to be of much use? Would it be more ethical to exercise restraint in asserting ethical authority and, instead, trust to the judgment of the responders? What ethical standards must be met by an ethical principle itself if it is to be given power over critical decision making?

Urgency in exploring, clarifying, and refining ethical positions has increased with heightened awareness of emerging threats. Public health experts have found that some lethal viruses can leap from one animal to another, and thence to humans. They have also found that viruses can mutate rapidly to become more contagious, more lethal, and less responsive to existing courses of treatment (Chettle, 2004). Even such measures as killing 100 million birds at risk for avian flu has not proven as effective as once believed: A global pandemic could break out at any time (Bradsher & Altman, 2004).

Perhaps this kind of threat should lead us to consider what might be called a metaprinciple of ethics: *The obligation to recognize and act upon ethical obligations.* None of the familiar ethical principles will do much good if they are bypassed when critical situations arise. There is a long and melancholy history of simply suspending ethical principles when the scent of disaster is in the wind. The initial SARS cover-up in Hong Kong is an example, but similar dynamics have operated time and again with respect to natural disasters, fire hazards, unsafe constructions, and pollution, as well as contagions. Who should recognize the threat? Who should warn? Who should prepare? Who should respond with steady focus on the main issue, rather than convenience or self-interest? Taking ethical issues seriously seems a prerequisite to choosing a particular ethical principle.

Garrett (1995) is among those who conclude that humans bear much responsibility for contagions already encountered (e.g., HIV/AIDS) and yet to come. She holds our species responsible for "a world out of balance." We have not only overpopulated the planet but demonstrated a "voracious appetite for resource consumption" and destabilized "every measurable biological and chemical system on earth" (p. 550). Others have observed that our forays into forests and swamps have brought previously unknown or rare diseases into global circulation. Holding ourselves responsible for our own misfortunes is not an attractive proposition, and not necessarily an incontrovertible proposition either. However, there is something to be said for increased thanatological attention to death writ large (Kastenbaum, 2004b; Wilson, 2002). This would include our possible role in hastening or delaying mass death from disease, starvation, ecological disasters, and human-inflicted violence. Is there an ethical dimension here?

The implicit ethical question might be put this way: Is it right to compartmentalize, if not deny, prospects of mass death, as society once did with the death of individuals?

THE FADING AWAY: ALZHEIMER'S DISEASE

Particular ethical issues arise in connection with particular terminal situations. With cancer patients, for example, the question of truth-telling emerged. With persistent vegetative states, it is the question of passive or active euthanasia. What about Alzheimer's disease? The situation differs markedly from both "the model case" of terminal cancer and the chaos of pandemic.

There are now more robust and long-lived adults than ever before—but also more people with or at risk for Alzheimer's disease. The number of Americans with Alzheimer's was estimated at 4.5 million at the beginning of this century. By the middle of this century, the total could be as high as 16 million (Hebert, Scherr, Bienias, Bennett, & Evans, 2003). Already, about 10% of the population reports having a family member with this condition. The burden on family members is enormous: the stress of seeing personhood fade away, knowing that further decline is inevitable; providing and funding care; difficulties in maintaining their other relationships and obligations—and fear that what they are witnessing might someday be their own fate. The magnitude of the problem will increasingly challenge society's ability and resolve to support quality care. There is already a cultural sanction in place: "Honor thy father and mother." But other ethical concerns also apply, closely related to the existing state of knowledge and management skills. Is the Alzheimer's patient "dying" and in need of "terminal care," or do we face a much different kind of situation?

The status of being perceived as "dying" had been the subject of discussion from several perspectives—until Medicare introduced coverage of hospice services. "This patient has 6 months or less to live" became the working definition of dying. At that point, the policy-makers obviously were not thinking of Alzheimer's disease. People can live 10 or even 20 years after they begin to exhibit Alzheimer's symptoms (Larson & Shadlen, 2004). Even if progression is more rapid, the time scale is much longer than for conditions to which the terms "dying" or "terminal illness" are usually applied. Palliative care was organized around the mission to relieve pain and suffering that would otherwise intensify over weeks or months. By contrast, patients with Alzheimer's seldom are wracked with pain and become less sensitive to both physical and psychological suffering as they approach the end phase of life. Should we then think of the Alzheimer's decline as "aging" rather than dying? No, respond the gerontologists who have been working hard at distinguishing inherent age-related changes from dysfunctions produced through illness or mishap. Moreover, the tell/don't tell question now occurs within a different context: Should people be given an early diagnosis of Alzheimer's because this would be truthful? Or should they be spared years of dread in advance of severe symptoms? Why impose painful knowledge when is no remediation is available?

Not an acute life-threatening episode. Not a quick trajectory from well-being to end state. Not aging (although including normal age-related changes). Something like HIV/AIDS in that a person can live with the condition for years—but not really like HIV/AIDS because people with Alzheimer's (1) are usually spared the siege of multiple physical symptoms in the end state; (2) will have diminishing awareness of their plight; and (3) do not scare off family and caregivers because of contagion fears.

And yet something—rather someone—is dying in Alzheimer's: the person we knew; the person who knew him- or herself. It is difficult to think about both the residual person who is still there and the essential person who is vanishing. The ambiguity can overload and paralyze. Furthermore, whatever we think we have understood about the patient's state of awareness is subject to vacillation and directional change. Is he or she "still in there"? Does the person experience only shallow and labile feelings, or are there deep emotions and keen sensitivities under the surface? Can this person still express decisions or at least preferences? Family caregivers and even professionals may not be certain about remaining capacity at a particular time. Unsure about facts, we find it difficult to be sure about the right thing to do. There may be a strong impulse to withdraw from this stressful situation, but also a search for authoritative guidance. We would more than welcome a confident principle about what is the right thing to do.

Here, then, is the place to propose a second metaprinciple: *The ethical use of principles requires us to accept responsibility for knowing as much as can be known and recognizing the limits of our knowledge.* To put it another way, it is less than ethical to impose an ethical principle on a situation without scrupulous attention to facts known, facts unknown, and facts in dispute.

We do not lack for ethical principles. We may need new principles as we confront new situations; perhaps we would be wiser to monitor more alertly the ways ethical principles are used and abused. The tensions inherent in life-and-death situations can intensify the tendency to use principles either as shields against personal twinges of mortality or as power moves in the service of an agenda. The unfamiliarity of emerging contexts of death could further contribute to a not very principled application of principles.

Alzheimer's disease also raises anew the question of "medical futility" that has been encountered under many conditions. These range from severely impaired infants to the "useless eaters" killed by physicians in Nazi Germany, the doomed victims of medication-resistant strains of tuberculosis or other contagions, and elders of sound mind whose bodies can no longer make use of transfusion or most other interventions. The diversity of conditions in which "medical futility" has been conceived as an issue is a clue to the protean character of this concept. It does not necessarily mean the same thing in all situations or from all perspectives. We can define our way toward or away from any particular course of assistance by manipulating this term, or leave one another in confusion by using the term differently.

Alzheimer's disease does have a distinctive profile: The individual often is physically able to survive for years, but with memory, competence, and personality in sad decline. How do we decide when medical treatment is futile? There is certainly an ethical dimension to this question, but it is lodged within a complex of other considerations. Our decision about the right thing to do could hinge on our beliefs about such considerations as (1) personhood, (2) sacredness as distinguished from quality of life, (3) continuing bonds and loyalties, (4) right use of limited resources, (5) priority on the individual versus avoiding stress and dysfunction of caregiving families and society, and (6) what constitutes "treatment" and what alternative course would follow if treatment were abandoned. We have choices with respect to each of these concerns. Furthermore, we have the challenge of taking all of these concerns into account in coming up with a comprehensive plan for responding to Alzheimer's.

Rather than examine these choice points in the detail they deserve, let me reflect on my experiences 30 years ago, as first a psychologist and then an administrator in a large state-operated geriatric facility. Alzheimer's disease was known in the late 1970s, but "organic brain syndrome" and "chronic brain syndrome" were the more common entries in the medical folders. It was a sad joke that we translated "CBS" into "cost/benefit syndrome." The prevailing attitude was that nothing could be done for "these people," and therefore next to nothing need be provided for comfort and dignity, let alone treatment. Their deaths were also regarded as insignificant—with the significant exception of staff members who had become close to them.

We found that many of these markedly impaired people could regain elements of their personhood through fairly basic interventions that gave them an opportunity to experience and renew themselves as persons (e.g., Kastenbaum, 1972; Kastenbaum et al., 1981). Almost all needed substantial assistance in living, but enough sparks of their previous selves came through to hearten both family and staff. Their eventual passages through end-of-life experiences were also more often accompanied by attentive family and staff. Perhaps this was as much the result of others having resumed the habit of regarding them as persons as it was of the patients' partial and fleeting returns to a higher level of function. Other gerontologists have also reported that geriatric patients with dementia often respond to a variety of humane interventions. Are such interventions "medical"? Sometimes they have been classified as such to fit into established reporting categories. Are they treatments—or just humane care? Are these efforts futile? Whatever we did, the patients would continue to age, decline, and die. Staff members often found themselves operating with a value scale different from that to which they had been accustomed. The "good" was not cure, return to the community, or substantial life prolongation. In fact, it was hardly anything that could be included in a statistical outcome report.

Later, as director of the geriatric hospital, I repeatedly encountered ageism and "mortalityism" on the part of government and community agencies. The neglect of aged and terminally ill institutional residents often was justified by the assumptions that they were less than human and that offering anything beyond minimal custodial services was a waste of resources. There was a corresponding reluctance to visit the facility and meet residents and staff. Privately, officials would admit it gave them the creeps to be around people who reminded them of their own vulnerabilities to aging and death. The cover story, though, was the familiar "medical futility" assumption and the admirably ethical resolve to allocate funds to programs of higher need and social consequence. I developed a skeptical attitude toward ethical platitudes that served merely to justify other motives. The "medical futility" proposition is likely to become even more salient as the number of people with Alzheimer's increases. There will certainly be a need to consider the challenges of expense, management, and exhausting demands on family and other caregivers. We can hope, however, that needs such as cost containment will be presented and examined as such, rather than packaged as purely ethical issues. It is just too easy to "discover" that what one wanted to do anyhow happens to be an ethical imperative.

THE MOMENT OF DEATH—GONE MISSING?

The moment of death was once indeed momentous (e.g., Aries, 1981, Comper, 1977; DuBruck & Gusick, 1999; Duclow, 1999; Paxton, 1990). In Christian tradition, the final moments of life were regarded as crucial for the fate of the soul. Those who had strayed from righteousness still had a chance to renounce sin and renew faith. Even the most pious would attempt to demonstrate their faith at the last moment. Depictions of the ideal deathbed scene were promulgated to serve as models (Bell, 2004). The prevailing mood differed markedly from early Christianity's jubilant belief that death had been conquered because it gives way to the blessings of eternal life. The optimism faded through the centuries as life remained very hard and deliverance seemed increasingly remote. The physical and spiritual agony of the sinner on the deathbed might be but a foretaste of torments to come. Hope and despair both invested the deathbed scene— a perfect recipe for life-long anxiety.

The cosmic drama of the deathbed scene had the effect of making the dying person Important. It was necessary to expunge weakness and sin, to purify the soul, close to the moment of passing. This concern for dying in grace carried over to rites for disposition of the body, and often to lighting candles and offering masses to protect the dead on their journey.

This tradition persists, but no longer in the mainstream of industrialized societies. There have been partial and short-lived revivals of engrossment with the moment of death. For example, some upholders of religious dogma saw the rise of science as threatening. In response, they invented "last words" and put them posthumously into the mouths of such rogues as Charles Darwin (Kastenbaum, 1993). The fear of being buried alive also had its moments (Bondeson, 2001). (This was a precursor to current controversies about definitions, signs, and criteria for death.) Fear of live burial stimulated people to take precautions such as designing escapable coffins and entreating friends to make sure they were really dead. Nevertheless, the deathbed scene gradually lost its salvation-versus-damnation theatricality.

Unfortunately, it would be some time before the dying person would again receive close and compassionate attention. Theologians retreated from the deathbed scene, but so did society in general. Commerce, industrialization, and nationalism were among the engines of change. "Holy dying" (Taylor, 1977) was to a large extent supplanted by the dismissal of the dying person as a loser, an acceptable casualty on the march of progress. Medicine, riding on a new wave of discovery and efficacy, had limited interest in care of the dying. Women devoted to religious service provided compassionate care for a few, but medical neglect was the rule until the establishment of the modern hospice movement (Clark, 2003a).

Many people's last moments passed unnoticed because they were alone, even in crowded institutional settings where an increasing number of lives came to an end. If last words were uttered, there was nobody to hear them. "Being with" a dying person was seldom a priority in hospitals and long-term care facilities. Families were rarely encouraged to visit. Allied health care professionals were seldom on the scene.

Other factors also contributed to the decline of the moment of death as a crucial spiritual and communal event. Emotionally barren institutional environments reduced the residents' level of awareness and cognitive function. Medications were too often administered with the intention of reducing custodial burden. Again, the result was to dull the mind and interfere with the ability to experience and share the last moments of life. Is there an ethical issue here? I think so, but in 40-plus years in this field I have yet to hear the question raised. It is true that many people have expressed their wish to slip away from life in their sleep; others, however, would prefer to take their leave with an intact mind and the company of those they cherish. The decline in opportunities for shared end-of-life moments can also be a source of distress for family members.

Not yet mentioned are two major trends that seem likely to become increasingly significant in the future. The borderlines between life and death have become blurred since "brain death," "clinical death," "persistent vegetative state," and related phenomena have drawn attention. At the same time, population aging and slow decline from multiple chronic conditions have more frequently resulted in cognitive and communicational impairments before the final phase of life. A very different and alarming pattern is increase in deaths by mass brutality and violence. "Ethnic cleansing" and genocidal massacres often exterminate people so efficiently that there is very little of a dying process involved, and frequently no one to share last moments. Perhaps even more inhumane are the slow, agonizing deaths of displaced people in Sudan and elsewhere. It is one thing to respond to the final moments of a person whose life is coming to its natural end, and quite another for parents to watch helplessly as their children die of starvation and disease. All of this is a long way from the ideal deathbed scene illuminated by faith and compassion. One fears that the future holds more of the same. How does this loss of personhood and connection with others affect our beliefs and hopes about a meaningful life in a humane society? If lives ending so horribly (Leviton, 1991) can become almost routine, where do we even begin to apply ethical standards?

Fortunately, there are positives as well. Cicely Saunders (Clark, 2003b), Elisabeth Kubler-Ross (1969), and other pioneer thanatologists showed the way to renewed compassion for terminally ill people from both the general public and service providers. The "moment of death" remains an elusive concept and is not clearly evidenced in all passages from life (Kastenbaum, 1999). Nevertheless, more people are now in a position to bring their own beliefs and values to the end-of-life situation.

Should the last moments of life again be regarded as sacred and profound, or has this ethical priority outworn its place in a radically changing world? The controversy is on—whenever we choose to begin. ■

Robert Kastenbaum has held major academic positions including those at Wayne State University, The University of Massachusetts-Boston, and Arizona State University, from which he retired and at which he is Emeritus Professor. Major areas of scholarly emphasis in his career include gerontology, life-span development, and dying/death/grief/suicide. He was editor of both the International Journal of Aging *and* Human Development *as well as* Omega, Journal of Death and Dying, *for almost 20 years. Former President of the American Association of Suicidology, GSA's Behavioral and Social Sciences section, and the American Psychological Association's Division 20, he is the recipient of numerous awards and honors. A recent award was Gerontological Society of America's Richard A. Kalish Award for Most Innovative Publication for his book,* Dorian Graying, *which also formed the libretto of an opera.*

A walk through Dr. Kastenbaum's many publications and their provocative titles tells part of the story of this remarkable career. 1963: "The reluctant therapist" in Geriatrics; *1966: "The mental life of dying patients"; 1967: "aged?"; 1989: "Old men created by young artists: Time transcendence in Tennyson & Picasso"; 1992: "Let's stay on speaking terms about death and dying"; 1995: "Cookies baking, coffee brewing: Toward a contextual theory of dying."*

References

Aries, P. (1981). *The hour of our death.* New York: Alfred A. Knopf.

Bell, R. J. (2004). "'Our people die well.' Death-bed scenes in John Wesley's *Arminian Magazine.*" Cambridge, MA: Harvard University, manuscript.

Bluebond-Langner, M. (1996). *In the shadow of illness.* Princeton, NJ: Princeton University Press.

Bondeson, J. (2001). *Buried alive.* New York: W. W. Norton.

Bradsher, K. , & Altman, L. K. (2004, July 9). Bird flu may be impossible to destroy. *New York Times*, p. A16.

Chan, F. M-Y (2004). Private communication.

Chettle, C. G. (2004). The Bird Flu (H5N1)— Infuenza A: What is it and why should we care? Retrieved on January 18, 2005, from http://nsweb.nursingspectrum.com/ce/ce341.htm

Clark, D. (2003a). Hospice in historical perspective. In R. Kastenbaum (Ed.), *Macmillan encyclopedia of death and dying. Vol. 1* (pp. 437–441). New York: Macmillan Reference USA.

Clark, D. (2003b) Cicely Saunders. In R. Kastenbaum (Ed.), *Macmillan encyclopedia of death and dying. Vol. 2* (pp. 743–745). New York: Macmillan Reference USA.

Colt, G. H. (1991). *The enigma of suicide.* New York: Simon & Schuster.

Comper, F. M. M. (Ed.) (1977). *The book of the craft of dying and other early English tracts concerning death.* New York: Arno.

Dodge, J. S. (1963). How much should the patient be told— and by whom? *Hospitals, 37,* 44–49.

DuBruck, E. E., & Gusick, B. I. (Eds.). *Death and dying in the Middle Ages.* New York: Peter Lang.

Duclow, D. F. (1999). Dying well: The Ars moriendi and the dormition of the Virgin. In E. E. DuBruck & B. I. Gusick (Eds.), *Death and dying in the Middle Ages.* New York: Peter Lang.

Emanuel, L. L. (1998). *Regulating how we die: The ethical, medical, and legal issues surrounding physician assisted suicide.* Cambridge, MA: Harvard University Press.

Florencio, P. S., & Keller, R. H. (1999) End-of-life decision making: Rethinking the principles of fundamental justice in the context of emerging empirical data. *Health Law Journal, 7,* 233–258.

Garrett, L. (1995). *The coming plague: Newly emerging diseases in a world out of balance.* New York: Penguin.

Glaser, B. G., & Strauss, A. (1966) *Awareness of dying.* Chicago: Aldine.

Glaser, B. G., & Strauss, A. (1968). *Time for dying.* Chicago: Aldine.

Grimes, R. L. (2000). *Deeply into the bone: Re-inventing rites of passage.* Berkeley, CA: University of California Press.

Hebert, L. E., Scherr, P. A., Bienias, J. L., Bennett, D. A., & Evans, D. A. (2003). Alzheimer's Disease in the U. S. population: Prevalence estimates. *Archives of Neurology, 60,* 1119–1122.

Kasper, A. M. (1959). The doctor and death. In H. Feifel (Ed.), *The meaning of death* (pp. 259–270). New York: McGraw-Hill.

Kastenbaum, R. (1972). Beer, wine, and mutual gratification in the gerontopolis. In D. P. Kent, R. Kastenbam, & S. Sherwood (Eds.), *Research, planning, and action for the elderly* (pp. 365–394). New York: Behavioral Publications.

Kastenbaum, R. (1993). Reconstructing death in postmodern society. *Omega, Journal of Death and Dying, 27*, 75–89.

Kastenbaum, R. (1999). The moment of death: Is hospice making a difference? In I. B. Corless & Z. Foster (Eds.), *The hospice heritage. Celebrating our future* (pp. 253–270). Binghamton, NY: Haworth Press.

Kastenbaum, R. (2004a). *On our way. The final passage through life and death.* Berkeley, CA: University of California Press.

Kastenbaum, R. (2004b) Death writ large. *Death Studies, 28*, 375–392.

Kastenbaum, R., Barber, T. X., Wilson, S. G., Ryder, B. L., & Hathaway, L. B. (1981). *Old, sick, and helpless. Where therapy begins.* Cambridge, MA: Ballinger.

Keyes, W. N. (1995). *Life, death, and the law* (Vols. 1 & 2). Springfield, IL: Charles C. Thomas.

Kolata, G. (1999). *Flu: the story of the great influenza pandemic of 1918 and the search for the virus that caused it.* New York: Farrar Straus Giroux.

Kubler-Ross, E. (1969). *On death and dying.* New York: Macmillan.

Lamers, W. (2003). Hippocratic oath. In R. Kastenbaum (Ed.), *Macmillan encyclopedia of death and dying. Vol. 1* (p. 414). New York: Macmillan Reference USA.

Larson, E. B., & Shadlen, M. F. (2004). Survival after initial diagnosis of Alzheimer's disease. *Annals of Internal Medicine, 6*, 501–509.

Leviton, D. (Ed.). (1991). *Horrendous death, health, and well-being.* New York: Hemisphere.

Moremen, R. D. (2003). Gender discrimination after death. In R. Kastenbaum (Ed.), *Macmillan encyclopedia of death and dying. Vol.1* (pp. 311–314). New York: Macmillan Reference USA.

Paxton, F. S. (1990). *Christianizing death: The creation of a ritual process in early Medieval Europe.* Ithaca, NY: Cornell University Press.

Taylor, J. (1977). *The rules and exercises of holy dying.* New York: Arno (original work published 1651).

Wilson, E. O. (2002). *The future of life.* New York: Alfred A. Knopf.

CHAPTER 18

Resources

Lisa McGahey Veglahn

The Hospice Foundation of America recognizes that decisions about end-of-life care are challenging and difficult. The following list can serve as a guide to meeting some of your needs when facing these complicated situations. You will find national organizations and resources that offer general information, disease-specific support, and bioethics information. And as always, your local hospice can serve as an excellent community resource. While the list below provides useful resources, be sure to look to those who have helped you in the past—friends and family, co-workers, your faith community, your family physician, and other care professionals. Whether you are facing these situations as a family member or as a professional caregiver, you don't need to struggle alone.

■

Access to End of Life Care
1351 24th Avenue
San Francisco, CA 94122
Phone: (415) 566-9710
Fax: (415) 566-9720
Web: www.access2eolcare.org

Access to End of Life Care serves as an advocate for end-of-life care that reflects a commitment to multiculturalism, and provides education about death, dying, and grieving from a multicultural perspective. The Web site includes online training opportunities and an extensive bibliography.

Administration on Aging (AoA)

U.S. Department of Health and Human Services
Washington, DC 20201
Phone: (202) 619-0724
E-mail: AoAInfo@aoa.gov
Web: www.aoa.gov

For over 35 years, the AoA has provided home- and community-based services to millions of older persons through the programs funded under the Older Americans Act. Two such programs are the Alzheimer's Disease Demonstration Grants to States Program and the National Family Caregiver Support Program. The latter provides a variety of services to help people who are caring for family members who are chronically ill or who have disabilities.

American Academy of Hospice and Palliative Medicine (AAHPM)

4700 W. Lake Avenue
Glenview, IL 60025
Phone: (847) 375-4712
Fax: (877) 734-8671
E-mail: info@aahpm.org
Web: www.aahpm.org

AAHPM is an organization of physicians and other medical professionals dedicated to excellence in hospice/palliative medicine and to the prevention and relief of suffering among patients and families by providing education and clinical practice standards, fostering research, facilitating personal and professional development of its members, and by public policy advocacy.

Association for Death Education and Counseling

342 North Main Street
West Hartford, CT 06117-2507
Phone: (860) 586-7503
Fax: (860) 586-7550
E-mail: info@adec.org
Web: www.adec.org

The Association for Death Education and Counseling is an international professional organization dedicated to promoting excellence in death education, care of the dying, and bereavement counseling and support.

Based on quality research and theory, the association provides information, support, and resources to its multicultural, multidisciplinary membership and, through it, to the public.

Careplanner.org

Web: www.careplanner.org

The Careplanner site is a decision support tool for seniors, caregivers, family, friends, and professionals. Funded by the Center for Medicare and Medicaid Services, the site includes downloadable worksheets and a step-by-step tool to help in analyzing living options and care choices.

Faith in Action

Wake Forest University School of Medicine
Medical Center Boulevard
Winston-Salem, NC 27157-1204
Phone: (877) 324-8411 (toll-free) or (336) 716-0101
Fax: (336) 716-3346
E-mail: fia@wfubmc.edu
Web: www.fiavolunteers.org

Faith in Action is an interfaith volunteer caregiving initiative of The Robert Wood Johnson Foundation. Local Faith in Action programs bring together volunteers from many faiths to care for their neighbors who have long-term health needs. Faith in Action volunteers come from churches, synagogues, mosques, and other houses of worship, as well as the community at large.

Hospice Foundation of America (HFA)

1621 Connecticut Avenue, NW, Suite 300
Washington, DC 20009
Phone: (800) 854-3402 or (202) 638-5419
Fax: (202) 638-5312
E-mail: info@hospicefoundation.org
Web: www.hospicefoundation.org

HFA is a nonprofit organization that provides leadership in the development and application of hospice and its philosophy of care. HFA's Web site and other programs are the foremost sources of information on caregiving and end-of-life issues for consumers, health care professionals, and the media. HFA produces an annual award-winning national teleconference on grief and publishes the companion book series, *Living with Grief*®, which includes this book. HFA offers a range of other resources, both in print and audio format, that offer guidance and support for laypeople and professionals facing illness, death, and grief. HFA is also the primary supporter of Hospice College of America, an online and home study program for clergy, nurses, social workers, and other health care professionals seeking further education in hospice care and bereavement.

The International Association for Organ Donation
P.O. Box 545
Dearborn, MI 48121-0545
Phone: (313) 745-2379
Fax: (313) 745-4509
Web: www.iaod.org

The International Association for Organ Donation provides dynamic educational and outreach programs and services to the general public, and particularly to vulnerable racial and ethnic minorities, ensuring their awareness of the need for organ transplantation and actively securing their commitment to become organ donors.

National Alliance for Caregiving
4720 Montgomery Lane, 5th Floor
Bethesda, MD 20814
Phone: (301) 718-8444
Fax: (301) 718-0034
E-mail: info@caregiving.org
Web: www.caregiving.org

The National Alliance for Caregiving is dedicated to providing support to family caregivers and the professionals who help them and to increasing public awareness of issues facing family caregivers. The alliance conducts research, develops national projects, and works to increase public awareness of the issues of family caregiving.

National Family Caregivers Association (NFCA)
10400 Connecticut Avenue, Suite 500
Kensington, MD 20895-3944
Phone: (800) 896-3650
Fax: (301) 942-2302
E-mail: info@nfcacares.org
Web: www.nfcacares.org

NFCA supports, empowers, educates, and speaks up for the more than 50 million Americans who care for a chronically ill, aged, or disabled loved one. NFCA reaches across the boundaries of different diagnoses, different relationships, and different life stages to address the common needs and concerns of all family caregivers. NFCA is committed to improving the overall quality of life of caregiving families and minimizing the disparities between family caregivers and non-caregivers.

National Hospice and Palliative Care Organization (NHPCO)
1700 Diagonal Road, Suite 625
Alexandria, VA 22314
Phone: (703) 837-1500
Fax: (703) 837-1233
Consumer HelpLine: (800) 658-8898
E-mail: nhpco_info@nhpco.org
Web: www.nhpco.org

NHPCO is the largest nonprofit membership organization representing hospice and palliative care programs and professionals in the United States. The organization is committed to improving end-of-life care and expanding access to hospice. NHPCO offers educational programs and materials for professionals and the public.

The National Hospice Work Group
c/o San Diego Hospice and Palliative Care
4311 Third Avenue
San Diego, CA 92103
Phone: 619.278.6449
Email: Tryndes@aol.com
Web: www.nhwg.org

The National Hospice Work Group is a professional coalition of hospice pioneers, executives, consultants, and researchers committed to increasing access to the palliative competencies of hospice care. For more than 25 years its members have made significant local and national contributions to the care of patients facing life-threatening illnesses, regardless of age or diagnosis. Through issues analysis, advocacy, best practice exchange, research, and education, they continue advancing a valued philosophy of care for people affected by the profound effects of aging, disability, and disease.

U.S. Department of Veterans Affairs (VA)
VA Hospice and Palliative Care (VAHPC) Initiative
c/o Diane Jones, Project Administrator, VAHPC and HVP
Phone: (856) 310-0051
E-mail: djones@ethosconsult.com
Web: www.nhpco.org/veterans

The goals of the VAHPC Initiative are to increase veterans' access to the continuum of hospice and palliative services and contribute to the palliative care education and training of VA staff and trainees. The Accelerated Administrative and Clinical Training (AACT) Program promotes the development, expansion, and improvement of hospice and palliative care in all VA facilities. AACT, along with the National Hospice-Veteran Partnership (HVP) Program, has helped form statewide and regional coalitions of people and organizations dedicated to ensuring access to end-of-life care for all veterans.

DISEASE-SPECIFIC ORGANIZATIONS

The ALS Association
27001 Agoura Road, Suite 150
Calabasas Hills, CA 91301-5104
Phone: (800) 782-4747 or (818) 880-9007
Fax: (818) 880-9006
Web: www.alsa.org

The Alzheimer's Association
225 North Michigan Avenue, Suite 1700
Chicago, IL 60601-7633
Phone: (800) 272-3900 or (312) 335-8700
TDD Access: (312) 335-8882
Fax: (312) 335-1110
Web: www.alz.org

American Cancer Society
1599 Clifton Road
Atlanta, GA 30329
Phone: (800) ACS-2345 or (404) 320-3333
Fax: (404) 325-2548
Web: www.cancer.org

American Heart Association
7272 Greenville Avenue
Dallas, TX 75231-4596
Phone: (800) 242-8721
Web: www.americanheart.org

American Parkinson's Disease Association
1250 Hylan Boulevard, Suite 4B
Staten Island, NY 10305
Phone: (800) 223-2732
Fax: (718) 981-4399
Web: www.apdaparkinson.org

American Stroke Association
7272 Greenville Avenue
Dallas, TX 75231
Phone: (888) 478-7653
Web: www.strokeassociation.org

Medline Plus Health Information
a service of the U.S. National Library of Medicine
and National Institutes of Health
Web: www.nlm.nih.gov/medlineplus

National Alliance for Children with Life-Threatening Conditions
113 Holland Avenue (111T)
Albany, NY 12208
Phone: (518) 626-6089
Fax: (518) 626-6128
Web: www.nacwltc.org

National Association of People with AIDS
8401 Colesville Road, Suite 750
Silver Spring, MD 20910
E-mail: info@napwa.org
Web: www.napwa.org

BIOETHICS INSTITUTES AND UNIVERSITY PROGRAMS

American Society for Bioethics and Humanities (ASBH)
4700 W. Lake
Glenview, IL 60025-1485
Phone: (847) 375-4745
Fax: (877) 734-9385
Email: info@asbh.org
Website: www.asbh.org

The purpose of ASBH is to promote the exchange of ideas and foster multidisciplinary, interdisciplinary, and interprofessional scholarship, research, teaching, policy development, professional development, and collegiality among people engaged in all of the endeavors related to clinical and academic bioethics and the health-related humanities. ASBH offers a Hospice and Palliative Medicine Affinity Group with an online discussion board.

American Society of Law, Medicine, and Ethics (ASLME)
765 Commonwealth Avenue, Suite 1634
Boston, MA 02215
Phone: (617) 262-4990
Fax: (617) 437-7596
E-mail: info@aslme.org
Web: www.aslme.org

The mission of ASLME is to provide high-quality scholarship, debate, and critical thought to the community of professionals at the nexus of law, medicine, and ethics. For nearly three decades, ASLME has fulfilled its mission by providing extensive opportunities for interdisciplinary education to its members. ASLME's membership comprises attorneys, physicians, nurses, ethicists, educators, allied health professionals, hospital and public administrators, risk managers, pharmacists, social workers, and students.

Bioethics.net
Web: www.bioethics.net

This is the Web site of the American Journal of Bioethics, which has editorial offices at the University of Pennsylvania Center for Bioethics and Stanford Center for Medical Bioethics. The site has a topic-specific index, including a section on Pain and Palliative Care. The site also has a section entitled "Bioethics for Beginners."

The Center for Bioethics and Culture (CBC)
P.O. Box 20760
Oakland, CA 94620
Phone: (510) 594-9000
Web: www.thecbc.org

Through educational resources, seminars, and conferences, CBC aims to train and equip people to understand issues in bioethics and to meet the needs of those wishing to rightly understand the ethical decisions all will face one day. The CBC Web site has an End-of-Life section with articles and other resources.

The Center for Practical Bioethics
Town Pavilion—1100 Walnut Street, Suite 2900
Kansas City, MO 64106-2197
Phone: (816) 221-1100
Fax: (816) 221-2002
E-mail: bioethic@practicalbioethics
Web: www.practicalbioethics.org

The Center for Practical Bioethics is a nationally recognized voice in aging and end-of-life care. Its Resource Center includes information on new ways to approach advance care directives, appointing a durable power of attorney for health care, understanding pain management, and helping families and communities meet the psychological and spiritual needs of loved ones at home, in the hospital, or in long-term care facilities.

The Center for the Study of Bioethics
at the Medical College of Wisconsin
Web: www.mcw.edu/bioethics

Duke Institute on Care at End of Life
Duke University Divinity School
Durham, NC 27708
Phone: (919) 660-3553
E-mail: Iceol@div.duke.edu
Web: www.iceol.duke.edu

The institute, which is dedicated to including previously underrepresented and diverse groups, seeks to learn how to best meet the end-of-life needs of all communities. The institute is committed to enhancing meaningful public dialogue around issues related to care at the end of life through education and the dissemination of information. The core faculty is drawn from theology, medicine, nursing, social work, and the humanities at Duke and other partnering institutions.

The Hastings Center
21 Malcolm Gordon Road
Garrison, NY 10524-5555
Telephone: (845) 424-4040
Fax: (845) 424-4545
E-mail: mail@thehastingscenter.org
Web: www.thehastingscenter.org

The Hastings Center is an independent, nonpartisan, nonprofit bioethics research institute founded in 1969 to explore fundamental and emerging questions in health care, biotechnology, and the environment. Its research projects are diverse, ranging from genetic paternity testing to newborn screening to palliative care. The work of The Hastings Center is to frame and examine issues that inform professional practice, public conversation, and social policy.

Kennedy Institute of Ethics, Georgetown University
http://georgetown.edu/research/kie/site/index.htm

MacLean Center for Clinical Medical Ethics
   at the University of Chicago
http://ethics.bsd.uchicago.edu

National Institutes of Health Bioethics Resources on the Web
www.nih.gov/sigs/bioethics/

Promoting Excellence in End-of-Life Care
The Practical Ethics Center at the University of Montana
1000 East Beckwith Avenue
Missoula, MT 59812
Phone: (406) 243.6601
Fax: (406) 243.6633
Email: excell@mso.umt.edu
Web: www.promotingexcellence.org

Promoting Excellence in End-of-Life Care is dedicated to long-term changes to improve health care for dying people and their families. It strives to address particular challenges to existing models of hospice and palliative care through demonstration projects and peer work groups.

The Stanford Center for Biomedical Ethics
http://scbe.stanford.edu//

Stop Pain.Org
Web: www.stoppain.org

Stop Pain.Org is a service of the Department of Pain Medicine and Palliative Care at Beth Israel Medical Center. The site has sections on management of pain and other symptoms, end-of-life care/hospice, and ethical and legal issues in palliative care.

University of Miami Ethics Programs
P.O. Box 016960 (M-825)
Miami, FL 33101
Phone: (305) 243-5723
Fax: (305) 243-6416
E-mail: ethics@miami.edu
Web: www.ethics.miami.edu

The programs feature education and research on ethics and policy across the professions, especially the health professions. The Web site includes a number of resources on the Terri Schiavo case, as well as curricular tools on ethics and geriatrics.

The University of Pennsylvania Center for Bioethics
http://www.bioethics.upenn.edu/

■ INDEX ■

I

N

R